D1016984

Will Teach for Food

CULTURAL ❦ POLITICS

A series from the Social Text Collective

Aimed at a broad interdisciplinary audience, these volumes seek to intervene in debates about the political direction of current theory and practice by combining contemporary analysis with a more traditional sense of historical and socioeconomic evaluation.

12. *Will Teach for Food: Academic Labor in Crisis*
    Cary Nelson, editor
11. *Dangerous Liaisons: Gender, Nation, and Postcolonial Perspectives*
    Anne McClintock, Aamir Mufti, and Ella Shohat, editors
10. *Spectacles of Realism: Gender, Body, Genre*
    Margaret Cohen and Christopher Prendergast, editors
9. *Cultural Materialism: On Raymond Williams*
    Christopher Prendergast, editor
8. *Socialist Ensembles: Theater and State in Cuba and Nicaragua*
    Randy Martin
7. *The Administration of Aesthetics: Censorship, Political Criticism, and the Public Sphere*
    Richard Burt, editor
6. *Fear of a Queer Planet: Queer Politics and Social Theory*
    Michael Warner, editor
5. *The Phantom Public Sphere*
    Bruce Robbins, editor
4. *On Edge: The Crisis of Contemporary Latin American Culture*
    George Yúdice, Jean Franco, and Juan Flores, editors
3. *Technoculture*
    Constance Penley and Andrew Ross, editors
2. *Intellectuals: Aesthetics, Politics, Academics*
    Bruce Robbins, editor
1. *Universal Abandon? The Politics of Postmodernism*
    Andrew Ross, editor

Cultural Politics, Volume 12

Will Teach for Food

Academic Labor in Crisis

Cary Nelson, editor

University of Minnesota Press
Minneapolis
London

The foreword and chapters 1 to 8 were originally published in *Social Text* 49 (volume 14, number 4, winter 1996). Copyright 1996, Duke University Press. Reprinted with permission.

Published by the University of Minnesota Press
111 Third Avenue South, Suite 290
Minneapolis, MN 55401–2520

Printed in the United States of America on acid-free paper

Library of Congress Cataloging-in-Publication Data

Will teach for food : academic labor in crisis / Cary Nelson, editor.
p. cm. — (Cultural politics ; v. 12)
Includes bibliographical references and index.
ISBN 0-8166-3033-X (alk. paper). — ISBN 0-8166-3034-8 (pbk.)
1. Graduate teaching assistants – Strikes and lockouts – Connecticut – New Haven. 2. Yale University – Faculty – Salaries, etc. 3. College teachers – Salaries, etc. – United States. 4. College teachers, Part-time – Salaries, etc. – United States. 5. College teachers – United States – Social conditions. 6. Teachers' unions – United States. 7. College teachers – Tenure – United States. I. Nelson, Cary. II. Series: Cultural politics (Minneapolis, Minn.) ; v. 12.
LB2335.845.U52N499 1997
378.746′8 – dc21 96–51992

The University of Minnesota is an equal-opportunity educator and employer.

Contents

Part II
Academic Workers Face the New Millennium

Figure 1. Jenny Schmid's drawings for the Graduate Employee Organization at the University of Michigan

Foreword
What Yale Is Teaching Us

Barbara Ehrenreich

I am writing very much as an outsider. I'm not part of the Yale community, and I'm not even an academic. But I have spent two days reading stacks of documents sent to me by Debby Applegate (a member of the Graduate Employees and Students Organization [GESO] at Yale) and by my daughter, who is a student at the Yale Law School: stacks of memos from the unions and the administration, correspondence from both sides, clippings. I've had a crash course in Yale and its unions. And the conclusion I have to offer as an outsider is that this is not a pretty picture. When an elite institution dedicated to scholarship and education uses strong-arm tactics to suppress its own graduate students, when it starts asking its employees to subsist on poverty-level or subpoverty-level wages, when it brings in a notorious union-busting law firm and security firm to make sure that employees will accede to its terms — well, this is more than a little disillusioning. It's like finding out that an elegant old gentleman you've always admired at a distance has a secret life as a mugger and a thug. It's painful to watch. But of course it's happening everywhere.

If you look at the real world, as academics call big business and finance, one widespread trend today is the practice of driving down the wages and living standards of people at the bottom and the middle. I'm not sure what to call this. An economist might call it hyper-capitalism, but I'll just call it the bandit economy. It begins with downsizing. And, if I may make a brief aside to Patrick Buchanan, this is not a matter of globalization. AT&T laid off forty thousand people, and it's not replacing them with forty thousand Mexicans or Malaysians; it's just getting rid of people. The bandit economy also entails cutting benefits, subcontracting work to firms with lower wage structures, and going from full-time workers to temporary workers with no benefits. It involves givebacks — like asking employees to accept lower wages than they already have — and things like constructing two-tier work structures, such as the one Yale offered its employees.

Because this has been happening for a number of years in the society at large, the results have become entirely predictable and familiar. Already apparent is a trend toward class polarization: the rich get richer, the poor get poorer, and the middle class gets smaller all the time. I'll give one example. I can't explain this in detail, since I'm not an economist, but there's a measure called the genii coefficient, a measure of the inequality in a society. And the United States has the number one genii coefficient among all the industrial nations. So we win; we're the most unequal. The top 2 percent of the people in the country control 20 percent of the wealth. The ratio of CEO earnings to the average employee's salary is 150 to 1. That's a huge gap, larger than any other nation. And it is far greater than it was in this country twenty years ago. So we have people who have more money than they know what to do with, a pretty large number of them in fact. And we have more and more people — a majority — who are scraping by, who work two and three jobs just to make ends meet. Some of these working people have to go on and off welfare; many have no benefits, no retirement, no health insurance. This is happening everywhere. It's even happening in the nonprofit sector, in the university.

But there is a difference when this bandit approach to management comes to the nonprofit service sector and particularly when it comes to the university. In the corporate sector, you can practice bandit management without altogether betraying your industrial mission. You can downsize, exploit your workers, and still perhaps produce a perfectly fine widget. Maybe the quality will suffer a little, but you're still making widgets, and you keep doing business in more or less the same way. In a nonprofit service institution, however, like a hospital or a university, this style of management, of exploitation, invariably changes the nature of the product. You are no longer making the same thing when you make it via bandit management. Hospitals, for example, are attempting to eliminate their nursing staffs. They eliminate educated nurses and replace them with people earning the minimum wage who are only minimally trained. You don't have the same health care when you do that. You have something else. It's not even *care* when you do that. It's a different product. I would say that whenever you underpay and underappreciate service workers — nurses, teaching assistants, and so on — you get a different product from them than you might have gotten otherwise.

In a university, something even more sinister happens. Here the justification for the cutbacks is that you'll get better education; you'll have finer scholarship if you reduce labor costs. But the nature of education changes when you do these things. It's not the same education. When Yale, in the name of finer scholarship, sets a goal of paying its food workers ten thousand dollars a year, and those workers have to go on welfare to survive their summers off, the institution is telling its students that their convenience outweighs the most basic economic needs of people around them, people they see every day. The students learn, in other words, that some lives are valued a lot more than others. And somehow, since it is such a fine institution making these judgments and treating its workers this way, it's all OK. So this is what students learn in a place that purports to teach the world's most noble philosophical traditions, that teaches the humanities while ignoring the humanity of its own employees and part of its teaching staff.

What you learn at Yale is the moral numbness of compartmentalization. You learn that ethics and fine ideals belong in seminars and in books but not in dining halls, laboratories, offices, or other places where people mingle. When Yale employs a notorious union-busting law firm and brings in a union-busting security firm, you learn that civil discourse and relationships of integrity end when the seminar is over. You learn that these values do not apply or extend to the great majority of working people around you. Yet these people are the majority of your fellow citizens.

Now maybe these are the lessons that you need to learn in order to function in a bandit economy — lessons of arrogance, lessons of moral indifference, and ultimately lessons of brutality. You could argue that the university's function is not to challenge the larger society but to mirror it and reproduce it, to produce another generation of morally numb and indifferent leaders who can graduate and do the same thing in the larger world. You could say that, no matter how cruel and exploitative that larger world becomes, the university should continue to mirror it. You could argue that a university in a bandit economy must produce the bandit chieftains who will carry on the work of further enriching the already rich without conscience or remorse. Now, if the purpose of the university is simply to mirror and reflect what's going on in the country, then Yale's treatment of GESO and Locals 34 and 35 (the unions representing, respectively, Yale's clerical and technical workers and its service and maintenance workers) is the right thing; it is teaching the right lesson. But I would have to say, as an outsider, as a person who can only look with envy at Yale's scholarly and intellectual resources, that it is an appalling shame to use such resources in that way. Why should the knowledge, creativity, energy, and brilliance that this institution contains be used to further an economic trend that is grinding down the majority of our fellow citizens (white-collar as well as blue- and pink-collar), keeping them slaves to economic anxiety, day-to-day financial stress, unmet needs, and, in an increasing number of cases, genuine poverty? Wouldn't it be more worthwhile for Yale to set an ethical example for the rest of the world by demonstrating what a community can look like if it's based on reason, mutual respect, and commitment to honor each individual's contribution, whether that contribution consists of grading papers, giving lectures, keyboarding exams, or cooking food in the dining halls?

I want to end on a personal note. A few years ago my daughter matriculated at Yale Law School, and I was very proud of her. I was proud to say, I will admit, that I have a daughter at Yale. Two and one-half years after she matriculated, Yale became engaged in a ruthless struggle against its own graduate students and employees, and my daughter became engaged in nonstop strike support. Witnessing that, I wasn't proud of Yale, but I sure was proud of my daughter.

Will Teach for Food

Figure 2. Poster designed by Trip McCrossin for a Yale teach-in

Introduction
Between Crisis and Opportunity: The Future of the Academic Workplace

Cary Nelson

> *"In the summer of 1995 I was diagnosed with breast cancer and had a mastectomy. As a part-time teacher paid per course, I had no health benefits that would enable me to take paid medical leave. I needed money to live on, so that fall I taught five courses at three different schools while taking chemotherapy."*
>
> —Long-term part-time college teacher

> *"We have people who've been teaching part-time for us for fifteen years. They still think they'll get a full-time job. I tell them, 'Don't count on it.' "*
>
> —Department head in 1996

> *These non-tenure track positions have always been problematic for us. The pay is poor, the workload heavy, the room for development and growth narrow, and the future prospects a dead end. Those in these positions have often become demoralized as well as frustrated and injured, especially when they hope, in vain, for the temporary positions to become permanent. Yet as long as people are willing to take these jobs at these salaries, and as long as the administration can see this, these positions will be with us.*
>
> —February 1996 English department memo from a flagship state university

As universities struggle with increasingly constrained budgets, the temptation to make ends meet by exploiting more vulnerable employees grows daily. Industry meanwhile provides a handbook of relevant strategies and techniques: make paying workers as little as possible a basic managerial principle and goal; deny employee benefits any time you can get away with it; disguise your responsibility for the most abused workers by subcontracting for their services; during contract negotiations offer nothing until frustration peaks, then make generous salary and job security offers to long-term employees on condition they agree to decrease their numbers through attrition; establish multiple tiers for compensation, hiring all new employees on substantially lower salaries; break existing unions and fight recognition for new ones; collude with other CEOs and governing boards to establish industry-wide standards for maximum exploitation; take advantage of any weaknesses in the local economy; minimize what different classes of employees know about each other's compensation; promote an ideology of loyalty, dedication, and service dependent on self-denial; establish a climate of vulnerability, job insecurity, and competing interests. Of course many financially healthy and successful corporations adopt these ruthless strategies simply to increase their profits. Here and there across the country a wealthy private college or university does the same; one of those, as we will show in the first half of the book, is Yale University, which impoverishes workers simply to raise its already comfortable profit margin and enlarge its five-billion-dollar endowment. Perhaps Yale should change the motto on its university seal to read "America's foremost robber baron university."

This is the dark underside of academic employment. Increasingly, that underside is becoming one of higher education's major modes of operation. Over the last two decades the percentage of college and university teaching done by underpaid part-time faculty across the country has risen to about 45 percent. Very few schools hire their own part-time faculty for permanent positions when they open up, so these part-timers instead become a permanent underclass. Meanwhile, the business community considers the extensive use of part-time or adjunct faculty to be evidence of good financial management. Bond-rating services express concern if colleges do not have a high enough percentage of part-time employees; they make for "flexibility," a code word referring to the ability to hire and fire employees at will to meet changing needs and changing budgets.

The gradual shift to part-time teachers has accompanied a gradual reduction in the percentage of tenured or tenure-track faculty, the only faculty members with reasonable guarantees of free speech and with a significant role in institutional governance. Across the country, many institutions that do not hire part-timers to teach introductory courses instead hire graduate assistants to teach them. What part-timers, graduate assistants, and adjunct faculty all have in common is that they are substantially less costly to hire. Their pay rate ranges from $1,000 to $3,000 per course; most beginning full-time faculty in the humanities receive from $5,000 to $9,000 per course.

What is clear from the national picture is this: higher education as a whole has become structurally dependent on a pool of cheap labor to teach its lower-level courses. The economic structure largely erases the status differences between part-timers and graduate assistants; economics thus also exposes the claim that graduate assistants are not employees for what it is: a cynical lie. Part-timers, adjuncts, and graduate assistants are filling the same role in the university — teaching the same courses — and doing so for the same economic reasons. Indeed, the long-term collapse of the academic job market means that most graduate students can no longer look forward to tenure-track jobs. When they finish their Ph.D.'s, they may actually have to turn to still lower-paid part-time employment. A University of Illinois graduate student, earning about $2,800 per course, received her Ph.D. in 1996 and went on to part-time teaching at $1,200 per course, well under subsistence level.

Although the shift to expendable teachers has the most serious academic consequences for higher education, it is actually part of a more general shift in campus employment patterns. Downsizing, subcontracting, outsourcing — all the terms familiar from news stories about American industry in the last decade — have made their way into campus discourse and administrative planning. Part-time maintenance and cafeteria workers are usually cheaper and less uppity than full-time workers in the same jobs. In addition to receiving lower wages, they may not get health care or retirement benefits. That all this can make colleges insecure, oppressive, and embittered places to work does not seem to trouble those who recommend these changes. When colleges are one of the major employers in a community, shifting to underpaid and disposable workers may set the pattern for the whole area, impoverishing all lower-paid workers and pervasively destabilizing family life. But

CEO-wanna-be administrators and board members can often see no reason to refuse these cost-saving opportunities.

Yet if the campus-wide adoption of marginal employment makes it an increasingly probable future for more and more of the higher education workforce, it also provides hitherto unrecognized grounds for building interested coalitions for resistance. Faculty members have long assumed a great gulf in status separates them from campus blue-collar laborers. But part-time faculty and cafeteria workers have a good deal in common. Moreover, even full-time faculty and workers lose relative authority when their numbers are reduced and their jobs are outsourced or given to part-timers. Permanent faculty, adjunct faculty, graduate students, secretaries, and maintenance workers suddenly acquire common interests and reasons to build working alliances. Improbably enough, the academy has become a place to build workplace solidarity that crosses class lines. That is the source of the "opportunity" referred to in my title. *Will Teach for Food* is a book devoted to both the deepening crisis and the increasing opportunity. Its title identifies the condition we urge everyone to resist. All the contributors believe those employees who cannot negotiate better salaries and working conditions as individuals should consider collective bargaining as an alternative. More than that, the contributors all see the debates over these issues as a way to revive critical reflection about the mission of higher education and the community responsibilities of individual institutions.

Indeed the two aims are interwoven. There has been a long-standing conflict in academe between individual and collective notions of identity, a conflict intensified when salary and reward systems are instituted and put into practice. In the decades since World War II, during the rise of the research university, academic culture at many such institutions has connected all collective action not only with debased forms of popular culture but also with the rejected mass political movements that swept across the 1930s. That this repugnance was partly a disempowering and self-deceiving ideology installed during the heyday of McCarthyism most academics seem willing to forget. Certainly the inability to evaluate collective action or distinguish one form of mass politics from another has often made academics ineffective. Meanwhile, the professoriat has been filled with middle-class people who do need to be concerned about issues like compensation; the days of the wealthy scholar who could care less about salary or benefits are long gone. More importantly, the general inability of faculty to act collectively now threatens the existence of the university as we know it; certainly it threatens any sustained commitment to the centrality of a liberal arts mission.

Must individual ambition and a concern for the common welfare always be unalterably opposed to each other? Judging from the public sphere one would think not; there is no lack of cases supporting both the mutuality and the incompatibility of these impulses. And certainly many classes in the academy send a different message. But a good many practices at our most prestigious institutions, including Yale, suggest these are warring impulses that cannot both be institutionally honored.

Many academic institutions now set salaries and rewards hierarchically — by a combination of disciplinary patterns, individual negotiation, and analysis of individual achievement and merit. At the same time there are numerous institutions where merit plays no significant role, and rewards are mostly universal. In the repeated (and continuing) constrained budgets of the last twenty-five years, there was and is often not enough money both to give everyone decent yearly salary increases and to recognize exceptional merit. So either an awkward compromise is made or the college decides to honor one principle and ignore the other. If collective bargaining is to make further headway at the most distinguished institutions, the special nature of academic labor needs to be recognized and new and better ways of balancing these two value systems need to be found.

At my own school, the University of Illinois, there are, for example, notable awards for outstanding teaching. In my own department alone, several faculty members have won a college teaching award that adds a six-thousand-dollar permanent increase to their salary. I would hate to see that form of recognition be abandoned. We also make a serious effort to reward scholarly accomplishments. I know something of the consequences of not doing so, because I know faculty members who teach under union contracts that allow no significant rewards for publication. To publish book after book with no institutional recognition is highly alienating. On the other hand, a ruthless merit system can leave some faculty members nearly impoverished. Indeed, where no collective forms of agency and action exist, even universal considerations like health care, retirement rules, child care, and other benefits may receive no effective advocacy. An administration committed to the idea that those stars who deserve salary increases will earn them and the rest need no consideration may not even make money for salary increases a high priority. A small pool of funds may be enough to fund exceptional merit if it is the only priority. Meanwhile, the loss of tenured faculty nationwide is undermining basic academic freedom and may shift curriculum control to administrators without disciplinary expertise. Collective action may be the only way faculty can continue to have an impact on the aims and methods of higher education. It is certainly the only way to prevent tenure from being undermined or eliminated.

Where all doubts about the conflict between individual and collective action should disappear, however, is over collective bargaining for those employees paid by group rates who have no power of individual negotiation. Underpaid, overworked, and undervalued, such employees may sometimes be deceived into thinking a better future and fair compensation are around the corner. But the collapse of the academic job market means that the overwhelming majority of graduate students, part-timers, and adjunct faculty will face either a worsening future or no future at all within the academy. It is time for them to secure a better present; *that* they can do only with collective bargaining. Without collective bargaining as an element in the decision-making process, even the most well-intentioned administrators will never shift enough resources to improve the lot of these marginal employees significantly. Too many other powerful constituencies have claims on the same dollars.

At my own institution, administrators, recognizing that teaching assistants (TAs) are underpaid, have regularly given them 1 or 2 percent additional salary raises. These administrators feel they have done all they can and that these TAs should be grateful. On the first point, the campus administration is correct: given present power relations that is probably all they can do, which is why TAs need to organize and gain a role in negotiations. As for feeling indebted, well, this pattern of increases might actually make a difference in twenty-five or thirty years. Until then, TAs will be unable to make it through the summer on what they earn for teaching the same number of courses as faculty; moreover, at their end of the salary scale the annual cost of rent and other necessities frequently increases faster than their salary does. Thus TAs often find their finances get worse each year.

Three years ago a new senior campus administrator approached me and asked what he could do to put a stop to the graduate student union movement. He had not been around long enough to know my history of support for unionization. Further, since I had published a presentable number of books and essays and held a named chair, he assumed I would be opposed to unionization. Rather than set him right, I decided to answer his question: "Guarantee all TAs a two-thousand-dollar summer fellowship." He nodded; the idea had come up before, and everyone had long since agreed that summer support for TAs should be a priority. It seems clear to me that if graduate students form a union, such a shift in priorities will probably occur.

Graduate students who become active in collective bargaining campaigns often find that they do not have to make a choice between pursuing their individual careers and committing themselves to the common welfare; it is possible to do both. They also typically discover new skills, strengths, and resources within themselves, capacities they take with them whatever they do next. Yet many part-timers and graduate students feel too vulnerable to make an overt commitment to collective bargaining. Others have been so fully positioned within the university's hierarchical and paternalistic culture that they feel they deserve only those benefits freely given by higher authorities. Some, finally, feel irrationally that their future identity as independent intellectual subjects and entrepreneurs will be compromised by taking on a collective identity now. They need to be approached by organizers from similar backgrounds, and often they need to be seen at home, not at work.

On the one hand, phone campaigns are not of much use in such efforts, nor is literature alone unless it is supplemented by close personal relationships with people committed to collective bargaining from the same department. On the other hand, good literature and compelling graphics can make a difference. Consider Gary Huck's clever cartoon on the cover of a brochure issued by the Campaign to Organize Graduate Students at the University of

Graduate Employees Need a Union

COGS

Campaign to Organize Graduate Students

Figure 3. Cover of an organizing brochure issued by University of Iowa students. Cartoon by Gary Huck for the Pittsburgh local of the United Electrical, Radio, and Machine Workers of America

Figure 4. Jenny Schmid's design for the Graduate Employees Organization at the University of Michigan

Iowa (fig. 3). A beleaguered TA grading stacks of exams or papers repeats in parallel seriality the absurd lesson learned from supervisors: "I'm not a worker. . . . I'm not a worker." Or consider Jenny Schmid's empowering image designed for the Graduate Employees Organization at the University of Michigan. A clenched fist, once employed by the Industrial Workers of the World and later adopted as the symbol of the antifascist popular front in the 1930s, is here adapted to academic unionism. It has been issued in a bold version visible from a distance (fig. 4) and in a more subtly modulated version for viewing on the Internet. There, arrayed like a constellation against the starry night, the fist becomes an object of political idealization: a clenched hand holds a pencil, and from it spring bolts of lightning made possible by collective action. And a series of clever GESO (Graduate Employees and Students Organization) posters by Kathy Newman adapt drawings from children's books to play New Haven's present less-than-utopian setting off against the collective dreams for change the union is proposing; one shows Alice grown

Figure 5. A fall 1994 poster from the Yale Graduate Employees and Students Organization

too large for Yale's fallen wonderland as she reaches outward for relief and freedom (fig. 5).

The next decade is certain to see increasing numbers of drives for unionization among graduate students and part-timers, and that is one of the reasons we have put together this collection — to help all concerned see the issues more clearly. The struggle can be a difficult one, in part because organizing efforts and legal battles can take years and new leaders must thus be regularly identified. They will have many hard lessons to learn, among them the lesson that intelligent and hardworking administrators will often be their antagonists in a union drive. They can expect misleading and threatening statements from the administration; they can expect opposition in court; and they can expect an especially ruthless antiunion campaign in the weeks just prior to a vote on collective bargaining. As a result of that pressure, a significant minority of those who sign union pledge cards will end up voting against representation. To protect against that danger, a 60 to 70 percent commitment from the members of a prospective bargaining unit is good insurance, as are repeated conversations with all who have signed. The more people who can be brought forward to make actual commitments of time, energy, or money, the more people who take public stands, the stronger will be the chance of success. Affiliation with a national union that has financial resources for organizing and perhaps for a strike fund is also often necessary. Graduate assistants at the Universities of Kansas, Michigan, Oregon, and Wisconsin have affiliated themselves with the American Federation of Teachers (AFT); those at the University of Iowa have chosen the United Electrical, Radio, and Machine Workers of America (UE); those at Rutgers University are represented by the American Association of University Professors (AAUP); and those at the University of Massachusetts at Amherst have selected the United Auto Workers (UAW). Graduate student unions on the campuses of the State University of New York (SUNY) system are affiliated with the Communication Workers of America (CWA). Meanwhile, graduate employees on the five University of California campuses — in a long-running recognition battle with their administrations — have signed up with the UAW.

Assistance is also increasingly available from national networks of graduate teaching assistants and postdocs with organizing experience. In the summer of 1996 the Coalition of Graduate Employees met in Albany, New York, and on July 27 they issued a document entitled "Statement of Principles Governing Academic Employment" to serve as a national bill of rights. They wrote:

> We the Coalition of Graduate Employee Unions stand together on this Day of Action to demand recognition of, and respect for, the work of academic student employees as teachers, researchers, and staff. We call on universities to honor the following principles:

- *The Right to Organize*
    - — Recognize the results of free and fair union election; honor other evidence of majority support among academic workers.
    - — The freedom of academic student employees and other academic workers to engage in union activity free from threats, retaliation, and other forms of interference
    - — The right to strike
    - — The right to good faith negotiations
    - — The right to an enforceable collective bargaining agreement
- *Fair Working Conditions*
    - — The work of universities can only be accomplished by teachers who are fairly compensated, who are fully included in university governance, and who are protected from discrimination and attacks on academic freedom through tenure or other job security provisions
    - — The right to a living wage
    - — The right to health care
    - — The right to child care
- *Affirmative Action and Equity*
    - — A safe workplace and classroom free from discrimination or harassment on the basis of gender, race, national origin, class, or sexual orientation
    - — The necessity of affirmative action in outreach, recruitment, retention, admissions, funding, hiring, and contracting
    - — Expanded affirmative action programs and additional mechanisms to protect the civil rights of academic student employees
- *Respect for International Students*
    - — Recognition of the value of the contributions of international scholars
    - — Fair and equal access to teaching opportunities

- — A safe workplace free from discrimination or harassment in hiring procedures, job allocation, employment criteria, salary, benefits, and training
- *Accessibility*
  - — Adequate support for public education to make it affordable
  - — Increased retention rates of graduate students
  - — Tuition waivers for all academic student employees

The distance we have to go in realizing these goals gives some indication of how troubled the academic workplace is. I like to think that there are some administrators who might secretly welcome being compelled to honor some of these principles. Certainly on my own campus a number of the upper-level administrators are honorable and talented. On many issues — such as the drive to improve the quality of the faculty — I have been their ally. But on the issue of graduate student unionization we part company. I cannot help but reflect on the fact that I am sending the manuscript of this book to the press the same week I am giving sworn testimony before the Illinois Labor Relations Board on behalf of the Graduate Employees Organization at my university, an act some senior administrators will not appreciate. I would rather see administrators align themselves with us in an effort to make the academy a model American workplace. Failing that, action and education are the only alternatives, and *Will Teach for Food* is one piece of that national effort.

The first section of the book offers an extended analysis of the widely publicized union conflicts at Yale University during the 1995–96 academic year, especially the graduate assistants' grade strike in December 1995 and January 1996. After some years of quietly negotiating job issues for graduate students, the emerging union there sought to open negotiations with the administration about the possibility of holding a vote for formal recognition as a bargaining agent. The administration refused to talk with union representatives; after months of unsuccessful approaches, the union decided to withhold the semester's grades as a protest. Taking a page from Ronald Reagan's decertification of the flight controllers' union, faculty and administrators at Yale made clear their intention of firing graduate assistants engaged in this rather modest job action. In one of the more remarkable documents of the season — a 1996 letter to all thirty-five thousand members of the Modern Language Association (MLA) — Yale English professor Annabel Patterson declared that Yale would have been willing to talk with the graduate students except for their willful transgression of a basic theological truth: they violated their professional identities by affiliating themselves with cafeteria workers. Apparently Patterson assumed MLA members would see this as a vulgar impropriety. Meanwhile, in a crude and obvious attempt to sway the membership against an MLA resolution condemning Yale, the MLA's national office forwarded Patterson's statement and five other letters attacking the union to all members. The packet of letters arrived the same week Pat Buchanan, temporarily off duty from his regular job of defending concentration camp guards and now instead running for the Republican nomination for president, heated up his populist rhetoric about unemployed and underpaid workers. As the Yale graduate assistants faced a jobless present, both the MLA and most Yale faculty were now proudly positioned to the right of Pat Buchanan.

Protest and analysis followed from around the country, and we present the first substantial gathering of it here. In the foreword, Barbara Ehrenreich opens the book with a brief but compelling warning about the pedagogical meaning of the Yale administration's union-busting efforts. Part I then opens with three essays by people deeply involved in Yale's union history. John Wilhelm, a Yale graduate who was a leading figure in Locals 34 and 35 in the 1970s and 1980s, provides some of the essential background to the current conflict, reviewing highlights of three decades of union history in New Haven. Then GESO members Corey Robin and Michelle Stephens offer an unusual personal account of how several graduate students reacted to organizing efforts; they talk about how these students' varied backgrounds helped shape their attitudes toward collective action and how over time their views did or did not change. This essay will help people understand how union organizing takes place among academics and will give others help with their own organizing efforts. The next essay also mixes political reflection with practical experience; Kathy M. Newman, another GESO activist, analyzes both the public image of graduate students and the union's efforts to intervene in that image and change it. Part of the essay also describes the way GESO uses graphic images to build solidarity and raise political awareness among its constituency. We move then to four focused position papers about the events of 1995 and 1996. Rick Wolff interrogates the social and economic aims and effects of Yale's corporate policy, while Duncan Kennedy reviews the legal and generational differences at stake in union organizing and collective action, Andrew Ross describes the larger aims of academic unionization, and Robin D. G. Kelley places the Yale struggle in a larger political, racial, and historical context. Michael Bérubé closes part I by providing the first thorough reading of the rhetoric and politics of widespread faculty antagonism toward GESO and its effort to gain recognition as a bargaining agent for Yale graduate students. The essay mounts an intricate analysis and condemnation of faculty reaction at Yale and should empower those encountering similar resistance elsewhere.

Part II reaches beyond Yale to address the general conditions of academic labor, mixing broad analysis with case histories. Stanley Aronowitz offers an opening overview of the history of and prospects for academic unions, setting academic unionization in the general context of the changing character of higher education. Daniel Czitrom reflects on his own experience in the Teaching Assistants Association at the University of Wisconsin, the first major U.S. graduate student union, and explores the impact the experience has had on his subsequent career as a faculty member. Aronowitz and Czitrom both also confront the paradoxes and ambivalences historically at stake in white-collar unionism and its struggle over group action versus individual achievement. Stephen Watt's carefully documented essay explodes the myth of graduate student apprenticeship and reveals the pertinence of the less flattering metaphor that compares academic life to life in a company town. James Sullivan's essay, "The Scarlet *L*," is an excruciating account of how one university created and filled positions for second-class teachers. Linda Ray Pratt and Karen Thompson describe the national situation for part-time or adjunct faculty and the potential they have to organize themselves. Pratt demonstrates how universities have used part-time employment as a management strategy, while Thompson identifies higher education's broad reliance on a reserve labor pool and reports on a successful organizing effort at Rutgers. Finally, Ellen Schrecker discusses the increasingly relevant question of how technological opportunities may affect academic workers in the future.

Although the conflicts in New Haven in 1995–96 have been widely publicized, it will be useful to review them briefly here. One of the notable effects of both the press accounts and the formation of networks of concerned faculty and students in the months leading up to the strike was the high degree of national participation in many of these events. In December 1995, for example, along with hundreds of other faculty members around the country, I wrote to Yale's president, Richard Levin, to urge him to negotiate with GESO, which was then trying to open a dialogue with his administration:

> I recently visited Yale to give a talk at the opening session of a conference on "the university in the public eye." Now Yale is very much in the public eye as it considers whether to honor traditional academic commitments to negotiation and dialogue and agree to talk with representatives of GESO, its graduate student employees union. In its last well-publicized experience with unionization — the long-running confrontation with its clerical workers — Yale opted to stonewall rather than talk. In that struggle Yale's president was part of the problem, not part of the solution. I am writing to urge you to show the vision and leadership to write a different story this time around, a story of cooperation and conversation.
>
> Higher education faces at least a decade of limited resources in which a depressed job market places extraordinary pressures on graduate education. The days when graduate students could eliminate $25,000 of debt after a few years of teaching are over, for many current graduate students will not find tenure-track jobs. As a result, pressures to treat teaching assistants as term employees will continue to increase. The real impulse toward unionization derives from the national economy and from social and political priorities in the public sphere; these things are outside your control. You cannot break the graduate student will to win recognition because its sources are nationwide. The problem you now face will not disappear. Yale has an opportunity to respond with humanity and thoughtfulness, to devote the rather modest resources necessary to address students' warranted concerns, and to establish a collegial pattern other schools can follow. Or Yale can once again teach us all a lesson the other way — by showing us once again how *not* to handle a labor dispute.

> When I was at Yale this September I had occasion to meet with about ten of the students active in GESO. I was struck that here was a group of articulate young men and women of diverse ethnic, racial, and economic backgrounds working together in a cause based on principle and a commitment to community. Future classes of students — not the organizers themselves — would be the most likely beneficiaries of their efforts. Meanwhile I was seeing the kind of multicultural alliance that not only higher education but also the country as a whole very much needs. Someone in authority at Yale needs to recognize that all of you have reason to be proud of GESO, not to demonize it.
>
> Finally, let me suggest that carrying out reprisals for traditional job actions like withholding grades would be the worst possible message you could send. I urge you to negotiate with GESO and help heal the Yale community, not fracture it further.

As anyone who follows the national news knows, Yale's president did not take the advice he received from faculty members all across the country. Indeed, he had strong local reasons *not* to do so, for the members of the powerful group that governs Yale, the Yale Corporation, Yale's aptly chosen name for its equivalent of a traditional board of trustees, along with the administration and the overwhelming majority of the Yale faculty were, as the faculty itself put it in a December resolution, "of one mind." The mind-set at the top of Yale's hierarchy in the winter of 1995–96 was never ambiguous: break the union and punish those who resist administrative authority. What some on the faculty were not aware of, despite their being of "one mind" with the administration, was that the administration and the Yale Corporation also intended to break Locals 34 and 35 of the Hotel Employees and Restaurant Employees International Union, the unions representing, respectively, Yale's clerical and technical workers and its service and maintenance workers.

The group of workers who would eventually become Local 35 had been organized and had been growing slowly in various incarnations since the late 1930s. Their relations with Yale were reasonably congenial until the university tried to break the union in 1968. A series of strikes, each longer than the last, followed through the 1970s, as the union tried to hold its ground. In 1977, however, the possibility of increased union strength arose when efforts to organize Yale's clerical and technical workers began. That drive gathered force in 1980 when Local 35 committed its resources and its business manager, John Wilhelm, to the organizing effort. Local 34 finally won a contract early in 1985, after a widely publicized ten-week strike had paralyzed the campus at the end of 1984.[1] Meanwhile, graduate teaching assistants at Yale had organized sporadically in small ways since the 1970s. By 1990, TA Solidarity, the emerging graduate student employee group, had changed its name to the Graduate Employees and Students Organization and had allied itself with Locals 34 and 35. GESO honored the picket lines Locals 34 and 35 maintained during their 1991–92 strikes. Throughout this time — from 1971, when Yale philosophy graduate students held a successful grade strike, to 1995, when GESO adopted the same strategy — the administration became increasingly unwilling to talk with graduate student union organizers and increasingly determined to crush all campus collective bargaining. In this struggle, the graduate students had much less support among faculty and undergraduates than did Locals 34 and 35. Still, GESO mounted its own grade strike in 1995,[2] and Local 34 went on strike early in 1996.

A brief chronology of labor history at Yale, emphasizing the most recent events, can be laid out as follows:

late 1930s	Yale's service and maintenance workers begin efforts to organize; this is the origin of Local 35. Groundskeepers affiliate with the United Mine Workers (UMW).
early 1950s	The Distributive, Processing, and Office Workers' Union fails in the first effort to organize Yale's clerical and technical employees.
1967–68	The Association of C&Ts (ACT) fails in its effort, underwritten by Local 35, to organize clerical and technical workers.
1968	Local 35, Yale's union of service and maintenance workers, which is affiliated with the Hotel Employees and Restaurant Employees International Union, goes on strike in response to Yale's effort to break the union.
1971	An independent group, the Yale Non-faculty Action Committee (YNFAC), loses a National Labor

	Relations Board (NLRB) election to become the bargaining agent for clerical and technical workers. Local 35 goes on strike again; its members are beaten in a New Haven police riot. Teaching assistants in philosophy withhold grades to protest low salaries.
1974	Local 35 goes on strike again.
1977	The Office and Professional Employees International Union (OPEIU) almost wins certification for clerical and technical workers in a close vote; Local 35 goes on strike once again.
1977–82	The UAW tries to organize clerical and technical workers.
1980–84	Local 34 works to organize clerical and technical workers, eventually winning full support of Local 35. Local 34 wins an NLRB election in May 1983.
Sept. 26, 1984	Local 34 begins a widely publicized ten-week strike.
1985	Local 34 wins a contract.
1987–88	Graduate students organize a group called TA Solidarity and plan a grade strike. They win concessions from Yale.
1989–92	TA Solidarity begins a new organizing campaign and affiliates with Locals 34 and 35, collectively known as the Federation of University Employees. TA Solidarity changes its name to the Graduate Employees and Students Organization in the summer of 1990. GESO sponsors a one-day walkout in December 1991 and a subsequent walkout from February 17 to 19, 1992, winning administration support for a teacher training program.
1995	April 3–7: GESO organizes a walkout in response to Yale's refusal to hold a union election. December: GESO mounts a grade strike; members refuse

to turn in the semester's grades until Yale agrees to negotiate. Yale threatens to fire (not rehire) striking TAs. The American Association of University Professors affirms graduate employees' right to organize and seek collective bargaining representation and warns Yale that reprisals are inappropriate. December 29: the Delegate Assembly of the MLA votes to censure Yale.

1996 Yale files disciplinary charges against selected GESO leaders. January 6: the Council of the American Historical Association passes a resolution warning Yale against reprisals. January 10: 133 protesters are arrested for blocking York Street on the New Haven campus on the first day of disciplinary hearings. January 15: the grade strike ends. Local 34 goes on strike. Summer 1996: MLA's members ratify the censure resolution passed earlier by the Delegate Assembly.

When Local 34 went on strike in the winter of 1995–96, Yale faculty member Hazel Carby went to President Levin to urge him to decide the issues on the basis of principles of social responsibility. Social responsibility was irrelevant, Levin replied; his decisions would be market driven. Members of the Yale Corporation were in fact incredulous that Yale gave some job benefits to its staff not offered by other New England employers. Cafeteria workers, for example, were employed year-round; the university found other work for them to do in the summer instead of letting them go on welfare. This practice, won by the unions after decades of struggle, gave such employees health benefits and job security that cost Yale money. The members of the Yale Corporation could see no reason to waste resources this way. Neither they nor Levin saw any merit in taking public pride in treating employees decently. Their notion of the university's mission did not include being a model employer and setting a humane example among regional industries. As one Yale undergraduate put it in a public forum, "The university is not taking dialogue seriously. When it comes to your pocketbook, discussion is out the window. The bottom line is the bottom line."

A majority of the faculty meanwhile considered such matters beneath their dignity and none of their concern. In their view, it is the administration's job to supply toilet paper, to heat buildings, and, apparently, to control the working conditions of all nonacademic employees *privileged* to work at Yale. For many faculty all these are equivalent matters; they can see no difference between them, no community principles at stake that might require that they listen to the voice of exploited nonacademic employees. But many of those who teach classes at the best and the worst of our institutions are increasingly being exploited in much the same way. One of the lessons of the Yale strikes has been the alliances some groups of academic and nonacademic employees have formed, the efforts they have made to support one another and understand their common interests. Such alliances, historically uncommon, are likely, as I suggested above, to multiply over the next decade. If they do not, higher education will be a diminished and less effective enterprise. The democratic, participatory organizations that university-based unions are building are critical to the future of American education and perhaps to American workers in general.

We are entering a period when labor and academia can help each another. That they have not done so for decades, however, is no accident. My own account of their relative estrangement would put some blame on both sides, but it would start with the late 1940s, when much of American labor began the wholesale purge of the Left from its ranks. It was not merely Communist Party members who found themselves violently cast out of labor's ranks in the 1940s and 1950s, though the purge took place under the banner of anticommunism, but all members allied with the Left. In the process, labor lost many of the idealists in its ranks, many of those who saw unions as forces to promote social justice and general welfare. Meanwhile, as the purge spread and became more complete, labor effectively became an agent of state power at its most repressive. The notorious bureaucratization of large-scale labor unions came about in part to facilitate the political control and cleansing of its membership. When, in the next decade, the Vietnam War buildup began and a campus-based protest movement gathered force, labor was ill-prepared to see the issues clearly. Steeped in anticommunism, many unions reacted to support for North Vietnam with the most visceral antagonism. Meanwhile, with many issues of social justice effectively red-baited, labor focused narrowly on salaries, workplace rules, and benefits.

Now all this has changed. The fall of the Soviet Union has made anticommunism irrelevant, and it has made it easier for labor once again to embrace the wider social mission that inspired so many of its supporters earlier in the century. And college students in turn are more readily drawn to a movement more widely devoted to the public good. Certainly the economic crisis in higher education justifiably motivates many, but economics alone has not made these new alliances possible.

Nor has labor's conservatism been the only impediment. For decades academe has fostered an idiot-savant culture among its faculty. A professor maintains eloquent expertise in a subdisciplinary specialization and comical ignorance about every other area of life. In boom times this worked well enough, but academe has not seen boom times since the 1960s. Now its fundamental commitment to academic freedom is being restricted to a smaller and smaller percentage of its workforce, as tenured and tenure-track faculty positions are decreased and as expendable part-timers, adjuncts, and teaching assistants are hired in their place.

Meanwhile, except for some small liberal arts colleges, most faculties have maintained no ongoing conversation about the nature and social function of higher education. In the current long-term crisis, that is a conversation we desperately need to be having. Interestingly enough, its only vital presence at large institutions may be among those involved in unionization movements. These groups are driven to ask the sorts of questions all of us need to raise: What is the mission of the university? How should increasingly scarce university resources be used? Does the university's mission encompass its employee relations, or are the two matters separate? Is it part of the mission of a great university to impoverish the community in which it is based? What does it mean for a university to talk about social responsibility in its courses and then refuse to practice it? These are questions *all* members of a university community need to confront; they cannot be left to administrators and the business leaders who often dominate boards of trustees.

Unfortunately, the response of administrators nationwide to such challenges has been either defensive or deceptive. When I met with the senior campus administrators at the University of California at

San Diego in 1996 as part of an outside evaluation team, the issue of teaching assistant working conditions came up for detailed discussion. Graduate teaching assistants had given us detailed reports about which courses and disciplines produced workloads substantially beyond the hours for which they were being paid; they made no overarching claims but rather specific complaints about particular problem courses and programs. Yet one senior administrator immediately responded by saying, "These graduate assistants have been trained by the union to lie about how many hours they work."

There has indeed been some deception in these matters, but it has come mostly from administrators. Universities persist in claiming graduate students teach as part of their doctoral training, not as employees, even though higher education is pervasively dependent on cheap instructional labor, with graduate assistants, postdocs, adjuncts, part-timers, or a mix of the above teaching exactly the same introductory courses on campus after campus. In the case of graduate teaching assistants, many of whom teach fifteen to twenty-five courses over six or seven years, the learning curve peaks years before the work ceases.

Campus debates or court cases in which administrators insist that graduate teaching assistants are *only* students, not employees, when they are self-evidently *both,* are thus debates conducted in bad faith. That bad faith lays the ground for long-term distrust and suggests to the general public that campus administrators lie like politicians.

Administrative bad faith, unfortunately, has been especially notable at Yale, both in actions taken and in statements disseminated. Consider, for example, the real and symbolic effects of the decision to hire union-busting security guards from Cleveland to police the New Haven campus during the 1995–96 year. At a February 1996 moratorium, history professor David Montgomery, a distinguished labor historian and long-time union supporter, reported walking to his car one day in February and hearing three of these hired thugs bragging that they had taunted one of the Yale workers until it provoked a confrontation. "That is the mission for which they have prepared," he added, "the mission for which they were hired. It's part and parcel of the university's negotiating strategy. The presence of hired guards symbolizes the atmosphere of intimidation and silence that the administration enforces." At the same February meeting a law student rose to offer a different sort of testimony: "I think we have more than a right; we have an obligation to ask for more of this university than prestige and resources. We have a right to ask for this university to be the thing that we believe it should be. Just because we are here does not mean we have to be silent."

Wherever one stands on these issues, it is clear that the conflicts at Yale have been especially stark and instructive. On the one hand, Yale graduate students, including those with essays in this book, have been consistently articulate about their experience. On the other hand, antiunion Yale faculty and administrators have been remarkably unembarrassed, resolute, and self-righteous in ways that are equally instructive. Yale, then, intensifies the audibility of problems that are emerging nationwide, which is why it is the focus of the first half of this book.

One element of Yale's situation, however, is atypical: the university is flush with cash; it turns a profit every year. That does not prevent its chief administrators from claiming financial crisis, but they are quite simply lying when they do so. In an ideal world, Yale might well be required to share some of its vast endowment with other worthy and more needy institutions of higher education. If the country is committed to income redistribution, why not endowment redistribution? Meanwhile, by treating its reinvested profits as *expenses* — a practice that could land individual taxpayers in jail — Yale manages to pretend it is broke when actually its financial health could hardly be better. The rhetoric sounds plausible because so much of higher education actually is in financial trouble, but in Yale's case it is a dishonorable and unconscionable lie. I choose those strong terms advisedly, because Yale uses this falsehood to justify impoverishing its workers and denying them benefits and job security. As a result, it throws all of higher education's public pronouncements into moral crisis.

For what? American unions rarely revolutionize existing structures; they tend rather to rationalize them. Certainly the educational and research values that faculty and graduate students share are in no threat from a graduate teaching assistants' union; they may even be enhanced by more democratic participation in the process of defining the university's mission and deciding how to distribute its resources. Existing campus unions have won better compensation and security for their members, and only a ruthlessly exploitative mentality finds that regrettable. Meanwhile, graduate students, secretaries, adjunct faculty, and maintenance workers alike have no way to improve their situations except to negotiate collectively. It is not, however, the ultimate desirability of unions that faculty and administrators must first accept, but rather the right these employees have to determine for themselves whether they want union representation.

It is only from one limited perspective, then, that Levin, the Yale Corporation, and their allies among the faculty would appear to have won. They successfully crushed the grade strike by making it clear they would fire all participating teaching assistants. With no strike fund and no savings, the TAs were completely dependent on their next paycheck; enough capitulated so that the strike became pointless. But from another perspective, all Levin won is the right to continue exploiting a labor force that is now even more alienated than before. GESO is back doing advocacy for graduate students in individual departments and organizing its constituency. And these are the very employees Yale must continue to depend on in the future. If the administration reduces wages and benefits for other employees, as it intends to do, then as New Haven's largest employer it will set a scorched-earth example for every other local firm. The city will become even less economically viable than it is now. Meanwhile, all Yale's unions will work toward another, inevitably more hostile, confrontation. It is no way to handle a labor dispute.

Part I ("A Yale Strike Dossier") of this book is very much a collaborative effort. Earlier versions of six of the essays were presented at Yale on February 28, 1996, at a symposium moderated by Debby Applegate and organized by her and other GESO members. At my request, she sent me those essays—by Ehrenreich, Wilhelm, Wolff, Kennedy, Ross, and Kelley—and I then contacted the authors and invited them to revise and expand their talks for publication. Meanwhile, Michael Denning at Yale made the first contact with Robin and Stephens to suggest they contribute to the project. Kathy Newman, who has been my regular GESO contact for several years, supplied me with videotapes of the February events for additional transcription. Andrew Ross and Bruce Robbins, *Social Text* editors on the front lines of the culture wars, have offered continual encouragement and advice, as has Lisa Freeman of the University of Minnesota Press.

Throughout the book, the contributors have aimed to provide both sustained analysis and practical advice. We support the effort to organize academe's exploited workers, and we want both to reflect on its progress and to offer readers help in their own local struggles. The stories people tell here about their own and others' organizing experiences should help ongoing organizing efforts across the country. This book makes no pretense, then, about being a neutral collection. Its analyses are reasoned and thoughtful, but they make no effort to give equal time to the conviction that it is morally acceptable to impoverish some groups of campus workers. A campus-wide commitment to fairness or exploitation eventually affects everything a university does — from its teaching and research to its groundskeeping and maintenance. No realm is exempt from the impact of a ruthless policy of impoverishing lower-grade workers. We offer *Will Teach for Food* as a call for increased involvement and moral responsibility. Students and faculty need to compel upper-level administrators to honor principles of fairness and justice in the workplace.

Does this mean that every selective budget cut should be resisted, that every job and every program should be protected? Some believe that across-the-board cuts in the face of decreased budgets make for equity and solidarity and are the only fair and non-divisive policy. There is no question that differential downsizing has great risks and provokes power struggles. But my own experience suggests that some units should be selectively reduced in size or terminated. At my own campus we recently closed a computing services division that had become obsolete after the campus mostly abandoned a decades-old mainframe system. The people in the unit had resisted shifting their allegiance to new technology such as personal computers. As a result, the university was paying several million dollars a year to fund a unit with a steadily diminishing role. It was time to use the money elsewhere. I raise this issue here because it is for the most part not relevant to the book as a whole. Our focus is not on the gradual alterations in job priorities that accompany social and technological changes but rather on the fundamental way that higher education does its business. We are concerned with the treatment of large classes of employees and with the impact employment policy has on the educational process.

Consider a different kind of example — two midwestern university campuses thinking about closing their car rental and repair operations and leasing vehicles instead. Both found they could save money that way, and the campus in a medium-sized city with low unemployment made the change without incident. But the campus in a small town met with protests. The difference was in the nature of the communities, the first a city where the job loss had little economic impact, the other a town where the jobs mattered. Thus, although there are issues subject to universal standards, like health care or the excessive use of part-time faculty, the ethics of downsizing can be somewhat relative. A university needs to make such decisions in the light of its relations to and impact on the community, and the community as a whole needs to be involved.

Most tenured faculty members have never thought about, let alone intervened in, such matters. Should they care that the college retirement plan leaves lower-paid workers with only a few thousand dollars a year to live on after decades of service? Well, one answer is that all employees are increasingly interdependent, that policies tried for one group of employees will eventually make their way elsewhere. The more difficult arguments to put forward successfully may be moral and ethical ones, though in higher education idealism and social responsibility also have links to self-image and self-interest. Of course the victims of exploitation in academe are increasingly aware of their situation, even if they persist in thinking that ever more exaggerated hierarchies are the normal order of nature.

Surprisingly, even popular culture — in the form of Gary Trudeau's September 1996 comic strip "Doonesbury" — has taken sharp and devastating notice of the new world of academic employment. Tenured professors may be in denial, but now the average newspaper reader can get the story succinctly. In the cartoon, an administrator expresses astonishment that Walden College's finances are in the black again: "How is this possible?" The answer: "Tuition hikes plus getting rid of tenure." "Amazing — and we can still attract competent faculty?" "Trust me, sir," comes the business manager's reply, "it's a buyer's market." Indeed it is. The overproduction of Ph.D.'s has made possible not only low salaries but also the potential for undermining tenure. In Trudeau's comic strip the dean heads out in a pickup truck to hire the academic equivalent of day workers. It's only the slightest exaggeration, since higher education does depend on a reserve labor pool for last-minute hires. "What are your requirements?" the dean asks a potential employee. "A living wage, and to be treated like a human being" is the answer, but those are excessive demands, and the dean moves on. "Okay, okay, forget the human being part!" shouts the "candidate." The only thing about this conversation that misrepresents the situation in academe is the frankness of the exchange.

Current economic conditions mean that we must not leave decisions about employment policy to campus administrations. Administrators are determined to continue taking responsibility for campus working conditions, but too often that now leaves students and faculty complicit in policies they might find socially, politically, or ethically abhorrent. Ignorance is no longer a convincing reason for silent collaboration. Students and faculty have an opportunity to reflect on what it means to participate in a certain segment of the economy, to work for a particular employer. They have a chance to insist that higher education either set higher standards than other industries or emulate the worst abuses of late capitalism. Whatever happens in the next decade, the stratification of higher education is likely to increase, and the nature of work in academe is likely to change. It is a watershed moment for an enterprise that has so far mostly held on to the expanded mission it took on after World War II. If we are to resist its degradation, we will have to change not only our practices but ourselves.

NOTES

1. See Toni Gilpin, Gary Isaac, Dan Letwin, and Jack McKivigan, *On Strike for Respect: The Clerical and Technical Workers' Strike at Yale University,* 2d ed. (Urbana: University of Illinois Press, 1995).

2. See Cynthia Young, "On Strike at Yale," *minnesota review* 45–46 (1996): 179–96, for a detailed chronology of the 1995–96 grade strike.

Faculty support for GESO is somewhat stronger than it appears, in that a successful effort to intimidate and silence sympathetic assistant professors was carried out at the departmental level, where these most vulnerable faculty were warned about the consequences of taking actions favorable to GESO. I have reluctantly concluded that free speech on this subject does not exist for untenured faculty at Yale. For these actions, Yale merits the most severe condemnation. I should add, in this context, that both here and in my forthcoming book, *Manifesto of a Tenured Radical,* where I talk about Yale in detail, I have restricted my sources to tenured faculty and graduate students.

One should also recognize the unusual stress suffered by faculty who did give GESO public support. They have to continue teaching at Yale while being not only wholly alienated from the administration but also in doubt about whether the university as a whole shares any of their educational values and beliefs.

Figure 6. Poster designed by Virginia Blaisdell

Part I

A Yale Strike Dossier

Figure 7. A 1985 poster commemorating the 1984–85 strike by Local 34 at Yale. Photograph from the 1984–85 strike by Virginia Blaisdell

Chapter 1
A Short History of Unionization at Yale

John Wilhelm

As we take up the union struggles of the 1990s and beyond, we have something to learn from our history. I cannot tell the story of unionization at Yale in full detail here, but I want to recall some of its highlights, so that we can all keep them in mind. Along the way I will also offer some observations about how Yale is governed and about labor in the academy.

In 1938, George Butler, a Methodist minister in New Haven, wrote a report on working conditions at Yale. His account contains surprising parallels with the struggles of the 1990s. Among the comments Butler made were these: "The maids, most of the janitors, and all of the gate men work a seven-day week. Practically all service employees work intolerably long hours. None receive adequate compensation. Since almost all maids and janitors are laid off for the entire summer vacation, the yearly wage is but $352.30. The head of New Haven charities told me that not only are Yale employees forced on relief during the summer months but that even during the winter some of those blessed with large families must receive supplementary relief."

That was 1938. What we now know as Local 35 at Yale organized incrementally, department by department, beginning with the Department of Heat, Light, and Power. This process lasted from the late 1930s until the early 1950s, when the departments that make up Local 35 were all organized together in one union. Those were years of tremendous struggle for recognition and for contracts acceptable in that era.

In 1968 the Yale administration seized what it saw as an advantage and literally crushed Local 35 during a six-day strike. The local survived as an organization, but the contract settlement was catastrophic. Then, as now, lower-wage workers, primarily women and minorities, earned only barely above the legal minimum wage. They were laid off at summertime, at Christmas, and at spring break. A third of them were on welfare even while working at Yale. Benefits were very poor.

The members of the union determined to rebuild, an effort that resulted in the strikes of 1971, 1974, and 1977. These were heroic, valiant strikes — tough, difficult strikes. The 1971 strike was actually an extraordinary civil rights struggle. I witnessed one of the most remarkable scenes of my life on graduation day at Yale in 1971, when — for the only time in the history of Yale since it moved to New Haven — the graduation procession was unable to walk down Elm Street, across the green, around Center Church, and up through Phelps Gate because of a police riot on Elm in which many strikers were beaten. The graduates had to scurry across Elm Street behind a large wall of club-wielding New Haven police who were beating the strikers. Major bloodshed was avoided only because of a Catholic priest, Father James Groppi, a civil rights activist from Milwaukee, who surveyed the scene, surveyed the police clubbing the strikers, and realized a significant portion of both the police and the strikers were Catholics like himself. So in a very big voice Groppi called out "Let us pray!" and he prayed at length, reminding us that, in his view at least, if Jesus had been around he would have been with the strikers, not with the police. That reduced the tension, but it was not an experience the Yale administration wanted to see repeated. Thus later, when the union said, "Let's do that again at alumni weekend," the strike was settled.

For those of us who had the privilege to be associated with the union during that time, these struggles were among the most important things happening at Yale, so it was always ironic to realize that what made Yale famous nationally was not the struggles of these workers or their accomplishments but rather the pronouncements by Kingman Brewster, then the president of Yale. Brewster, while refusing to make any sympathetic gesture toward his own employees, did pronounce that a black revolutionary, in his opinion, couldn't get a fair trial in America. The irony of the president's liberal stance and reputation, sustained while workers were being beaten in his front yard, was not lost on those of us associated with the union.

Despite the opposition of supposedly liberal administrators like Brewster, Local 35 made enormous progress during the 1970s and 1980s, not only in wages, benefits, and rights for workers on the job but in particular on one issue raised throughout the 1970s and finally resolved by the early 1980s — year-round work. Many Yale employees, especially those working in dining halls or providing custodial services, were traditionally laid off during student break periods. It was true in 1938 when Butler wrote his report, and it was still true in 1970. Many of these workers had to go on welfare, since under Connecticut law a person cannot collect unemployment during such a layoff. Over several contract negotiations Local 35 was finally able to persuade Yale that these employees should be assigned other required work during break periods — painting, heavy cleaning, groundskeeping, and so forth. It was clear that there was plenty of other work to be done at Yale during breaks, so the struggle was over whether these employees *should be entitled to that work*. This became known as the alternative work program; it turned these jobs into year-round positions (something that had great relevance to the 1995–96 struggle), which meant that people in these lower-labor-grade jobs could have more stable lives. They didn't make any kind of big wages, but they had year-round work with benefits and could think seriously about raising a family. That gives a pretty good indication of what impact these different labor practices have on people's lives and on the community. It was an extraordinary accomplishment, and it has echoes today.

Each of those four strikes was longer than the one before, revealing a growing struggle for power. All of us associated with the unions felt that there needed to be a little bit better balance of power in New Haven. Yet I don't think anybody in the unions really had the idea that there ever would be a true balance of power at Yale; it is much too powerful and too wealthy an institution for that.

During the same period efforts were made to organize the white-collar employees — the clerical and technical workers. Rick Wolff, who also has an essay here, was involved in one of those early efforts — the Association of Clericals and Technicals in the late 1960s. There were two labor board elections during the 1970s in attempts by the clericals and technicals to unionize. In the late 1970s and into the early 1980s, Local 35 and what became Local 34 decided to join together to enlarge the scope of unionization at Yale, which finally led to a successful labor board election — the third one — and the now-famous strike of 1984.

It was an extraordinary chapter in American labor history and in the history of the struggles of working women, one that foreshadowed what the labor movement should be, and needs to be, if there is going to be a viable labor movement in the United States. It is thus relevant to speak just for a moment about the university's strategy in that extraordinary strike. The university's strategy was founded on its belief that the members of Local 35 were all white men who were skilled tradesmen. There was certainly a strong, militant leadership in Local 35 drawn from that group, but equally strong leadership came from women and minorities, lower-labor-grade workers, semiskilled people, and unskilled people. So while Local 35 was actually made up of a diversity of people, Yale's administrators believed the members of Local 35 were white tradesmen who would never back up the women in Local 34. After all, the women in Local 34 had crossed the union's picket lines for years before they were organized. Just to make sure, Yale sent a telegram to the home of every member of Local 35 the night before the Local 34 strike began in September 1984 threatening to fire any worker who respected the picket line. But the members of Local 35 stayed out anyway. Yale's strategy failed.

The members of Local 34 — men and women, though women predominated and were the leaders — struck for ten and one-half weeks. They defeated Yale because they were organized and because there was unity between Local 34 and Local 35. And that strike led to major improvements for Yale employees. We tend to forget that the average salary of clerical and technical workers at Yale before that strike was around sixteen thousand dollars, while today it's between twenty-four thousand and twenty-five thousand dollars. Not a lot of money to live on, but enormous progress. We tend to forget that the only increase in pension benefits in the history of the nonfaculty pension plan at Yale University came about because of the 1984 strike. We tend to forget that it was only as a result of the 1984 strike that Yale finally paid health benefits for workers' families; that retirees' medical, which the university is now trying to take away, was finally paid for; that people in the clerical and technical ranks finally had the opportunity to bid for promotions, to bid for upgradings, to stand up and say, "Wait a minute, there's something wrong here." All that came out of that extraordinary strike.

The strike also exposed one of the great contradictions of Yale. The Yale Corporation has always been dominated by big-business types. For instance, in 1996, Henry Schacht, the chairman-designate of one of the three corporations into which AT&T is being divided, was a member. And I'm sure that Mr. Schacht, having just laid off forty thousand people, undoubtedly said to himself and his colleagues on the board, "Why — I don't understand this — we laid off forty thousand people in my company. Why can't we get rid of a few hundred people at Yale?" That same board has also had people who purportedly have stood for something better. In 1984 two of the prominent members of the Yale Corporation were Eleanor Holmes Norton, who had made her reputation on gender-equity and race-equity issues as the chairperson of the Equal Employment Opportunity Commission under the Carter administration, and Bishop Paul Moore, one of the great liberal leaders of the Episcopal Church in America. But neither was to be found or heard from when the issues that each supposedly cared about so deeply were being fought about in the streets at Yale. Today, Kurt Schmoke, the African-American mayor of Baltimore, an extremely progressive political leader with enormous political ambitions, is on the board, but he won't meet with the unions, won't talk publicly about these matters.

The 1984 strike went way beyond arguing about wages; it was a struggle for people's freedom. It was a remarkable coalescing of people who formed a successful alliance. Following that strike, then, what happened? In 1988 and 1992 there were peaceful settlements for both unions. And in the 1992 contract negotiations for Local 35 a groundbreaking labor-management committee was created and instructed to deal with questions of productivity, service delivery, costs, effectiveness, subcontracting, and so on. It was a joint committee where consensus had to be reached. And for two years, both sides took it very seriously, and it was working.

Then something happened at Yale. A new group of people showed up on the scene, a new group of Yale Corporation members, particularly big-business types, along with a new president and a new vice president for finance and administration. First they decided to abandon the university's support for and participation in the joint committee. Then they decided to turn back the clock in other ways. Initially, I thought they were trying to turn back the clock to 1970, but after reading Reverend Butler's descriptions, I realized that 1938 might be the date they had in mind.

They want a permanent two-tier wage system — beginning with a four-dollar-an-hour cut for new workers, for labor grades that are predominantly occupied by women and minority members. They want to do away with the alternative work program, so that the workers would go back to thirty weeks a year, would go back to welfare, assuming that welfare payments for people laid off in the summer will continue to be available on a recurrent basis, something the 1996 welfare legislation makes highly unlikely. They want to ruin the retirement system too, such as it is. And they want increases in "subcontracting" — a nice term! What does it mean? Subcontracting means that you get rid of a custodian or a dining hall worker or a physical plant worker who's eking out a halfway decent living at Yale and you bring in somebody working for the minimum wage with no benefits and no fixed schedule of hours, who works when the boss calls him in — that's what subcontracting is. That's where they want to go.

And this from an institution that, in 1984, when the strike occurred, had an endowment of $1.1 billion and today has an endowment of $5 billion, growing at the rate of $1 million a day — that's profit, not money they use to pay expenses. This is $1 million a day in *gain* — but they don't call it profit; they reinvest it and call it an expense.

I used to think, and probably many union members used to think, that Yale could learn, could learn that people shouldn't have to go through this kind of struggle in order to earn a living serving the university. But I have reluctantly concluded that that is not so, that this kind of division — and I've been observing Yale one way or another for thirty-three years now — seems to be intrinsic to Yale's structure and its outlook. After all, the structure and style of the institution are certainly not fundamentally democratic: students have no democratic rights at Yale. The faculty has no democratic rights at Yale.

I think it's troubling to Yale, and in the end unacceptable to the institution, that the people with the least status and the least prestige presume to come to the administration and the Yale Corporation as equals and say, "We want to talk with you about the conditions under which we work." That concept doesn't make any intuitive sense to the university, and I think that is at the core of the problem. Certainly it's part of what's going on in America. Perhaps because of these national trends, Yale is now proving bolder and more vicious than it has been in the past. For the first time the administration has threatened to cancel employees' medical insurance while they're on strike; they never did that particular inhumane thing before. They've even resorted to hiring a goon squad from Youngstown — a professional strike-breaking firm operating on the Yale campus. Bolder, more vicious.

It was particularly instructive for me to return to New Haven in the winter of 1996. I was invited back by the leaders of the unions, and I was delighted to be there. It's interesting to me now in part because I can see that Yale employees who are union members, who have engaged in these extraordinary struggles, aren't different from anyone else in America. Yale employees want to have a tolerable standard of living; they want to partake in what we were raised to believe was the American dream; they want to be able to go about their lives and raise their families and have days off.

In short, union members at Yale feel, "We've proved ourselves. We've earned the right to be treated halfway decently here. We've earned it with a lot of sacrifice and pain and struggle. We shouldn't have to be engaged in a year-round, year-in and year-out struggle in addition to the time we put in on the job." And so, because the settlements in 1988 and 1992 came without strikes, people in the union have come to believe cooperative negotiation will be the norm, that they have a right to expect it. The membership has come to believe a definition that goes something like this: "Collective bargaining is what it should be in the textbook — it's a business deal. We talk about what we need; they talk about what they need; and we work it out." That's a little different from a cause, a struggle, a movement; thus I think the unions have been put to sleep by recent experience and the expectations it has led them to adopt.

The history of unions at Yale reveals that periodically they have been put to sleep by such assumptions. Indeed they *ought* to be able to look at collective bargaining that way. They shouldn't have to say to the people who work at Yale, who are trying to raise families and get along in America today, "No, no, you have to spend all your free time and all your days off fighting this institution." Yale has perceived that the unions have become a little complacent — and they ought to have the right to be a little complacent — and so Yale is saying, "Let's take it all back!" They think the unions have gone to sleep.

But in the weeks I spent in New Haven in 1996 I saw people being forced back into a fighting mode, forced to look at the relationship between Yale and its employees once again not as a business deal — because Yale doesn't look at it that way — but as a cause, as a struggle for justice, as a movement. At first I think everyone in the unions found that discouraging — they shouldn't have to do that full-time. They should be able to live a regular life. But I think they're moving past discouragement. They're realizing: this is their future they're talking about; this is their families' future; this cause is *their job.*

No job at Yale is safe from subcontracting and downsizing and two-tier wage structures. So the union movement is once again turning into a struggle for justice; it's not just an argument over a business deal. And when that happens (and it is happening), then Yale, as it did in the 1940s, as it did in the 1970s, as it did in 1984, will once again lose! Because all of Yale's wealth and its power can't hold back a struggle for justice by workers who are organized, who have a plan, who reach out to allies and friends and supporters, and who expose the hypocrisy of this kind of institution.

I think there will be some very concrete results from this reawakened struggle. It'll take a while, but I think the union members will get over the discouragement and taste a little bit of the joy and the freedom and the power of that kind of struggle. Some of us have had the privilege to have gone through it before; some are new to it. It's very liberating.

I also think Yale will get less from its workers than it could have gotten by treating them as human beings worthy of respect and worthy of talking to as equals. I think the institution will once again suffer extraordinary long-term damage. The history of Local 35 began with a little department: Heat, Light, and Power. What is now Local 34 began in the School of Epidemiology and Public Health, with a group of 110 workers. And I think that's what's happening again. Those clerical and technical employees who are not part of the struggle in 1996 will eventually come to join it. Graduate teaching assistants will continue to organize themselves and will be successful. So-called casual workers, who are no different from anybody else except that they have even lower wages and no benefits and no rights at all, are joining the movement. Yale New Haven Hospital workers are learning; one of the remarkable things about the 1995–96 strike was the number of hospital workers who saw union members on the picket lines and said, "We need to do that, too."

In the sixty years since Reverend Butler made his observations, the change has been incremental, but it's been real. That's what's happening at Yale now. And the tragedy of it all is that Yale — the university that many people imagine is devoted to justice and humane values — ought to be celebrating what has happened.

People in our society are being driven apart by race, gender, class, citizenship status, sexual orientation, and all the other means of division that exist. What's going on in the union movement at Yale? The opposite of that! It ought to be celebrated. Where else in America do you see a scene like you would have seen at Yale in February 1996 if you were in the Methodist church across from the intersection where the union offices are? On the first floor was the membership meeting of Local 35 — blacks, whites, young people, old people, men, women all talking about how to deal with the latest challenge from Yale. On the second floor, members of Local 34, clerical and technical workers, were talking about dealing with the challenge from Yale. On the third floor, graduate students and undergraduate students — a whole bunch of undergraduate students — were calling alumni, talking about what a mess Yale had become.

That ought to be treasured. And if the administration won't treasure it — and I don't think it will — then those on the side of justice can!

Chapter 2
Against the Grain: Organizing TAs at Yale

Corey Robin and Michelle Stephens

In December 1995, approximately 250 teaching assistants (TAs) at Yale University undertook a grade strike, demanding that the university recognize the Graduate Employees and Students Organization (GESO) as their collective bargaining agent. In mid-January, after the grade strike was well underway, 137 TAs — along with other employees and students at Yale, residents of New Haven, and graduate students and faculty from area universities — were arrested in an act of civil disobedience while protesting the university's selective punishment of three striking TAs. These events garnered banner headlines around the world. Behind the journalistic accounts of a new group of organized workers using innovative tactics at a prestigious, wealthy Ivy League university lies an even more surprising story of individual graduate students struggling to overcome their own personal fears and pushing the boundaries of what they considered to be legitimate action. Many of these TAs came to Yale thinking they had chosen a life of the mind and would never involve themselves in collective struggle. In becoming union activists, they engaged in acts they previously would have scorned or feared. As a result, their political assumptions, their relationship to their work and their advisers, their personal attitudes and beliefs, and their everyday conduct and actions changed.

This essay details and analyzes some of these stories of individual transformation.[1] The first section briefly recounts the changes in two individuals who participated in the grade strike. The second section analyzes the institutional culture at Yale that led such individuals to become more involved in the union. In the third section, we look at how GESO "organizers" mobilize graduate students. In the last section, we contrast these accounts of individual transformation with an account of someone who did not strike. In analyzing the union drive at Yale, we hope that readers will gain a day-to-day sense of how a union is built, how antiunion graduate students can become prounion, and how an organized movement can tap into the surprising potential of men and women for collective struggle.

Prologue: Ellen Martinez and Thomas Cummings

Ellen Martinez, a Cuban-American student of ethnic politics in America, grew up in Los Angeles and came to Yale with a prestigious fellowship and a degree from Berkeley.[2] Her political work in the Latino communities of both Los Angeles and the Bay Area and her family's involvement in the teachers' union of Los Angeles distinguish her from most graduate students at Yale. She has stated:

> I didn't find the idea of unionization strange. My mother is a teacher. She's always been in a union. My sister [is also a teacher]. . . . There was a strike in '91. My sister went on strike and my mother didn't. My mom ended up staying home — because my sister guilted her into it. She wasn't on strike, but she didn't go in. She didn't cross the picket line. It caused a lot of family strife. . . . I felt my mom was totally nuts. I mean your group decides to go on strike, and you don't?

Martinez felt "very conflicted" about coming to Yale. "This is the bastion of everything I hate about this country," she says. She calls Yale a "white male *Yanquí* institution." She adds, "It's been very hard for me identity-wise to deal with being here. It's like José Martí said, 'It's like being in the belly of the beast.' The other saying is, 'To defeat the enemy you have to know him from within.' That's part of the rationale of why I came here. Know the mainstream so that you can criticize it." Despite the stereotype of politically correct academics running amok in the Ivy League, such sentiments are rare at Yale. Few students would voice their political or cultural identity as deeply or as viscerally as Martinez does.

Yet Martinez shared many assumptions with her classmates. "I wanted to go to a school that had a name," she confesses. She opted for Yale over Harvard because the attitude of the graduate students at Harvard was " 'Well, this is Harvard, of course you're going to come here.' " Yale offered her reasons "other than the name" for going there. "I thought Yale was what its reputation was." She imagined a vibrant intellectual community where faculty and graduate students asked and tried to answer the vital questions of the day. "I wanted a space where graduate students and faculty could think about things and talk about things." Her vision of graduate school was of a haven for public intellectuals who would serve as "the conscience" of the nation. In addition, she had high expectations of the faculty:

> I had seen so many of my friends at Berkeley flounder without attention that I wanted to be taken care of at this point. I wanted to know that I had access to people. I wanted to know there were faculty I could talk to and bounce all my crazy ideas off, that they would actually listen to me. That's what the Yale reputation implies — they have the resources to care about education and the production of intellectuals in this country.

Despite her political radicalism, her experience as an undergraduate activist at Berkeley, and her criticisms of Yale as a white-male institution, Martinez still subscribed to a paternalistic model of education. Like many graduate students, she imagined an intellectually engaged and benevolent faculty who would use their prestige, their education, and Yale's resources to help her foster and refine her own ideas and skills. She believed in the institution and in its mission; for her, that's what the Yale reputation meant.

Thomas Cummings, a philosophy graduate student, arrived at Yale with a different background and set of expectations than those of Ellen Martinez. Cummings grew up in a small town in Georgia, halfway between Athens and Atlanta. His father is a chiropractor, his mother "a housewife." Both of his parents are practicing Christians. Growing up, he was part of a "culture of Christian fundamentalism that is very right-wing politically." Cummings attended religious schools and a small religious college in Kentucky. As a graduate student, he remains committed to Christianity and still "reads Scripture." During the interview, Cummings repeatedly referred to "my Christian faith."

Prior to coming to Yale, Cummings had never participated in a rally or a march; the only political activity that he can recall participating in is voting. Instead, his major preoccupation was to attempt to understand "the very basic tenets of historic Christianity without all this political junk and cultural war stuff" that he had learned at his fundamentalist secondary schools. Also, unlike Ellen Martinez, his expectations of the faculty did not play a central role in his decision to come to Yale. His vision of the academy was one of solitude and quiet reflection. "I'm naturally a person who just wants to have peace and tranquillity and read my books."

When Martinez and Cummings first arrived at Yale, they shared little in terms of ethnic or regional background, political sympathies, cultural sensibilities, or intellectual assumptions. Because of their divergent experiences and outlooks, they had no reason to trust or identify with each other. They certainly had no reason to believe they had a stake in each other's lives. Cummings embodies Martinez's worst nightmares about Yale: "It's weird to come from California and sit in a classroom where everyone is white. It's bizarre. It's beyond bizarre. It's shocking in a way I never expected." Conversely, Martinez represents the politicized academic that Cummings eschewed. "I'm not a loud person," he admits. He thinks of radicals as "people who are very emotional, very confrontational." His first association with the word "radical," in fact, is people "who set people on fire in the '60s."

The basis of a union is solidarity, common identity, and mutual commitment, and thus — because Cummings and Martinez seemingly shared so little — it might seem improbable that both would join. Cummings was initially introduced to GESO when he visited Yale as a prospective student. An organizer told him, "There's an exciting labor movement here, and that's a good reason to come." His reaction was "that's *not* a good reason to come. . . . I guess my general attitude when he was talking about this exciting student-labor struggle was: ugh, this sounds like (*a*) a headache, and (*b*) I have no initial positive feelings about this sort of thing anyway. That was sort of where I was coming from." He grew up thinking of unions as "groups that didn't know when to stop, when to leave well enough alone." He recalls watching a television documentary that detailed the intimate links between unions and the Mafia. He was taught by his parents that "the world is such that people get what they deserve. If people weren't doing well financially, it was because they weren't working hard enough." Cummings's views are not atypical. In our own work recruiting new members, we have found that many Yale graduate students will openly state their deeply held belief in a meritocratic hierarchy and their suspicion of unions and the working class in general.

Martinez, coming from the other end of the political spectrum, was also not an automatic candidate for membership, for two reasons. First, although she was different from other Yale graduate students in many ways, the one belief she shared with them was an abiding faith in the faculty and in the intellectual value and prestige of the institution — the very ideology that prevents most graduate students from getting involved in the union. True, she did arrive at Yale believing TA unionization was "logical," and she was not hostile toward unions. Yet in our organizing experience we have found that many graduate students come to Yale initially supporting the idea of unionization but sour on it after seeing how antiunion the faculty and administration are. Second, her suspicion of other graduate students' ethnic backgrounds and her disagreement with their more mainstream political views made her less likely to want to get involved with them. "For me, the most frustrating thing was not only that it [her classmates and the faculty at Yale] was this homogeneous group, but that that homogeneous group wasn't willing to open up a space, to talk about other things. The range of discussion was so limited that I often didn't have anything to talk to people about." She was "frustrated by the level of politicization of my colleagues." She saw her classmates' shortcomings reflected in the union. GESO's goals, in her eyes, "were too narrow and too diluted." Martinez's activist past and radical politics were no guarantee of her commitment to graduate student unionization.

Despite their differences and deep suspicions, Cummings and Martinez found themselves on strike together in December 1995. Both were arrested. Both engaged in heated arguments with friends and family and stood up to varying degrees of faculty and administrative pressure. Both were radically transformed in the process. Martinez's growing involvement in the organization forced her to engage and argue with many of the same graduate students she had initially distrusted and disliked. "I've had to defend a lot of things," she says, and as a result, "my sense of politics is more well defined." "I trust my own instincts more than when I came here."

She also feels much more powerful. "I take less shit than I used to," she says. "I was not raised to respect my own opinion or to voice it, especially when I was challenging an area of authority. My old reaction was to feel something and not say anything, and I've gotten a lot better about that." Not all of these changes were positive. Ellen became deeply disillusioned with the faculty. She now calls them "scared little insecure people" who live in "fear" and always want "to toe the line." She no longer respects them as parental figures. This disillusionment, however, forced her to take her education into her own hands. She says, "I feel like I've grown intellectually despite this place; it's not because of [the faculty]. . . . The stuff I'm interested in was not included in what I took courses in, and so I had to learn it all by myself." Far from being crippling, her disillusionment with the faculty and the university seems to have strengthened her resolve and sense of herself. While she is not sure if she will stay in the academy, she says that she is more "committed to not giving this place the satisfaction of getting rid of me." At the same time, she is secure in the knowledge that she has many other options: "I have a lot more ideas than I used to about how to organize powerless people, how to start community organizations, how to get people involved and be proactive."

Cummings's transformation from a shy, nonconfrontational person is even more striking. During the grade strike he repeatedly confronted authority figures. He wrote a letter to the dean justifying his participation in the grade strike. A professor who will probably supervise Cummings's dissertation counseled him against striking. In response, Cummings explained that he was striking out of a sense of solidarity with his fellow graduate students who had put themselves at tremendous risk. The professor, a renowned ethicist, called Cummings "hyper-conscientious" in his concern for his fellow graduate students, but Cummings stood his ground. His parents called him in the middle of the strike to warn him not to jeopardize his career; he cheerfully informed them he had been arrested. As he says, there were "lots of firsts in this whole thing." Cummings has become someone who says, "I'm now involved in a labor movement. I think it's a good thing to be doing. A year ago I would never have thought that." He continues, "My views about the legitimacy of the complaints unions have about what the world is really like have changed. I've seen what the market really does, and I've seen that morally we have to try to work to balance it. I think labor unions are a way to do that." Despite growing up with Horatio Alger stories and ideologies, Cummings says, "I have become aware that there are people in the world who have a great deal of privilege and power and that their position is often sustained by other people having very little privilege or status." He justifies his own confrontational actions by saying, "I think the world is screwed up enough so that sometimes you have to do something against the grain just to be heard, to open possibilities for justice — just to make people aware of them."

Martinez's and Cummings's stories are not rare. Every GESO organizer can recount stories of this sort. Despite their disparate backgrounds and ideologies, graduate students at Yale have come together and engaged in actions that few academics would ever dare. There are two reasons for this. One is the nature of Yale itself and the frustration graduate students experience upon arriving there. Second is the kind of union organizing TAs and other workers have been engaging in at Yale over the last two decades.

Yale University: Corporate Power in the Ivory Tower

With its $5 billion endowment and three-hundred-year history, Yale University has educated the children of the nation's power elite for centuries. Fourteen members of the Continental Congress and four signers of the Declaration of Independence were Yale alumni. In this century alone, Yale has produced two U.S. presidents. Its law school has trained another president and one chief justice of the Supreme Court. More than a few senators and representatives have received their education at Yale. Yale has also produced the leaders of corporate America. Among Yale's many wealthy alumni is Sid Bass, reputed to be one of the richest men in the United States.

From Yale's Gothic towers, built by poor Italian immigrants during the Great Depression, the nation's future leaders can survey the desolate urban sprawl of New Haven, the seventh poorest city in the United States. As one of the largest employers in the city, Yale has always played a prominent role in the local economy. It has relied on New Haven as a source of low-wage labor for decades. Up until the 1960s, one-third of Yale's employees were collecting welfare benefits. Despite the presence of strong unions that have raised the wages of these workers, this relationship between Yale and New Haven continues into the present. The undergraduate newspaper is full of stories of New Haven's poor and homeless lining up behind the garbage dumps of the university's dining halls, looking for work. Because of Yale's nonprofit status, the city cannot tax the bulk of its wealth. As a result, one of the worst school systems in the country and one of the best universities in the world stand just a few city blocks from each other. In recent years, Yale has further insulated itself from the city by buying several New Haven streets. High Street, for example, is now called Rose Walk (named after a family of alumni donors).

The university's board of trustees is called "the Corporation." This most secret of Yale's secret societies includes a former U.S. senator, a perennial candidate for the Supreme Court, and industrial magnates like Henry Schacht, one of the chief architects of AT&T's recent layoff of forty thousand workers. In its fantastic capacity to contain dissent and co-opt opposition, the Yale Corporation has also absorbed prominent progressives like Baltimore mayor Kurt Schmoke, an outspoken campus militant during his youth. Other Yale Corporation members who have stamped the seal of liberal approval on Yale include *Nation* columnist Calvin Trillin and civil rights leader Eleanor Holmes Norton. A photograph of the Corporation membership might be the perfect image for the Yale of the 1990s. It offers a tableau of corporate wealth, political power, and progressive, multicultural leadership.

Although members of the Corporation are seldom seen on campus, their power and arrogance are reflected in the university's day-to-day treatment of its staff and graduate students. Because the university understands its mission to be the creation and education of the country's elite, university officials represent Yale as a gentleman's college. One of their favored images is that of the learned professor thoughtfully lecturing on the subtleties of canonical works to a rapt audience of ten or so young undergraduates. In this portrait, there is no room for graduate student TAs. The realities of a large, modern research university where tenured faculty do little of the teaching must be denied completely. Hence university president Richard Levin's repeated assertions to the news media that graduate students do only 3 percent of the teaching at Yale. In fact, graduate students at Yale are responsible for teaching more classroom hours than the tenured and nontenured faculty do.

Whenever graduate students make their presence felt by making demands of the university, they threaten to disrupt this idyllic picture. In response, representatives of the university — both administrators and faculty — have made it clear over the years that graduate students are unwelcome or, at best, are tolerated guests of the university. Invoking the classic icon of the pariah, the noncitizen, former graduate school dean Jerome Pollitt told an undergraduate magazine that graduate students lead "a gypsy life in New Haven." Investing money in the graduate school, according to Donald Kagan, former dean of Yale College, was like "throwing money down a rat hole." Any request from these pariahs for more resources takes on an extravagant quality because noncitizens and unwelcome guests are not entitled to anything. When English department graduate students lobbied for guarantees that they would be allowed to teach in their third and fourth years, for example, Professor Bill Jewett compared their request to graduate students asking for "personal helicopters." During the recent grade strike, the director of graduate studies in one department whisked away a striking TA with the comment, "I don't get paid enough to talk to you."

Graduate students sense this disdain the moment they arrive in New Haven. Jonathan Perry recalls his first encounter with the director of graduate studies in his department: "We all get together on the first day, and he says, 'In the next week or two you should make an appointment with me and we should talk about your own program.' So we all make these appointments. I go, and he says, 'Yeah, so what do you want?' He said that to others, too.... That meeting lasted for about three minutes." Perry also remembers a forum he attended in his first year with graduate school dean Thomas Appelquist. The forum had been billed as Appelquist's chance to meet and hear directly from graduate students:

> He seemed resentful that he had been drawn there and resentful that he had to be accountable to graduate students. He basically said he wasn't going to do anything [to improve the graduate school]. I just remember [another graduate student in my class] was sitting two seats down from me, and she jumped up and ran up to the microphone.... She was so angry.

Perry, whose father is a dean at a small college, was surprised that administrators did not even appear interested in graduate students' concerns. He recalls repeated encounters with indifferent administrators and faculty:

> You get a sense that you go into these meetings, and there isn't going to be anything that comes out of them.... They're not really sitting there hoping to help you find some sort of constructive solution, some middle ground.... They're not interested in what you have to say, and they're not interested in you being in their office, but they'll tolerate it for the time being.... That was a different experience for me, in talking to faculty, from where I went as an undergraduate.

In our interviews and in our organizing, we have found that graduate students come to Yale with high expectations and spend their first few years there coping with disillusionment and the frustration of those expectations. The graduate students we interviewed criticized the institution for lacking a critical intellectual community, for inadequate faculty mentoring, for not providing enough resources to meet the educational needs of both the undergraduates and the graduate students, and for generally failing to offer a rigorous vision of intellectual life in the 1990s.

Most graduate students come to Yale with a strong sense of the moral purpose of education and the cultural value of a critical intellectual community. Regardless of their political views, they view their particular academic pursuits in a moral framework; all of the students interviewed were concerned about the ethical dimension of their disciplines and their work. They looked to the faculty for models of the morally engaged intellectual. By contrast, Jonathan Perry was disappointed to find many faculty who "get caught up in what I find to be useless debates that are only in the literature and in the discipline and have very little relation to what's going on in the world.... It wears you down after a time." Because of his experiences with a highly professionalized professoriat speaking to other highly professionalized professors and disavowing a larger public audience, Perry is now "less enthusiastic I guess in general, and I do view [graduate school] much more instrumentally than I did coming in." He found it difficult to pursue his "real world" political interests within academe. "It does seem like a number of graduate students who have those interests have steered clear of them in the work they're doing."

Graduate students have found an even greater reluctance by the faculty to engage in a dialogue when Yale itself is the issue under discussion. Kate Kidjuski, a literature graduate student who is agnostic on the union issue and continues to be a reluctant member of GESO, comments on the failure of the Yale faculty to think critically about the university: "There's no critical attitude about the system at the top, which surprised me a lot. My experience as an undergrad was that tenured professors were very critical of the system, and that's what kept it alive in a way." In 1995, she tried to speak with her department's faculty about Yale's subcontracting of union jobs, an issue that surrounded the recent strikes of the other two campus unions, Locals 34 and 35. "You would think the faculty would feel a tension between the nonprofit mission of the university and the way that it keeps itself afloat, which is nothing short of corporate. Essentially they have all this money that they can invest. It's like investment banking, money made out of other money." Instead, she says, "everyone was saying, 'These are slim times; . . . everybody is tightening their belts.' " The faculty did not deal seriously with the contradiction between Yale's nonprofit educational mission and its proposed downsizing measures, which would have hurt poor, predominantly minority New Haven workers. "These are things I would have thought faculty members would have been considering. But they weren't. It was all about hierarchy and Yale as it is, Yale as this gigantic institution."

A first-year graduate student, Loni Cartwright, tells how one day she was standing outside of an area restaurant, urging customers not to patronize the restaurant because it was participating in an antiunion program with Yale. One of her professors

> stormed right by us and walked very determinedly into Au Bon Pain with a student, and I said, "Are you sure you want to go in there?" Very friendly . . . And he said, "I'm so sure I want to go in there, that's exactly why I'm going in there, and I have very good reasons for it, too." And I said, "I would love to hear those reasons." Again, politely, because we're out there to talk with people, and I had good conversations with people on the leaflet line. I was sad that this faculty member wasn't willing to talk. After I asked what the reasons were, he said, "Well, I don't want to tell you." Like a three-year-old,

> more immature than some kids I baby-sat, and I said, "But I want to learn from you," and he didn't know what to say. He just stalked in, and that was pretty upsetting.

Besides the general lack of a critical intellectual community and dialogue, graduate students pointed to the university's failure to allocate sufficient resources to fulfill its educational mission. An oft-invoked anecdote among Yale graduate students is Deputy Provost Chip Long's comment that TAs could save time (and Yale's money) if they did not read books assigned to their undergraduates that they had already read in college. Countless administrators have recommended that instead of paying TAs more money to do their jobs well, faculty should make fewer writing assignments or substitute short-answer exams for written essays. Long, for example, told an undergraduate newspaper, "It would surprise me if there weren't courses out there which could fruitfully, usefully, responsibly reduce the amount of writing they require from students." An infamous memo from the English department's administrator of Yale's only undergraduate course devoted solely to writing urges TAs to read undergraduate essays only once; the memo further instructs that "no written comments are allowed." These measures are accompanied by reminders that it is the TA's "responsibility . . . to sustain the student's desire to write." What particularly upsets graduate students about these incidents is the university's use of the rhetoric of excellence to justify anti-education measures that are solely designed to save money.

Loni Cartwright had a particularly personal response to Yale's lack of commitment to graduate students:

> My dad teaches at . . . a small liberal arts college where I grew up. The whole reason why I wanted to be a professor was because of my dad's experience with his students. The door to his office is always open. People always walk in; he doesn't have office hours. He has a million students who work for him, with him; he does research with them. These are undergraduates, mind you. They come over to the house for dinner. They call him [by his first name]. Imagine my surprise when I got here. . . . I thought that we [graduate students and the faculty] were going to be friends. It was going to be supportive. . . . You wouldn't feel bad about going to someone's office hours or taking up twenty minutes of their time. What is up with that? It's unreal. My academic experience here has been really

> bad, with bad teachers and overcrowded classes and feeling worse about taking up time than I did as an undergraduate. It's been really, really disappointing to me.

For graduate students, all of these actions and statements add up to a picture of Yale as a cold, uncaring institution that is, in reality, not committed to its most basic mission of education. Ellen Martinez says, "The fact that a place like this, that has the resources, chooses not to be what it could be, to me means there's something really wrong with this picture." Jonathan Perry claims:

> Yale has no vision of education. All they seem to want to do is increase their endowment. When I was an undergraduate, there was much more creativity in how courses were taught and things like that. Here, there's no institutional push for innovation. The incentive is to go into your office and work on a book. . . . Where's the sense of excitement around here, about anything that's new?

Thinking Collectively, Acting Confrontationally

Although the culture at Yale and the attitude of the university toward its graduate students are intimidating and unjust, more than Yale's actions and policies led Ellen Martinez to join Thomas Cummings on the picket line. Many large, bureaucratic institutions exhibit similar attitudes and behaviors toward their employees. In our age of downsizing and manufactured scarcity, Yale is certainly not unique among universities in fostering an attitude of indifference and, on occasion, outright contempt toward graduate students and other employees. What does distinguish Yale from other universities is a decades-long tradition of progressive, grassroots organizing within the university community.

The other two unions at Yale, Locals 35 and 34, represent the service and maintenance workers, and the clerical and technical workers, respectively. Many of their activists have years of experience dealing with the university. They are veterans of long, bitter strikes, especially the famous 1984 strike that brought Local 34 into existence and made Yale the focus of national attention around racial and gender discrimination for ten weeks. These two unions have been crucial in the formation of GESO. They have provided necessary resources and a vision of collective power. They have also trained several generations of graduate student organizers, who in turn have provided graduate students with leadership that turns daily disappointments and frustrations into powerful, collective demands.

Across the country, many aspiring teachers and scholars arrive at graduate school with high hopes and expectations that are quickly dashed. The gap between expectations and reality that we described above is probably relatively common. What has made the difference at Yale are the graduate student organizers who have lived through this process and have learned that disappointment and alienation are not the only options for graduate students. For organizers, disillusionment and coming to terms with Yale's institutional indifference are not the end; they are steps toward mobilization, empowerment, and fighting back. As Jonathan Perry explains, "I could have seen myself walking away, and there were certainly times when I considered just getting out of graduate school. I don't think GESO organizing has kept me motivated to stay here, but, on the other hand, something like that . . . I was more inclined to fight than to be just complacent." Loni Cartwright says:

> My dad thinks I'm dissatisfied with graduate school because I've become involved with a bunch of political radicals who are skewing my perception, because Yale is such an unpleasant place now with the strike that's going on [by Locals 34 and 35]. He says I'm spending too much time [on this], blah, blah, blah. I think that, sure, my dissatisfaction with my academic studies has been influenced by my involvement in GESO, to the extent that it has shown me there is an entire other world out there that I'm good at, and excited about, and would really like to be involved in working in.

Graduate student organizers have transformed sadness and disillusionment into indignation and a desire to fight because they approach graduate students bearing several assumptions in mind. First, organizers try "to meet people where they are at." Many of our conventional images — on both the Left and the Right — of radical leaders involve stereotypes of agitators or elites going out to persuade the masses to think in completely new categories, categories that are uncontaminated by the ideological trappings of people's current existence. Radical theory, in this formulation, precedes radical action. Our experiences and observations of graduate student organizing do not bear out this assumption. Successful graduate student organizers have tried not to force people to believe in partisan or alienating ideologies. Their goal in their first conversation with a nonmember is not to talk *at* that person for hours about the history of the labor movement or the need to join the ranks of the working class. Rather, organizers try to talk to graduate students in terms to which they can relate. Organizers try to get graduate students themselves to talk about their own issues of concern and to articulate their own agendas. The mismatch between graduate students' desires and Yale's intransigence has provided more than sufficient material to demonstrate why graduate students need a union, why nonmembers need to join, and why we need to act collectively. The organizer's goal is to mobilize people based on their own experiences, needs, and convictions, rather than on the organizer's ideological agenda.

Second, organizers learn that people often change their minds about controversial ideas. A graduate student's initial rejection of the idea of unionization does not mean he or she will never join GESO; it certainly does not mean an organizer should give up and never speak to that person again. For many graduate students, joining a union is a difficult decision and requires many hours of discussion and reflection. "Going back" to those who are indifferent and continuing the conversation about joining the union has been a central motif in GESO organizing, particularly since many of us who are actively involved were initially skeptical of GESO, if not downright hostile to its aims and goals. Our own personal experiences have convinced us that if we can change our minds about unionization and collective action, everybody else can, too. Linda Gershwin describes her own transformation as "a process of becoming more awake, becoming more conscious." She tries to keep that process in mind when she organizes other graduate students. "One of the things I thought I did well as an organizer was let people tell me their doubts; then I would say, 'You know, I was in the same place you are in a while back; this is how I thought myself out of it.'" Loni Cartwright has only recently started organizing. When she talks to other first-year students or nonmembers, she tries not to have the attitude that they are radically different or not yet part of the "elect." Instead, she tries "to make them comfortable and [tries] to make them think that [I'm] not a weirdo but that [I'm] listening to them, [I'm] with them, and that if I can do it, so can they. Because really I am not anything different from those 'meek' people who don't want to do anything. It's just that I've been convinced." Gershwin and Cartwright believe their job as organizers is to understand where people are coming from, draw them out, and then get them to see what they themselves already know about their experience of Yale.

Third, organizers assume that while people do not need to subscribe to a radical ideology in order to join a union, they do need an analysis of their experience as individual graduate students that enables them to see what they share with their fellow students. Organizers help graduate students see how their sense of personal frustration and disappointment is tied to the university's policies and priorities. Linda Gershwin says, "I felt so isolated, and I didn't think that my problems were collective problems. I thought that it was just my personality, mostly, so I didn't see it as this broader thing. . . . I think GESO . . . helped a lot in terms of making me think more systematically and institutionally." Organizers help people focus on how Yale actually works, how Yale treats graduate students in a collective fashion, and how we need to respond as a collective force. Although Thomas Cummings remained unconvinced about the need for a union — he thought that the "contract idea was neither here nor there" — he says that the "history presented to me [showed that] Yale almost always maintained the status quo, even when the status quo was pretty bad for us." Despite his hostility to unions, he came to see the university as a "big dinosaur that just wouldn't move, wouldn't offer the things we needed. It was clear that the things I was most interested in changing were not things I could go to some individual and talk about." Once Cummings began to see just how intransigent Yale could be — whether through its hostility to graduate student demands or out of mere bureaucratic inertia — he was convinced that the only thing that could force Yale to change was concerted, mass public action. Having demonstrated the collective nature of graduate students' problems, an organizer will then try to show that these problems can be addressed through collective action. In changing someone's mind from an antiunion position to a willingness to consider joining, organizers try to focus on facts and stories that show that collective action works. Heated ideological debates ensure that people remain divided and fighting one another. Emphasizing how Yale has stymied more conventional attempts to effect change and redirecting the conversation back to the goals that unite graduate students — smaller classes, more teacher training, health care benefits, and higher pay — enable apolitical and even conservative graduate students to consider seeing themselves as part of a larger movement.

Fourth, organizers assume that people change through small, incremental steps. For some graduate students, going to a union meeting is a scary thing to do. They imagine they will be the lonely voice of reason amid a crowd of belligerent, intimidating radicals. Good organizers can understand these sorts of personal fears. They try to persuade a nonmember to take the small step of going to a meeting so that he or she will see that union members are not crazed activists but reasonable people with real grievances. These small encounters have offered epiphanies to previous skeptics or merely have helped put a face on some of the many injustices graduate students have heard about but may not have experienced directly. Thomas Cummings recalls a meeting of a few GESO members that he attended during the summer after his first year of graduate school:

> There was somebody from another department at this meeting who has a family. He's a graduate student, and when he teaches, roughly half of his income goes back to Yale for health care. I just thought, "That is ridiculous. That's just unjust. . . ." This was at a point in time where we were beginning to see on the national political scene the possibility that a lot of the educational funding, the student aid that people have enjoyed for a long time, was going to be cut. So I sat there thinking, well, to the extent that we minimize the cost of graduate school to graduate students — and this is something that GESO is in a lot of ways advocating — particularly in an environment where there's less aid from the government, we make it more open to people who don't already have a privileged background. That became a crucial thing for me. That point and the health care thing with this student began to get into a moral level with me. I began to think there really are issues of justice here. GESO has the moral high ground; it's not just Yale trying to do what's in their interest and we're trying to do what's in our interest.

For other people, going to a forum with a dean has been the first of many steps toward recognizing that Yale administrators are not the friendly deans they imagined in their undergraduate days. Perry recalls how the forum with Dean Appelquist mentioned above started convincing him during his first year that graduate students needed a union:

> Up to that point, my impression of the graduate students in my department [who were in GESO]...was that they were really whiny. All of us come to graduate school thinking we're pretty bright. So I looked at these guys and said, "They just don't know how to get something changed, or they just want to sit around and whine...." Had they worked through the proper channels? Couldn't they just go meet with these people?...I thought, "Maybe if these whiners came to me, I wouldn't want to [help them] either; maybe it's just that kind of approach." This forum helped turn that around in my head, this sense that, gosh, it's not them, it's this guy [Appelquist]. What he stands for is the real problem.

While these small encounters and meetings may seem trivial, they can ultimately lead people to a point where they are willing to take significant risks.

The decision to become an organizer is itself a step that can change people significantly. When Perry first heard about GESO, he was in no position to join, much less strike. Even after attending the forum with the dean, he would not have struck. During Perry's first semester at Yale, his ambivalence went unnoticed by his organizer, who "was always apologetic about calling me....He never did a good job of trying to invest me in the problems or getting me to think it would be worth being a member." Perry did not join. During his second semester, however, a new organizer started working with him. "I just told her all of these problems I had with how I had been treated [by my first organizer], and she was completely sympathetic and said we can change those things — if you get involved." He then joined. His new organizer continued to encourage him to change things in the organization by urging him to take a more active role in making those changes himself:

> My agreement was to come to an organizers' meeting that summer. She and, I guess, [another organizer] ran it. I was a real asshole for the whole meeting. They had one agenda and I had another. I said, "This is what we have to focus on and do all of this." And they were very responsive. They said that, on the one hand, they could help

> do some of that stuff, but that I also had to do some of it myself. I was receptive to that.

Perry started to take on more responsibility as an organizer in his department. This involvement and increased role strengthened his commitment to the organization and his willingness to fight for its recognition:

> I initially wasn't so keen on the idea of other people knowing I'd become a GESO organizer. . . . That's really changed. I didn't want to lead meetings in the department, that kind of stuff. It wasn't just seeing the problems [with Yale that changed my mind]; it was also my sense that the other people associated with this effort were good people. I started attending the coordinating committee [the governing body of the union] and saw these other people who seemed very reasonable and thought this was the right thing to do.

Only after taking increasingly more initiative and leadership in the organization was Perry ready to make the decision to strike. In fact, his growing role led him to become one of the key leaders and planners of the grade strike. He was the principal speaker on behalf of the motion to strike at the membership meeting, and he helped formulate much of the subsequent press and negotiating strategy. As he now says, "My first year, I wouldn't have been ready to do a grade strike, much less stand up and advocate it."

The final assumption of an organizer is that the goal is to get people to act. Participating in a union is different from being in a seminar. A union is not primarily a space for idle speculation or bemused, detached inquiry. The point of a union like GESO is to accomplish specific goals and win for graduate students a greater role in the university's decision-making process. This requires more than thinking radical thoughts; it necessitates radical acts. Graduate students exercise power not by making particularly cogent or sophisticated arguments nor by inventing newfangled strategies for fighting the administration. Power comes from coming together with other graduate students and forcing the institution to change through concerted, mass public action. Because of GESO's six-year-long record of successful collective action, organizers can point to many examples from recent history to prove this.

Kate Kidjuski remembers her first realization of the power of collective action. In the spring of 1995, 70 percent of the TAs, including Kidjuski herself, stopped teaching for a week:

> We [the graduate students in her department] had a big meeting... right around the time of the job action, and I know that they [the faculty] were told by members of the administration, "Ease up on the graduate students." And why? It was because of GESO,... the atmosphere of graduate students really being dissatisfied. Something bigger may happen, so give it to them now. None of these changes would have happened otherwise. I'm convinced of that.

After that meeting and the strike, the department made far-reaching reforms in the TA hiring process. "We had been talking about it for months and months. But that was the time when it actually happened. Why? Because suddenly things were happening on campus."

After an earlier strike in 1992, the TAs won a 28 percent pay raise, the largest pay raise in the history of the graduate school. Such experiences — more than any book or classroom discussion — taught graduate students that collective power could create possibilities and change what seemed to be unchangeable. Linda Gershwin says of that strike, "I felt that graduate student collective action was really important, especially when I realized we actually achieved what we set out to achieve.... I could see a concrete result. That was a turning point for me." We have found that these assumptions, that people's ideological beliefs change less through persuasion and more through a process of increased participation in forms of collective struggle, are counterintuitive to graduate students. New organizers often believe that they need to engage in polite discussion and change people's minds before they will act. While intellectual persuasion and argumentation are certainly crucial to the process of organizing, people's ideas often change as a result of action, and not vice versa. Even when people have certain ideas about the world, only when they act — whether by directly confronting the university or by confronting their fellow graduate students — do they really come to understand the tensions, complexities, and integrity of those ideas.

Kate Kidjuski's struggle over whether or not to do the grade strike, for example, helped provide her with a deepened understanding of Yale's power structure. While she had had some vague intuitions about the hierarchy at Yale, her confrontations with her advisers and with the Yale administration brought the disparate strands of her thinking into a coherent whole:

> I had thought to myself, "At Yale everything's very hierarchical; everything depends on position within [a] department; everything depends on who you know and who you can get along with." And then I thought, "No, no, look, people are really nice to each other. Everyone is human, right?" And then something like this [the grade strike] happens, and you realize there really is this extreme structure, that the university is structured not just like a corporation; it's worse than a corporation. That was a huge awakening. It didn't matter if I said, "Professor So-and-so, I just think this is right, so I'm going to do it."

Difficult actions force people to confront themselves, to ask themselves difficult questions, to push and test the limits of their ideas and commitment. Through that process, they come to apprehend their reality with a much more discerning, critical eye. Wishful thinking and vague theorizing become genuine conviction and concrete analysis. Linda Gershwin's decision to organize forced her to start dealing with both her own and other graduate students' fears. She says that "people were quite recalcitrant initially; it was really tough." Dealing with other people forced her to understand the idea of unionization more clearly. "I was confronting my own ignorance in the process of doing this, so I think that what was actually good about organizing was learning from it, the way that you never really learn a subject till you teach it." As Jonathan Perry says:

> A lot of people in graduate school have this sense that you just come in with an ideology and a sense of what's right and what's wrong, . . . not just in the case of GESO but in most things, but that's just not going to be good enough in life. You have to be willing to act on your convictions, and if you're not, then you just can't expect that anything's going to change.

Organizers show that things can change—and have changed—when graduate students act collectively. They push members to act on this analysis by coming to meetings, paying dues, getting more involved in the union, and ultimately by taking an increasingly confrontational stance toward the university — going to rallies, demonstrations, and perhaps even participating in civil disobedience and striking. Organizers then help members cope with the confusion and self-doubt that come when graduate students confront powerful authority figures or when parents and family members challenge their decision to be active in the union. All of this organizing work happens through long, often hard conversations over coffee, over the telephone, after class, or late at night in apartments.

Organizing in GESO is built on one-on-one relationships between members and their organizers. Every organizer is responsible for talking to roughly five members. This kind of rank-and-file activism, based in departments, is central to the strength and militancy of the organization. Organizers are leaders in their departments, and they develop strong relationships with members. One-on-one organizing is often difficult work, partly because graduate students often come to Yale with deeply antiunion ideologies and suspicions. Linda Gershwin, who became an organizer during the first wave of GESO's organizing drive, remembers how negative many people initially were to the idea of a union:

> A lot of people were very anti-union. They thought it was antithetical to what they were doing in graduate school. They felt they were members of a privileged elite.... You had to combat people's sense of isolation and individualism and snobbery and also just their sense that this was a futile thing, all the kinds of reactions that I had had to TA Solidarity [GESO's precursor] initially.

Many graduate students have never participated in a union, and their only acquaintance with unions is through media representations of wealthy union bosses or unimaginative bureaucrats who never leave Washington. Jonathan Perry recalls that as a first-year graduate student, "I hadn't had an experience with unions. My family isn't in unions. It just wasn't something I was familiar with. So I didn't come into it with that sort of mentality." Linda Gershwin remembers one particularly hard but successful conversation with someone very much like Jonathan Perry in his first year:

> I remember speaking to this woman who was not poised to be thinking collectively, and I actually was able to convince her. I remember that she made a lot of headway in the conversation and that that was a big deal, because I hadn't thought I'd be able to talk to

> her at all, and I was really nervous. But that was hard, . . . the whole process of talking to people face-to-face. I remember afterwards thinking back nostalgically to it because I felt like that was really what was necessary and that was how we had built the initial phone tree. Everything was from the ground up, having these hard, nitty-gritty conversations with people.

Even when graduate students understand all of the logic behind unionization and know all of the history of Yale's treatment of graduate students, they may still be reluctant to join the union or participate in more militant action. The fear of confronting powerful authority figures at Yale is pervasive. Some graduate students fear outright material retribution. They are nervous that their adviser may not write them a positive letter of recommendation or that they will be denied a teaching position. After the grade strike, when the Yale administration made it a formal policy that participating in a union action would be considered legitimate grounds for preventing graduate students from teaching at Yale or for not recommending them for future academic careers, this fear cannot be dismissed as groundless. These fears of concrete retribution are often tied to the feeling that any action that would provoke such retribution must be wrong. If it were not wrong, why would the faculty or administration respond with such hostility? Jonathan Perry says, "There was a certain level of guilt associated with confrontation in the beginning. Am I creating this, or am I doing more than is appropriate?" As a result, in the early phases of his involvement with GESO, Perry would go to meetings where graduate students confronted the faculty, and he found himself "kind of wanting to sit in the back and not have to say very much and just sort of observe."

Other graduate students are nervous about incurring a more diffuse form of disapproval. They are concerned about standing out and being noticed as someone who is different or political (even though the majority of graduate students are members). Kate Kidjuski says, "The main thing that I didn't know was: Is it safe? Will my name be plastered up on the wall somehow? . . . Will all the professors know that I joined? . . . I had no idea." Graduate students worry about appearing too impassioned and not sufficiently skeptical, or they are scared they will get a reputation for being anti-intellectual. Kidjuski says:

> You don't want to be different because you want to fit in and not be an impostor. If everybody is living a life of the mind and not thinking about money or practical considerations, then you don't want to be that person. Because then it will be like: "Oh, yeah, Kate — all she thinks about is politics, and not about art." I think that has a lot to do with why first-year students are loathe to join GESO.

Many graduate students remain quite concerned about what their parents and friends outside of the university will think of them. One graduate student we worked with did not want to join during her first year because her father had access to her checking account and would see that she had paid union dues. During the grade strike, parents and other family members exerted a tremendous amount of pressure on striking TAs. Kidjuski says:

> I can tell you, my parents, the day after grades were due, called me up and gave me a long, I would say talking-to — except that the volume was a little bit higher than [a] talking-to — over the telephone. . . . They said, "Hand in your grades, idiot. Don't be stupid. This is crazy. . . ." They felt I was ruining my career, that I was not taking it seriously enough. Believe me, I was taking it seriously. I don't think I slept all night for a month. I just couldn't decide what to do. . . . There was a neighbor of my parents who is now in administration in a community college. He used to be a union worker; he used to teach at reform school. He was one of the people who started the union there. He had been on both sides, and he told me to hand in my grades. . . . At home, I met with him several times. . . . He said to me, "You have to decide why you're at Yale. Are you at Yale to get a degree, or are you at Yale to change the world?" . . . He gave me all these scenarios. He said he thought the consequences were pretty serious.

In the face of these countervailing fears and pressures, organizers must be able to marshal more than mere logic and rhetorical persuasiveness. Graduate students — like most other people — will not risk their careers and take on people who hold their futures in the balance merely because it is the right thing to do. They need to feel some deeper connection and commitment to the other graduate students who are in their position. They need to believe that their action will accomplish something and that other graduate students are completely depending on them to participate in the action. This accountability is both moral and practical. Graduate students must feel an obligation not to let other people down. If they feel that way, they will have a greater sense of other people's commitment to them. This solidarity gives them a sense of strength and fearlessness, and it ultimately becomes their strongest source of protection.

Because graduate students do not work together, they do not often develop any sense of workplace solidarity or have any direct experience of collective power. They are used to thinking of themselves as individuals and are taught that they can get ahead through their own cleverness and skill. They are not taught to depend on other people. If anything, they learn to distrust other graduate students and view them as antagonists in seminars, at conferences, and in the job market. Many of the graduate students we interviewed spoke of the "combative" nature of the classroom, and that feeling of being embattled does not make for much trust or solidarity.

Organizers serve as crucial links between graduate students as a whole. They help reinforce people's sense of commonality, and they try to remind people that collective struggle carries far more benefits than antagonistic and distrustful bickering. But even more important, when organizers push people to take confrontational steps, they convey to members a sense of confidence and collective power that is absolutely essential. Organizers' sense of confidence and commitment, their willingness to break through their own fears and push beyond their own limits, is one of the few indices that a graduate student has of the potential for and the possibilities in collective action. As Loni Cartwright says, "I think there has to be a level of expectation, but not of dogmatic forcing."

At this level of organizing, relationships can be severely tested and strained. Organizers have found themselves engaging in painful, soul-searching discussions, where graduate students are forced to ask themselves difficult questions, questions they would seldom face in their daily lives. Jonathan Perry speaks at great length about how organizing one of his closest friends tested their relationship:

> It's very awkward with [my friend] when I fight with her about doing stuff for GESO. That's a strange position to be in. . . . I don't argue with her to come over to have dinner or argue to go see a movie. It does put you in a weird position. I can be as kind as I want to be, but you're starting to ask for very hard things, and you're asking for

things that aren't for you. You're not usually in a position where you have to ask people to do something. . . . If it was for me that she was coming over for dinner and she didn't want to come, I'd say, "Don't come." But for a collective effort like this, it's not like that. That does create an uncomfortable situation.

Organizers grow more comfortable confronting members in this fashion when they have developed a long history of struggle with their members. For this reason, Loni Cartwright says, "I think one of the most important things is really developing a good relationship with the person you're organizing, so that it isn't somebody who you really never talk to or who you only talk to about this [GESO], and there's lots of tension."

Organizers are much more than bureaucratic representatives of the organization. They serve as a crucial lifeline, a supportive but firm voice that helps people through incredibly difficult experiences. Cartwright remembers one instance when someone she knew "was upset about the job market, her involvement in the grade strike, and the DGS's [director of graduate studies] response to that, and what that would mean on the job market. It was the time . . . to say, 'I know this is scary, and, in fact, I'm not going to tell you that you're going to be fine, because I don't know, but I think you're doing the right thing.' " Cartwright adds, "I don't like the idea of whitewashing things." Organizers try to help people cope with very real obstacles and fears. They cannot wish these difficulties away or pretend that there are no risks involved. They can lend a sympathetic ear, acknowledge what the person is going through, and remind that person that everyone must stick together and that there is something fundamental at stake in what that person does. In the context of extreme confrontation and, on occasion, paralyzing fear, that kind of individual intervention can make the crucial difference between one person's defiance and another's capitulation.

Because of the intensity of the conflict with Yale, and the corresponding conflict that that engenders among union members, many graduate students develop close relationships with their organizers and attribute many of their transformations to them. Individual organizers have made fundamental differences in people's lives. Thomas Cummings says of his organizer, "I wouldn't have done the grade strike if it wasn't for him. . . . He just kept asking me questions and confronting me with my own principles. . . . He was making me take my own principles seriously and think about the situation at hand from that perspective." Loni Cartwright says her organizer "does what she thinks is right." Graduate student organizers have often replaced the faculty as essential role models for other graduate students. Cartwright says, "It's so important to me that I can become one of those people." She explains why with a story about her organizer's behavior during the grade strike:

> In the German department after the grade strike people were trying to get their jobs back. A bunch of us were standing there to try to get [one of the striking TAs] back her job. . . . The faculty came out and started yelling at us. I have never lost so much respect so quickly for any authority figure. . . . I was watching these people yell at [my organizer], and she was quite calm. . . . You know, she didn't get angry back. She just really calmly and firmly said, "I'm sorry you feel that way. [The TA] feels threatened, and she'd really like to have me in there to talk with her." And she was calm, she was firm, and she went in. . . . And that's who I want to be.

The Other Side: Elise Neely

We have recounted here primarily the success stories of organizing — stories about individuals who participated in the union and emerged with a heightened awareness of the university's limitations, an expanded imagination about the possibilities for transcending those limitations, and a strengthened sense of themselves and their power. Yet as we mentioned earlier, organizing is hard work. It does not always succeed. For every successful transformation, there is potentially a failure. Elise Neely is one example of an organizing "failure."

Like many of her fellow graduate students, Neely chose to come to Yale out of a particular moral conviction about the value of education and the centrality of the university to society's cultural development: "I had very idealistic ideas about enlightenment and spiritual growth and community, about the way in which a discussion of a high-minded set of ideas can bring a group of people together and make them function as a group." Neely eloquently defends her ideal of a university. It has shaped and guided her research, her teaching (she won one of the university's top teaching prizes), and her personal quest for self-definition. She sees herself as a "kind and gentle" scholar whose teaching and commitment to undergraduate education are crucial to her sense of Yale's (and her own) educational mission. "Teaching is a very intimate experience, and it works to the extent that people believe in each other."

Neely quickly found that her vision of Yale was somewhat at odds with how it actually operated. First, her notions of intellectual community and scholarly collaboration ran counter to the "combative" culture of the classroom: "It's not about just simply sharing what you know.... It's about advancement. People don't often share what they know. There's a sort of secretiveness about graduate study, and people are very private about showing their work. And it makes people anxious because they know that they are going to be judged." Second, she did not anticipate the "boundaries" and the "distance between faculty and students" that shape scholarly engagement at Yale. Unlike Ellen Martinez, who expected the faculty to use their intellectual power to help her develop her own ideas, Neely was surprised to find out that "when you go to talk to a professor about a paper, they won't tell you what to write about." She initially found this quite jarring because she had expected more guidance. Third, she realized that the university was a business, which she now compares to General Motors and IBM. She talks at great length about administrators who subscribe to "the idea of the university as a business because that's the way to make it profitable." They are not, she says, "particularly sympathetic to graduate students who are concerned about finding jobs and finding a place in the world." These people have set a tone for the scholarly community at Yale, a tone that valorizes the efficient, but uncaring, production of research:

> The more capable you are as a businessperson in the sense that you can get your work done on time, that you can define a limited project and pursue it in a coherent manner, [the more you will succeed].... But I had an idea about the more poetic kind of scholar, more haphazard in method, but kind and gentle, and I found out that it was not really all that kind and gentle.

Neely found that teaching was not rewarded in such an atmosphere. Education was "certainly not what academic publishing is about, or getting papers accepted, or getting a job." Her discovery of the grim realities of the university was "kind of disappointing."

Despite her unhappiness with what she found at Yale, Neely refused to embrace the idea of unionization as a means to redress these shortcomings. Several considerations led her to avoid participating in the union. First, she found the members of GESO and its precursor, TA Solidarity, "a very angry group, and I didn't really understand what they were angry about." She was "frightened" of them. What particularly made her nervous was their commitment to the union and the extent of their involvement in the organization. "They seemed to me kind of stuck in their own graduate careers, not writing their dissertations, not getting on, and I basically thought, 'Wow, I really don't want to end up like that.' That was my first response, . . . just aversion."

Unlike other graduate students such as Jonathan Perry, who had similar initial reactions to GESO but soon realized that members of the union were serious about their academic work and that being in a union was not antithetical to being a scholar, Neely continued to view GESO members as she had in her first encounter:

> I've always had ambivalent feelings about GESO. It's not always been clear to me whether I've been responding to GESO's actions or to my own fears about getting distracted, based on that first initial experience, and then also based on my witnessing other graduate students ahead of me [in my department] get really involved in GESO and not write their dissertations. . . . To my infant eyes, I just saw them spending a lot of time on this organization and not spending a lot of time writing.

Nonetheless, for a small period of time, she did get involved in the union. That experience, however, only left her more ambivalent about unionization. Membership meetings and large crowds of people united behind a common goal made her nervous:

> It's very frightening to get up in those meetings and actually disagree because typically there's a strong and coherent platform that's been offered. Organizers will get up to the queue and speak very poetically about the issue at hand, and oftentimes the people who disagree really haven't thought very clearly about why they disagree — so there's the first problem with them being inarticulate.

> Then the second problem is that it's just difficult to stand up in a room that seems to be all of one mind, and I'm not quite sure it does seem that way, but it certainly has to me.

Probably more important was her fear of confrontation. "It was never the middling actions or just simply the spirit of talk that bothered me. It was the aggressive actions... like strikes,... which I just felt were going to make people angry." Neely could only understand confrontation as an angry, hostile act by a group of embittered, hostile people. More important, she felt that it would provoke hostility from the faculty or the administration. As we mentioned earlier, this fear of the faculty can involve fears of retribution, or it can entail a fear that the faculty will think less highly of a union member. In Neely's case, the latter seems more relevant:

> I thought that as soon as people began to get angry and began to really feel threatened, that in some way our battle would be lost paradoxically, and that we'd end up actually just sort of screaming and ranting and not being listened to, and worse yet being perceived as adolescents acting out against our parents and not as thoughtful academics in a discussion about high-minded ideals.... [I wanted to] focus on developing a discourse and creating a very academic approach to the question or a very intellectual approach to the question.

Neely feared that if she participated in union actions, she would be thought of as a child and was worried that she would not be perceived as a serious, thoughtful academic.

As Neely explains it, she is more comfortable with discussion and conversation. One of the few GESO events she has enjoyed in the past few years was a one-day academic moratorium in February 1996:

> I thought that the moratorium was an excellent, excellent achievement because that to my mind fostered discussion and was about really thinking through the implications of the situation, not just for Yale but for the country at large, and it was not confrontational. It wasn't about confrontation at all; it was simply about education, about thinking, and there was no action attached to it besides the actual thought.

Neely fears that when graduate students mobilize and confront the people who can actually implement the changes that they (and she) seek, a collective mind-set takes over, and only nasty conflict will ensue. "I'm a really conflict-averse person," she says. In her eyes, collective action is not about the achievement of a common goal. She refused to participate in the grade strike, she says, because it was "an unkind use of power." Her discussion of collective action is rich with this sort of imagery. "The undergraduates were at our mercy, and I don't like being a dictator in that way."

The combination of Neely's dissatisfaction and disappointment with Yale and her unwillingness to act collectively in order to transform the institution has left her in a difficult situation. She wants the university to change, but she cannot readily imagine how it will or who will bring it about. In the last year or so, as she has struggled to find a job in academe, she has grown even more concerned and increasingly embittered about Yale's failure to adapt and change to the realities of a downsized academic job market. "I'm frankly furious that I have received so little help figuring out what is going to happen afterward," she says. Nonetheless, her refusal to accept the need for concerted, mass pressure prevents her from acting.

Instead, Neely remains confident in the administration's good will and benevolence. She readily admits to her "desire to preserve intact a power structure that I could trust." As she explains, she has always believed in the authority of the institution: "I've been incredibly lucky. I'm one of those kids who got into every school I applied to, then got into the right graduate program and went to Yale. It seemed to me that, you know, trust in God and he will lead, trust in the Ivy League and things will follow." She longs for the university to respond to her concerns and to look out for her best interests. As she begins to face an increasingly uncertain future, her desire for a nurturing, protective institution has increased. She wistfully recalls how helpful and caring her undergraduate university was: "I went to college for four years, and there was a huge career services office that would give me as much time as I wanted and one-on-one appointments and hold my hand as I struggled to figure out what to do." These memories spark her imagination today and inform her hopes for Yale: "Wouldn't it be comforting if we had a person who would tell us about how to become an academic dean, a person who would tell us how to get involved in a think tank, a person who would tell us how to get involved in any of the numerous foundations that exist?" Despite the intensity of her desire, she carefully insists on framing her concerns in polite, nonconfrontational terms: "I like to frame it as a question: Well, what can we have? Not as a demand—we deserve this—because I don't think we do deserve anything in particular. We need more information about what it is that we can expect."

The conflict between her heartfelt needs and legitimate concerns about the future and the university's unwillingness to deal with them has not led Neely to question the legitimacy of the power structure at Yale. Unlike the other graduate students we interviewed, who found themselves posing increasingly confrontational demands on the university and challenging the authority of deans and the faculty, Neely insists that the problem is merely the administration's lack of information. When they have the correct set of facts, she believes, they will respond in a more helpful manner. The issue is not power, who has it and how it is used, but perspective: "The administrators aren't really familiar with this situation either. It's as new to them as it is to us. Maybe it's new to them because they're still seeing through eyes that saw a different world. We don't have access to their perspective. I think in a certain way we need to educate them." Her belief in the administration's ignorance of the facts is closely tied to a concern that graduate students not offend them or make them feel bad. She is worried that graduate students' assertiveness may ultimately be hurtful and cruel:

> I've always felt a little bit bad for some of the administrators who are operating under the same assumptions they've always had and feel like they're getting clobbered and they didn't study for the test. Somehow they came to school one day and somebody had rewritten all the questions. It's almost like we need to explain to them what it is that's going on in a way that makes clear that they're not responsible for it, because I don't think they really are. They're just older than we are, and that's basically why they're where they are.

Neely's relation to the authority of the administration and the faculty is nonetheless ambivalent and full of contradiction. At one point, she openly acknowledges the structural nature of the conflict, and she seems to accept the struggle that inevitably comes with change. "We want to reorganize the world that people have grown comfortable in and reshape it to make it more comfortable for more people. But that's necessarily less comfortable for people who are accustomed to it the way it is." At the same time, she cannot give up on the hope that "real creativity or maybe more patience or more understanding" will ultimately bring about the necessary changes without "the kind of anger that [change normally] generates." In another instance, she admits that her faith in the Ivy League has been badly shaken. "Frankly, it [her faith] doesn't seem to be that true anymore," she says. But rather than moving on from her disillusionment to challenge the administration to do better and fight for change, she believes she must adjust herself to a new reality. She says that she must come to terms with "the real terrifying prospect of not knowing what the next step for me will be." At the same time, however, she cannot really accept that reality, so she hopes that Yale will change its ways: "If they really do believe in our skills enough to have us instruct the undergraduates during our training period, I don't see why our training period needs to end." She concludes on a wistful note: "I don't know how they could fund [continuing to pay graduate students as TAs until they receive a job elsewhere], but I would certainly like it if they could."

Neely's inability to conceive of herself as part of a collective movement that would not just hope for change but actually bring it about is tied to an abiding faith in the power of individuals. Her conceptions of change and power often are drawn from the classroom, where she imagines students wielding a remarkable control over their destiny:

> To teach someone how the language works is to give them an ability to shape the world that they live in. What could be more exciting than to be actually able to understand your existence in the world as something that you could frame, something that your ability to wield English in any particular shape or form will allow you to . . . choose? I still think that's incredibly exciting and that that's something in my power.

Even though her actual experiences at Yale have called that faith in the ability of individuals to shape their destiny into question (she used to believe, "You can do [graduate education] any way you want, and you can end up somewhere," but now says, "In fact, you can't do it any way you want and end up somewhere"), she still believes in the power of each person to remake her or his world.

Again, the classroom is her model: "Teaching is a place where I can make the world that I want to live in appear as if by magic or maybe by sheer force of will."

This faith in the power of the individual — as opposed to the collective — has a negative side to it, however, for it would seem to imply that Neely is facing the prospect of unemployment because she has not sufficiently mastered the skills of being an academic. Although she is aware that the "success of the previous group [of graduate students who graduated before her and got academic jobs] was arbitrary" and she knows "that life doesn't necessarily reward hard work or talent," her interview is full of self-doubt and self-criticism for her failure to find an academic job. "If I don't get a job as an academic, I'll think clearly I didn't learn how to make it a career."

The only way Neely can imagine herself to be powerful as an individual is when she thinks about what Yale owes her in her status as a consumer of education: "I just honestly can't understand if this is a business, why it is they're basically not taking care of the customers." She is careful to say that "I don't think that Yale owes us a living. While I wish that Yale would have us teach, I don't think they owe that to us at all." She eschews any sense of entitlement that comes from being a worker, but she feels somewhat confident that she has paid for an education and, therefore, "they owe us a Ph.D." This language of consumer rights is ultimately as disempowering as the language of the classroom is. It emphasizes the power that comes from money — not from a sense of right, not from making a contribution to society, and not from being part of an organized group that is committed to changing the academy. "Wonder" — not "demand" or "insist" — becomes the operative term: "I think what we can do is identify our desire not just as graduate students wanting a living from the university, but as people getting a degree granted by a university. As customers, we'll wonder what it might be that this degree can buy."

Beyond Fear

As universities continue down the path of downsizing and rely increasingly on part-time teachers, the choice for graduate students, and indeed for all adjunct instructors, becomes clearer: either we hope for the best and depend on the good intentions of those who are driving these trends, or we organize ourselves into a concerted, national movement that will force administrators across the country to make the necessary reforms. Our experience at Yale has demonstrated that there is an almost one-to-one relationship between graduate student collective action and progressive improvements in the graduate school. Almost every reform in the last six years—whether in the form of pay increases, better health benefits, fairer academic policies, or greater democracy in the institution itself—has come on the heels of some specific action by graduate students. Needless to say, we believe that the success of collective action at Yale argues overwhelmingly for our choosing that option rather than the politics of wishful thinking.

Beyond the crucial impact of collective action on the university's treatment of its teaching workforce, we must bear in mind the transformation of those individuals who have protested and struggled, who have fought for progress and challenged powerful elites. We believe that these changes are the most far-reaching and significant results of the union struggle at Yale. The members of GESO have emerged from their battle with the university as powerful men and women, prepared to continue their struggles at Yale and at other universities and institutions. Graduate students have learned necessary skills and developed critical faculties for launching and building an organized movement. As the country falls increasingly under the thumb of a smaller and smaller number of people, these skills and faculties will prove crucial to any movement that challenges the dominance of these elites.

The formation of GESO has left a lasting imprint on those who have fought for union recognition. Educated into the mores of a university culture, most academics learn the values of politesse, cooperation, and just plain getting along. Words like "struggle" or "confrontation" are frowned upon; they carry the stigma of popular and, as it is so often assumed, anti-intellectual movements. They are not part of the accepted vocabulary of serious or legitimate scholars. The stigma associated with these words reflects more than the conventions of a university community. They are part of a system of rules and regulations that teach people powerlessness, timidity, and an excessive solicitude for the opinions of those with power over us. Those rules and regulations are the tools of trade for those bent on fostering a culture of servility. They are antithetical to democracy, and they are antithetical to the values of intellectual life.

Through organizing and struggling for a union, graduate students at Yale have confronted what is the most essential dilemma for any genuine teacher and scholar: how to be a thoughtful, independent intellectual in the age of academe. Instead of succumbing to the easy conventions of the university community, the graduate students who have fought for a union have acted out of a more strenuous, and more elemental, conviction about the purpose of that community. They have acted on the belief that values and principles are more important, and more powerful, than pedantry and careerism. They have faced serious tests of their intellectual integrity and commitment, and they have passed those tests. In doing so, they call to mind Max Weber's famous address, "Politics as a Vocation," to the students at Munich University in 1918. "It is immensely moving," Weber wrote, when an individual "is aware of a responsibility for the consequences of his conduct and really feels such responsibility with heart and soul." That individual "then acts by following an ethic of responsibility and somewhere . . . reaches the point where he says: 'Here I stand; I can do no other.' That is something genuinely human and moving."

NOTES

1. For this essay, we conducted about twenty in-depth interviews with graduate students who participated in the union at various levels. In addition, for the last three years, both of us have been responsible for directing all of the organizing in the union. In our roles, we have worked in twenty-six academic departments with hundreds of rank-and-file organizers and members. The conclusions in this article are based on both our interviews and our organizing experience.

2. For the sake of protecting graduate students' privacy, we have changed their names.

Figure 8. A December 1994 poster designed by Kathy Newman

Chapter 3
Poor, Hungry, and Desperate? or, Privileged, Histrionic, and Demanding? In Search of the True Meaning of "Ph.D."

Kathy M. Newman

A few years ago I heard the novelist Tom Wolfe speak to a group of graduate students and faculty at Yale University. Wolfe, a 1957 alumni of the Yale American Studies Ph.D. program, started his talk with a few stories about his graduate school days in New Haven. But his stories were few, he explained, because graduate school is painful to recollect and difficult to represent. As evidence for his argument, he noted (with some mirth) that there has never been a novel written about graduate school.

At the time of Wolfe's talk I was writing a paper on representations of higher education in the genre of the college novel (made famous by such classics as F. Scott Fitzgerald's *This Side of Paradise* and Owen Johnson's *Stover at Yale*). Beset by Wolfe's questions, and armed with a descriptive bibliography of 425 college novels, I determined to find out if he was right and if, in fact, there was no extant novel about the trials and tribulations of graduate school.[1]

I discovered that Wolfe was wrong — at least technically. There are some absurd and delicious novels of graduate life, my favorite being *Doctor's Oral,* published in 1939. I love it because the principal drama — at least one hundred pages of the novel — is set in the oral exam itself. The plot revolves around two crises: on the morning of his English department oral exam the protagonist learns that his girlfriend (also a graduate student) is pregnant. Next he gets a telegram informing him that if he passes his orals he will be awarded a job at a nearby college. At the end of the exam the seven faculty on his committee are divided about whether they should pass him. Ironically, it is the guest examiner from the economics department who, out of appreciation for the student's reading of Theodore Dreiser's novel *The Financier,* breaks the tie in his favor. Our hero passes the exam, gets the job, and keeps the girl — not to mention the baby.

But in a more general sense, Wolfe was correct. There is no ur-novel of graduate student life, no graduate student equivalent of Owen Johnson's "Dink Stover" or Fitzgerald's "Armory Blaine." In light of recent attention heaped on other professionals in training, graduate students seem especially slighted. If medical students have their Michael Crichton, and law students have their John Grisham, no equivalent bard has exposed the sad life of the graduate student.

The few times graduate students do appear in popular culture, they seem either sad or pathetic. Dustin Hoffman plays a graduate student whose nickname is "The Creep" in the 1976 drama *Marathon Man.* In *Terms of Endearment,* Debra Winger's lousy, cheating husband is a graduate student at the beginning of the film and has an affair with one at the end. In the horror film *Candyman,* a white, female graduate student in sociology — who studies urban legends in Chicago's Cabrini Green housing project — encounters the fierce, black Candyman of urban legend and is soon accused of his flesh-eating crimes. Less monstrous, but equally sinister, both the male and female graduate teaching assistants on the series *Beverly Hills 90210* (as well as the short-lived *Class of '96*) seduce their first-year students.[2]

While I cannot deny the terrific humor (and horror) of these images, I do not offer them merely for laughs. Rather, I see some connections between the negative representations of graduate students in popular culture and the problem of their political representation in universities. As graduate students have been appearing with greater frequency and prominence in popular culture, they have simultaneously been appearing with greater frequency and prominence on college campuses, demanding, among other things, better pay and more power. The relationship between these twin upheavals in representation might be difficult to pin down. On the one hand, if there is a "crisis" in the cultural representation of graduate students, it is a crisis as old as graduate schools themselves. On the other hand, the crisis in the political representation of graduate students seems relatively new, as graduate students across the country have been organizing for greater control over university decisions that affect their lives — primarily by forming teaching assistant (TA) unions.

My stake in these problems of representation — and unionization — is personal. I have been a graduate student in the American Studies program at Yale for six years, during which time I have been one of the leaders of a drive for a graduate student union. As part of this effort I have tried to improve both the cultural and the political representation of graduate students at Yale. In the process, I have discovered that the issues are closely related. As we have struggled for greater political representation in the university, we have had to struggle against (and sometimes within) the negative and conventional representations of the graduate student — representations available not only in the broader popular culture but also on campus in undergraduate newspapers, cartoons, and literary magazines, as well as in the rhetoric of university administrators.

Using the Yale union effort as a case study, I would like to explore the relationship between the cultural and political representation of graduate students more thoroughly. First, I will examine some of the popular depictions of graduate students from the last twenty-five years, with the goal of trying to explain what the conventions are and what they mean. Second, I will show how university officials, undergraduates, and faculty have used the dominant (and negative) cultural images of graduate students to discredit their attempts to gain greater political force within the university. Third, I will examine some of the representations of graduate students that have been produced for the TA union drive at Yale — to show how some of these images play with, or reshape altogether, the dominant cultural stereotypes. Finally, I will speculate about the effect that the graduate union movement at Yale — along with those at universities around the country — has had on the dominant image of graduate students in the popular press and beyond.

The Paradox of the Graduate Student

Horror movies and *Beverly Hills 90210* episodes aside, the most prevalent image of the graduate student — inside and outside the academy — is the student wearing the black graduation robe and mortarboard. We see this image in cartoons, in the newspapers in June (when everyone is "a graduate"), and as an icon in university brochures. But as simple and as common as this image is, it raises a question. For which graduation is the graduate student dressed? On the one hand, if the robe and mortarboard signal the student's college graduation, then throughout her graduate student career she is stuck in the past, forever reliving the triumph of her collegiate rite of passage. On the other hand, if the robe and mortarboard signal some future graduation, in which the Ph.D. will be awarded, then this too is a depressing scenario. The graduate student is not looking backward but instead is waiting: all dressed up and six years to go.

The paradox of this image is resolved, perhaps, if we interpret it to mean that the graduate student is suspended *between* graduations. The student must graduate from college to go to graduate school, and she must remain a graduate student until the second graduation — the Ph.D. graduation — is complete. Graduation from college begins the graduate student's career. Graduation from graduate school will terminate it.

The problem is that six to eight years turns out to be a long time to be suspended between anything, let alone graduations. There are probably close to a half-million graduate students in the arts and sciences in this country, and the median time to degree for the humanities is 8.3 years.[3] While this is a lengthy and arduous process for the students themselves, it is unfathomable for the greater public. How could anyone be in school for so long? What could possibly take so long to learn? Indeed, the length of my degree program has been a source of great angst and confusion, not only for myself but also for my mother (*When* are you going to finish?), her friends (*What* will you do when you are done?), and my grandmother (*When* are you going to get married?).

The matriarchs in my family (and their friends) are not alone. If popular culture is any measure, the public is aghast at how long it takes to get a Ph.D. For this reason, I think, the graduate student in popular culture is often depicted as a social misfit or a loser. After the mortarboard, probably the most prevalent image of graduate students is the classic nerd: thin and hunched, with glasses and a pocket protector. Smart, but awkward. Especially with the ladies.

This image was perfectly embodied by Dustin Hoffman in the 1976 classic, *Marathon Man*. Hoffman's character, Thomas Levy, is training to run a marathon and is also writing his dissertation on tyranny in American politics. He is drawn to this topic for personal reasons — his father killed himself under the scrutiny of a political scandal during the McCarthy era, and Levy is determined to prove his innocence.

But when Levy's brother shows up on his doorstep, stabbed to death, Levy is drawn into a complicated web of intrigue that involves a sadistic Nazi dentist, a safe-deposit box full of diamonds, and the U.S. government. Slowly and painfully Levy learns that his brother was a secret agent and that his new girlfriend (whom he picked up in a library reading room!) is a diamond courier for the Nazis. At the end of the film he realizes that the Nazi dentist killed his brother, and, in a vengeful rage, he goes one-on-one with the aging sadist, preventing him from escaping with a suitcase full of diamonds taken from Holocaust victims. Graduate school was never this exciting, and the dissertation gets lost in the shuffle.

While Dustin Hoffman's character succeeds in his crusade to avenge his brother's death, overcoming tyranny in real life, the dominant image of the film is still Levy as a rumpled, stringy, huffing and puffing marathon runner whom Latino neighbors call "the Creep." He may be able to track down a famous Nazi, but his sweatshirt has holes in it. Worse still, his room is a mess. What is he learning? What will he contribute, except to himself? Even his mentor, a professor named Biesenthal, questions the use-value of a Ph.D., telling his graduate students that he hopes they all flunk: "[T]here is no shortage of historians. We grind you out like link sausages, and you are every bit as bright. Well, I say, enough! I say, let you find harmless employment elsewhere." We don't find out if Levy does find employment elsewhere — after all his heroic running and chasing we never see him on the university campus again. The film ends as it began, with Levy running around a reservoir.[4]

It is no accident, I suspect, that this film appeared in 1976, just as the stays were beginning to tighten around the expanding postwar research university.[5] Though the number of Ph.D.'s produced per year in this country tripled from 1963 to 1974, this production peaked in 1974 and actually decreased until 1988, when the number of Ph.D.'s produced per year finally reached the 1974 level and began to increase again.[6] Throughout the 1970s, with the decreasing production of Ph.D.'s and the shortage of academic jobs, the image of the graduate student as a taxi driver became a cultural symbol of the new postindustrialism — an image as clichéd as the corner apple-cart in the Great Depression. Popular economists, writing for magazines like *Newsweek* and *Time,* began to decry the overproduction of Ph.D.'s, as well as other kinds of graduates. If the economy is shrinking, they argued, why should we devote our surplus resources to educational degrees of questionable use-value?[7]

Since the 1970s, the dominant image of the graduate student has played on this question as to what (if anything) graduate students produce. Moreover, these images have played off the fear that graduate students might actually pose a danger to society, not as producers, but as reproducers out of control in their role as researchers and, increasingly, in their role as teachers of undergraduates.

The image of the graduate researcher out of control is best captured by the actress Virginia Madsen, who plays a sociology graduate student in the horror film *Candyman.* As a student of the urban legend, she finds out that the mythical black Candyman is no fairy tale and that he will appear if she says his name five times while looking in the mirror. She conjures him, and he does her bidding, which includes making a delicious meal out of her philandering professor husband and his undergraduate girlfriend. She is accused of Candyman's brutal murders, and though we know she is innocent, we are left feeling that she bears some responsibility for the terror. Once a producer of knowledge, she ends up as a reproducer of monstrous deeds, with Candyman acting as an extension of her deadly unconscious.

Popular culture also figures graduate students as evil reproducers in the classroom. Increasingly, on such television shows as *Beverly Hills 90210,* graduate student TAs are cast as manipulative he- and she-devils who seduce their students. The most she-devilish of them all is a ravishing anthropology graduate student who brazenly publicizes her "open" marriage to a sociology professor and who is probably the first character on television to use the term "ABD" (all but dissertation). She teaches a class on cross-cultural feminism to the women on *90210,* while in her home she seduces their boyfriends, the freshman Brandon Walsh and rebel-without-a-career Dylan McKay. While all that is taking place, the studious Andrea is seduced by her male TA, a nerdy, long-haired, and "politically correct" guy with questionable teaching mores.

Though these graduate student seductions do not lead to actual reproduction, the implication is that graduate students might have dangerous influence over their students, inside and outside the classroom. Moreover, all these graduate student characterizations are negative. When not explicitly feminine, they are feminized, like the wimpy character played by Hoffman and the long-haired TA. But more than feminized, they are demonized. The message to the public is chilling: beware of graduate students—they might study something useless, kill you, or seduce your children.

Indeed, university folklore is replete with stories of real killer graduate students — there was a math graduate student at Stanford who killed his adviser with a hammer, and by now everyone should know that the Unabomber won the prize for the best math dissertation at the University of Michigan in the 1960s. But hammers and bombs are not the tools of choice for the average graduate student in real life, no matter how resentful we might feel, and thus it still must be asked: Why are the conventions of reproduction, horror, and slackness used to represent graduate students? What makes graduate students in popular culture so pathetic? And so dangerous?

One answer to these questions, suggested to me by Yale professor Michael Denning, is that graduate school is the place of domestic reproduction within the academy — the institution through which the university itself is reproduced. This makes the graduate school different from all other professional schools within the university: only the graduate school trains students for a life within the university's ivory towers.

Thus negative representations of graduate students have something in common with the negative image of the university as a whole. If universities are threatening or dangerous places that anoint the ruling class or waste and misuse the social surplus, then graduate students are at the heart of the university's dangerous uselessness. If, in the words of the Marathon Man's mentor, history professors are as useless as link sausages, why should the public fund another study of tyranny in American politics or another study of urban legends? What is the use-value of academic research, and who should determine it?

Universities also come under attack not just as places of questionable knowledge production but also as places of dangerous social reproduction, especially in the realm of undergraduate education. Though graduate students did little university teaching twenty-five years ago, they are now admitted in numbers that reflect each school's teaching needs rather than the demands of the faculty job market. As one state-level labor-hearing officer put it, when determining whether or not graduate students should be classified as employees for collective bargaining, "the university clearly hired teaching assistants more for economic reasons than academic ones."[8] But this fact is also a sore spot with tuition- and taxpaying parents: Why should graduate students be teaching undergraduates when professors themselves appear to lead such slack and cushy lives? From the point of view of taxpayers and parents, everything that is wrong with graduate students is wrong with the university, and vice versa.

Graduate students may get a bum rap in popular culture, but hardly anyone, except graduate students like myself, would even notice this pattern, let alone consider it a real crisis: there is no Anti-defamation League on the lookout for distorted and misleading images of the graduate student. A quick scan of graduate student activism across the country suggests, however, that there is a real crisis of graduate student *political* representation on a growing number of campuses. These graduate students are increasingly unhappy about material issues, such as TA compensation, teacher training, professional development, health benefits, and the collapsed job market. But the greatest controversies are over issues of representation and power. Graduate students have been demanding more control over the university decisions that affect the quality of their life and work.

At the same time that graduate students have been heating up the pop-culture screen, real-life graduate students have been heating up campuses through union recognition drives. TA union drives have become the dominant form of graduate student activism in the 1990s, with actions that include union elections, rallies, demonstrations, teaching strikes, and grade strikes. Today there are thirteen campuses with recognized unions and many more with drives in process.[9] Though these activities rarely make it into the narratives of popular entertainment, recent strikes, especially the Yale grade strike, have garnered a great deal of attention in the popular press.

Graduate student representation, even of the cultural variety, is thus a significant campus issue; long before these controversies make it into the *New York Times,* they are widely debated on campus. Graduate students who are fighting for a union thus have to combat a more pernicious form of negative representation than the lecherous TAs of *90210:* the negative images of the graduate student circulated by university administrators, undergraduates, and faculty. In the section that follows, I examine some of these images and offer interpretations of the university's contribution to the stereotype of the lonely, monstrous, and oversexed graduate student.

The Revenge of the Deans

At the end of my first year of graduate school I was initiated into the union movement with horrific tales of the "Kagan-Pollitt Plan." Named for the deans who proposed it, this plan made sweeping changes in the graduate school funding structure — initiating a 30 percent cut in the teaching budget, adding a modest dissertation fellowship, and limiting the length of Ph.D. registration. According to the new rule, graduate students would not be allowed to register beyond their sixth year. While they could submit their dissertation later, they would be denied such privileges as subsidized health care, deferred loans, and library use.

This was a devastating change, since even graduate students who finished in six years rarely found jobs in their first year on the market. The modest dissertation fellowship did not offset either the hardship inflicted by the sixth-year rule or the cutback in the total number of TA positions. Though graduate students had already started to organize for a union, when the Kagan-Pollitt Plan went into effect, they mobilized as never before, with rallies, petitions, an active membership drive, assorted strikes, and the formation of the Graduate Employees and Students Organization (GESO).

More devastating than the plan itself, however, was the attitude of the administrators who invented it. Donald Kagan, former dean of Yale College, and Jerome Pollitt, former dean of the graduate school, often spoke of graduate students with disdain. In explaining the rationale behind the sixth-year rule, Kagan claimed that graduate students should be hurried along because "money is being thrown down a rathole." Jerome Pollitt added that he wanted to help graduate students finish their degree "rather than lead a kind of gypsy life in New Haven."[10] With deans like these, it could be argued, who needs enemies?

These remarks, I soon learned, did not represent an isolated incident but rather a pattern. There is a culture of meanness toward graduate students at Yale, which, while difficult to document, has fueled the continual anger of graduate students there, as well as the continual drive for unionization. Some of the stories about this meanness are imbedded in the oral culture, passed down from one generation of graduate students to the next. One associate dean of the graduate school has been known to tell graduate students who come to him with financial troubles that if they are concerned about money they must be "mercenary" and that "Yale is not a breadline." Almost everyone I know who has met with this dean has left his office in tears.

These incidents affect the whole community: if it didn't happen to you, it happened to someone you know. These confrontations with mean deans — often in the midst of real crises over money, health care, or registration — make us wonder why we are at Yale. If they do not like us, then why did they invite us to come? Indeed, while popular culture's attacks on graduate students may reflect general resentment of universities, it would be hard to argue that Yale's attitude toward graduate students comes from populist anti-intellectualism. But then where *does* it come from?

One answer is that graduate students do not fit into the collegiate culture that makes Yale distinctive. In a long-standing attempt to distinguish itself from Harvard, Yale advertises itself as an intimate liberal arts college for undergraduates that also has a world-class faculty. University administrators make undergraduates feel enormously special and encourage them to believe that everything good about Yale is good for them, created exclusively for their happiness and education. Most of my students, for example, do not know that a graduate school is the institution that differentiates a university from a college. Many of them do not even know that we are paid for our teaching. It is a carefully guarded secret at Yale that the professors are here because they want to direct graduate research, as well as to have their teaching load lightened by graduate student service in the classroom.[11]

But this does not fully explain the larger problem of disrespect toward graduate students that exists at Yale and beyond. Examining some of the images of graduate students that are circulated on the Yale campus, however, will help account for the conditions that lead graduate students to unionize and administrators to fight back. Surprisingly enough, the rhetoric that Yale administrators use to describe graduate students resonates with the popular conventions of representation that I outlined in the first section. In the eyes of Yale administrators, graduate students, and especially *unionizing* graduate students, appear as lonely misfits and uncontrollable he- and she-devils.

Yale administrators have homed in on one principal explanation for the graduate student union drive at Yale: graduate students at Yale are lonely, and the drive for a union is really a search for community. This statement was first made to the parents of Yale undergraduates in the fall of 1995, as Yale president Rick Levin and dean of Yale College Dick Brodhead tried to explain to puzzled parents why hundreds of graduate students (and other campus workers) were marching, yelling, and demonstrating all over campus during Parents Weekend.[12] The antidote to this loneliness, the administrators explained, was in hand, and it was *not* a union. Instead, they promised to build a cultural center for graduate students that would solve the problem. If graduate students had access to a community center, perhaps they would put down their picket signs and bullhorns, and perhaps their complaints would melt away.

But at the same time that administrators have raised this concern about our loneliness, they have also raised concerns about our capacity for sexual reproduction. Over the last six years, each successive dean of the graduate school has claimed that the high price of graduate student health care is the result of graduate students having more and more babies. According to the deans, these babies are very expensive, and they make the overall cost of graduate health skyrocket. This was recently asserted by current dean of the graduate school Tom Appelquist in a 1995 meeting with GESO leaders. His statement raises an interesting paradox. Are graduate students lonely? Or are they having too many babies? Can they be both terribly lonely and terribly pregnant?[13]

Yet the administration has offered a way out of this rhetorical corner. In the spring of 1996, during a week-long strike of Yale teaching assistants, graduate school administrators began to use the phrase "entitlement program" to describe the funding for graduate students. In an interview with the campus press, Associate Dean Jonas Zdanys claimed, "It's free to go to graduate school at Yale," and Dean Appelquist said, "It's incredible. It's an entitlement program."[14] This was a slick and effective rhetorical move. By using the word "entitlement," which has powerful associations with welfare, Appelquist made it possible for graduate students to be both lonely and pregnant, since no one could be more lonely, or more pregnant, than the she-devilish welfare queen.

While it might be going too far to say that administrators see graduate students as the welfare queens of the leisure class, I think their statements conjure up the standard images of the graduate student — images of lonely misfits and lecherous teaching assistants — for several reasons. First, when it comes to public relations, universities are in a bind on the subject of graduate study. If universities try to argue that graduate students are merely students, then they have to explain why most graduate students, unlike undergraduate students, do not pay tuition. They have to justify their "entitlement program" to parents who do not understand why their children are paying up to thirty-five thousand dollars a year for school while graduate students pay almost nothing for tuition and often receive stipends as well.

Second, if universities try to justify the fact that graduate students receive extra support because they do extra work — namely, teaching — then they must admit what few universities want to admit: that graduate students do the bulk of the intensive one-on-one teaching and much of the grading in the modern research university. One recent study of graduate teaching at Yale found that graduate students spent more hours per week in the classroom than full-time tenured and ladder faculty.[15] At state universities the numbers are even more startling. For example, Cary Nelson estimates that at the University of Illinois at Urbana-Champaign it would cost more than $4 million a year to hire full-time faculty to replace the teaching done by graduate students in the English department alone.[16] Even smaller schools, like Wesleyan University in Middletown, Connecticut, allow professors to outsource their heavy exam and paper-grading work to graduate students at neighboring universities like Yale.

This heavy dependence on graduate teaching, coupled with the dismal job market, turns graduate school into something like a "Teach for America" program for the benefit of undergraduates. Graduate students are often gifted and dedicated teachers, but their teaching experience in graduate school, even when combined with their Ph.D., will not guarantee them an academic job — or any other kind of job.

Administrators cannot admit this to the public, to the graduate students they recruit, and perhaps not even to themselves. In a downsizing economy, their job is to cut at the margins, and graduate students are an easy target. The number of students applying to graduate school increases every year and so do universities' teaching needs, making graduate students vulnerable to financial cutbacks. Graduate students do not have even the limited assembly power of professors or the potential earning power (and thus the potential alumni-donating power) of undergraduates who go on to become doctors, lawyers, and management consultants. When graduate students vie for more power by forming unions, the easiest counter for administrators is to claim that graduate students want to form unions simply because they are monstrously privileged social misfits — a view that popular culture will corroborate.

Yale administrators have added a few more images to this rogues' gallery, painting graduate students in GESO as ungrateful apprentices and greedy children. Yale undergraduates immediately seized on the latter image, since they enjoy representing their union-happy teaching assistants as whiny, ungrateful stepchildren of the great Mother Yale. In one particularly graphic cartoon (see fig. 9), GESO is pictured as a rattle-holding, screaming toddler. Perhaps undergraduates relish this kind of representational power-reversal because they are often the ones who cry — quite literally — over their grades. It is also easier for them to criticize GESO than to criticize Yale. They have invested their futures in the reputation of the university, and they are terrified that graduate students threaten to

Figure 9. Cartoon by Jon Lucas from the *Yale Herald*

expose Yale's hollowness with our street-oriented, press-garnering marches, rallies, and strikes.[17]

The treatment of graduate students in the undergraduate press at Yale is so mean that many graduate students refuse to read the undergraduate press at all. In another cartoon, published when Yale graduate students refused to turn in grades at the end of the term, GESO is pictured as a huge, masked, bare-chested, and hairy executioner, holding a knife that reads "GRADE STRIKE," which is pointed at a trembling "John Q. Undergrad" (see fig. 10). The undergraduate in this cartoon has one knife stuck in him already, left there by the other two unions on campus, who tried to end a popular "flexible" meal plan for undergraduates involving local restaurants. But the clear villain in this cartoon is the masked executioner, GESO, who asks naively, "Why don't you guys like us?"[18] Though this cartoon presents a terrifying visage, the executioner's question is one GESO members frequently ask. Why don't the undergraduates like GESO? Though we have adjusted to the fact that our teaching is not appreciated by our employers, we would like it to be appreciated, or at least not *scorned,* by our students.

Both images can be linked to popular culture's stereotypes of

Figure 10. "Slap-Happy" by David A. Moore. Cartoon from the *Yale Herald*

graduate students: if the baby is the abandoned misfit, then the executioner (he is so fat he has "breasts") is the crazed, feminized killer. There are various reasons for tapping into these conventions, but for Yale undergraduates the cruelty of these images is fueled by two factors: graduate students' power over their grades and their fear that their future might be as bleak as our reality. Many of them want to go to graduate school, or at least to professional school, but if they acknowledge the legitimacy of our grievances, then they must admit that their future could turn out like ours. They too might become lonely misfits or the welfare queens of the leisure class. They too might need a union.

In addition to harboring this fear of and resentment toward graduate students, many Yale undergraduates subscribe to the administration's view of graduate teachers as cheap labor, available to do their bidding. At the height of the grade strike controversy, the masthead editorial of the *Yale Daily News* charged graduate students with treason, insisting that "[g]raduate students who take part in such a strike have no place in the classroom, and do not deserve the privilege of grading Yale undergraduates."[19] This astonishing statement suggests that undergraduates see graduate students as their educational servants and grading as an exalted pleasure.

What they do not seem to realize is that grading is among the most tedious kinds of work in the academy — so tedious, in fact, that many of the senior faculty do not want to do it, or at least not very much of it. This is the dirty little secret that Yale graduate students let out of the bag by withholding grades. The grade strike, unlike the previous day-long and week-long teaching strikes, revealed how little control Yale professors have over the educational bullion that matters most to the central administration *and* to the students: the almighty grade. Most senior faculty have little contact with the undergraduates in their lecture courses, and the grade strike touched a raw and defensive nerve in the Yale professoriat; it raised questions about who "owns" the grade, as well as the papers and exams. Does the grade belong to the undergraduate, the faculty member who chooses the books and gives the lectures for the course, or the TA who comments on the papers and gives the final mark? Many professors said to their TAs, "You can't withhold the grades. This is *my* course." But the strike showed what little ownership professors had over these courses when the task of grading was divided up into teams of as many as sixteen teaching assistants.

The helplessness of the faculty in the face of the grade strike brought the culture of meanness at Yale to new heights. Until then the faculty at Yale were neutral to discouraging about the prospect of a teaching assistants' union. But once jolted to attention by the grade strike, they flocked to faculty meetings, shouted among themselves, issued a host of threatening memos, and held one-on-one meetings with their graduate students, during which they alternated between pleading with them to stop the madness and threatening to ruin their academic careers. These threats, however, were not the least bit farcical. The French department issued a memo telling graduate students that if they participated in the strike, they would never teach in the French department again. Three professors singled out their students for disciplinary hearings. The dean of the graduate school issued a memo saying that striking might legitimately be used by professors in negative letters of recommendation for the academic job market.[20]

Out of this unorganized but angry crackdown emerged one final, and enduring, image of the graduate student. The faculty, shocked that the grievances of their advisees might actually impact them, or worse still, implicate them, decided that the complaints of their teaching assistants were not that severe. This attitude was best articulated by Yale comparative literature professor Peter Brooks, who told the *New York Times* that Yale graduate students were among "the blessed of the earth." This was an effective rhetorical turn, at once erasing the university from the mundane world of labor relations and repositioning it as a temple of learning in a sacred otherworld.[21]

This image of graduate students as "the blessed of the earth" does not fit any of the pop-culture conventions — no one would single out Dustin Hoffman in *Marathon Man* or the *90210* TAs for such biblical distinction. But like the administration's suggestion that graduate student fellowships constitute an "entitlement" program, this image plays into public resentment of the educational dole. From this point of view, any group of students that gets free tuition, stipend support, *and* a degree has no right to complain.

But what this quote really shows is that the faculty, like the administration, is in a precarious position on the subject of graduate students. If, on the one hand, they admit how much of the teaching and grading we do, they expose the fact that we are employees and that our teaching is of greater benefit to our students than it is to us. This might also expose the fact that professors do other kinds of work *besides* teaching and grading — research, grant writing, committee work, and so on — that the public might not want to support. If, on the other hand, professors insist that graduate students are the blessed of the earth, they contribute to exactly the kind of public resentment of universities that leads to cuts in public funding for higher education. If graduate students are the blessed of the earth, then what are professors? Are they not also blessed? Perhaps, in the eyes of taxpayers, too blessed? The distance between "grad-scam" and "prof-scam" is short indeed.

Taken as a whole, these varied and condemning images of the graduate student — the graduate student as lonely misfit, as seductress, as welfare queen, as whiny child, as subservient teaching stooge, as blessed of the earth — suggest that no one inside or outside the university has been able to come to terms with graduate students. The attitude of the larger culture is one of fear and resentment, mostly because few outsiders understand what graduate students do, and when they do understand it, they raise legitimate questions about whether or not it is valuable. Ironically, the attitude of administrators, faculty, and undergraduates toward graduate students is also one of fear and resentment, but this is because they know exactly what we do and how much power we have on campus. These insiders are worried that if they acknowledge our contribution, they will have to supply us with more resources and more respect — two commodities that are in short supply in a downsizing academy.

Not a single one of these images contains an affirmation of the role that graduate students play in the university or in the larger culture. Though we are at the heart of the university — as products of the university and as producers in our own right — we are feared, resented, and misunderstood. For the audience outside the university, our work is hard to explain. For those inside the university, it is easy to explain away.

In the context of these negative representations, graduate students at Yale and elsewhere have fought to offer positive accounts of their research and teaching. We have struggled to convince our-

Figure 11. GESO button

selves, despite the negative images, that the contribution we make to the university is valuable. In the process we have generated a collection of images and texts that counter the negative representations of graduate students prevalent in the wider culture and the campus press. In the following section I present some of these images with the hope of showing how graduate students have fought for respect — with actions as well as with pamphlets and computer graphics.

Getting a Voice, Getting a Life

When I arrived at Yale in the fall of 1990, GESO was a relatively new organization, recently evolved from a group called TA Solidarity. The new GESO slogan, available on buttons and T-shirts, was "Get a voice" (fig. 11). This was a catchy and efficient phrase, suggesting in a few words that what we really wanted was more say on campus, as well as someone to listen to us once we had it. But it also had a flip, potentially self-deprecating quality, which I realized when I saw a version of the "Get a Voice" button that a friend of mine kept hanging in her bathroom: she had crossed out the word "Voice" and replaced it with the word "Life."

The perception that graduate students do not have a life is so widespread and so internalized that many of us accept this pathetic popular image as an explanation for our own lives. Indeed, the stereotype of the lonely misfit is not entirely a fiction. Graduate school is a place of insecurity and self-doubt, replete with arbitrary tests of intellect, flaming hoops, and skyscraper hurdles, with very little feedback and paltry rewards. Many graduate students *are* lonely, absurdly so, since the expectation is that everyone has come to the academy to retreat. The life of a scholar, our mentors tell us, is a solitary one. Embrace loneliness and get your work done. I was prepared for this before I came to Yale. I knew that my friends in graduate school were unhappy and that this would be my fate unless I found a way to fight the conventions.

The unionization drive at Yale has offered graduate students a very tangible way to fight such alienation. In the first place, the union has given us a way to name the shared properties of our misfortune. If we are lonely, voiceless, or misrepresented, once banded together it becomes clear that we are lonely, voiceless, and misrepresented *collectively,* rather than individually. At Yale, the recognition that isolation is something we suffer as a group has been important in learning how to build a collective movement as well as a collective identity.

Looking back over the range of posters, buttons, and literature that GESO produced between 1991 and 1996, there is evidence of a kind of "collective loneliness" stage in the organizing message that dominated the 1991–92 union recognition drive. In September 1991, GESO held a rally to protest the closing of the Yale graduate student cafeteria, known as "Lords." In a poster (fig. 12), a lone graduate student eats lunch beneath an imposing and overwhelming row of columns, out in the cold. The theme of the rally, "Let them eat cake!" (borrowing from French history), is written by hand over the computer image. Though striking, this poster sparked a controversy when it was first produced. There was a heated debate about whether the pictured graduate student was too lonely—the antithesis of the empowered and active image of the graduate student that we were trying to invent and project.

Yet it makes sense that our early posters and literature incorporated and confronted the most widely accepted stereotype of the graduate student: the lonely misfit. Social movements that have "identity" as one of their components often use self-deprecating humor to show how certain depreciated qualities (like loneliness, nerdiness, and alienation) might be the result of external forces. The pathetic image of the graduate student, used in the context of a union drive, raises the possibility that if graduate students

Figure 12. GESO poster regarding the closing of the graduate student cafeteria at Yale

are lonely misfits, this may be because they are unappreciated, underpaid, and undervalued.

This is the message that some of the early GESO posters convey with an economy of words and images. In the "This Is You/This Is You in GESO" poster (fig. 13), loneliness and disrespect are the problem, and GESO is the solution. The slogan is a parody of a popular antidrug commercial that showed a man holding an egg ("This is your brain") and then the man cracking the egg into a frying pan ("This is your brain on drugs — Any questions?"). The GESO poster reverses the negative trajectory of the drug ad: you're better off in GESO than outside it. First, you will be part of a collective that will stand up with you. Second, you will have a voice.[22]

In addition to playing on the convention of the lonely graduate student, the posters from the 1991–92 union recognition drive played heavily on our role as students and by extension on our role as consumers of university services, such as libraries, health care, and cafeterias. We used this focus to make links with undergraduates — as well as with faculty — on such issues as library

Figure 13. GESO poster

hours and academic freedom. We used a context for the poster on library hours, "Football isn't the only way Yale is losing to Princeton" (fig. 14), that we thought undergraduates would appreciate: football and competition. And though library hours are not a traditional union issue, recent cutbacks in library hours and services (as well as a hike in library fines and photocopying)

DOES YALE MEASURE UP?

Football isn't the only way Yale is losing to Princeton.

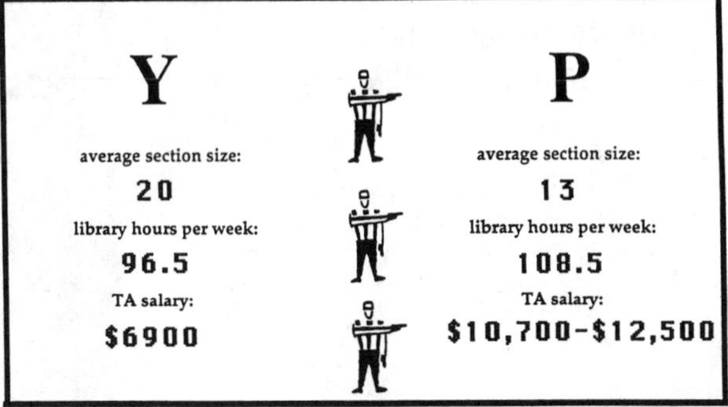

Average section size gathered from departments of History, Economics, Biology, Political Science, and English at Yale and Princeton. Library hours reflect open hours for CCL, Sterling, and Princeton's main library. Salary figures based on a 15-20 hour per week workload (TF3 at Yale). Princeton's figure provided by the Office of Graduate Admissions. The Yale figure is from the *Teaching Fellows Handbook* 1991-92.

Support GESO, the Graduate Employees and Students Organization working for academic excellence at Yale.
For more information about GESO, call the union office at 624-5161.

Figure 14. GESO poster

made the library a focus of activism throughout the 1991–92 school year.[23]

Similarly, our posters raised the matters of union recognition and negotiations as free speech issues, in an attempt to appeal to professors for whom academic freedom is at the heart of the mission of the university. The "Free Speech?" poster (fig. 15), which demonstrates the irony of administrators refusing even to "talk" to GESO represen-

Figure 15. GESO poster

tatives while still claiming to value freedom of expression, was very popular among graduate students and faculty alike. The poster's message was part of a larger strategy to create a broad coalition that could encompass graduate students, other campus employees, undergraduates, faculty, and even the New Haven community — with the overall goal of isolating the Yale administration.[24]

This broad, utopian strategy helped us to plan a one-day strike on December 4, 1991, which was framed around the administration's refusal to talk with our elected negotiating committee. The other two unions on campus, the service and maintenance workers' union (Local 35) and the clerical and technical workers' union (Local 34), honored our picket lines, and this unusual three-way strike made it onto the front page of newspapers like the *Wall Street Journal*. But our student-centered rhetoric made it hard for us to claim the power of the action in terms of our teaching. After much discussion, we declared that the name for the action would simply be "December 4th" because we did not have agreement to call it anything as aggressive as "strike," "walkout," "boycott," or "job action."

After December 4, the administration started to negotiate with GESO, but the negotiations soon reached an impasse. In early February, GESO authorized a short "academic strike," during which we called for a cessation of graduate student teaching, as well as a boycott of classes. In one of the posters for the action (fig. 16), the reasons for the strike were listed in terms that could appeal to faculty ("Who slashed the faculty budget?"), workers ("Who is threatening to force the workers out on strike?"), and undergraduates ("Who slashed the library budget?"), making graduate students into defenders of the true values of quality education and fair treatment. This was not a poster that focused on the unique contribution of graduate students; instead, it portrayed graduate students as leaders of a broad coalition of concerned consumers and workers.

At the end of the 1991–92 campaign we learned that the union model could be used to foster widespread support among graduate students across disciplines, as well as some (soft) support from faculty and undergraduates. After December 4 and a three-day "academic" strike in the spring, we did win a 28 percent pay increase and an end to the much-loathed sixth-year rule. But at the same time we realized that the teaching strike was a more powerful tactic than the boycotting of our own graduate classes. We realized that our contribution to Yale as consumers, in the form of tuition and fees, is much less than our contribution as teachers of undergraduates. Thus our threat to withdraw our consumption of Yale's educational facilities, while symbolically powerful, did not have a

Who slashed the library budget?

Who slashed the TA budget?

Who slashed the faculty budget?

Who has neglected TA training?

Who is threatening to force the workers out on strike?

Who is betraying their "professional responsibility" and the "central mission of the University?"

It is because we care that we must act.

Academic Strike

Figure 16. GESO poster

corresponding bottom-line punch. Yet the power we had to disrupt teaching at Yale, even for three days, was of serious concern to the university.

With this realization intact, as we charted a new strategy for a unionization drive that would focus more on our role as teachers, I began to research the history of teachers' unions in search of visual

Figure 17. GESO button, 1994

inspiration. What I found, to my dismay, was that teaching, especially as a form of unionized labor, is very difficult to represent. Teaching, like other kinds of service-industry work, is a process, something that takes place between a teacher and a student, and is therefore hard to reduce to an icon. What few icons there are for teaching — pencils, pointers, rulers, and apples — are reminiscent of elementary school and seemed unsuitable.

In April 1994, GESO sought the help of a local progressive artist named Virginia Blaisdell. She helped us design a series of posters and buttons for a large rally and open forum, to which we had invited the dean of the graduate school. The most popular image from this event was a sporty button (fig. 17) that said "I'll be there!" Five hundred graduate students actually were there, and at this event we presented the dean with over six hundred TA union cards that called on Yale to sponsor a TA union election.

For this event, and others that followed, Virginia devised a playful and enduring icon that reshaped the direction of GESO's public image: the compact, angular, graduate student (with mortarboard) who can hold up calls for recognition with great enthusiasm (fig. 18) and go on strike (fig. 19). This GESO icon, which is a clear advance in representational confidence over the alienated graduate student from our early posters, is a symbol of the greater self-consciousness and power of our current movement. This confidence comes in part from GESO's longevity but also from our greater focus on the power of teaching as well as our focus on the power of *not* teaching.

For example, though the "Teach in/Walk out" poster from the

Figure 18. GESO icon (GESO-Joe/GESO-Jane) rally poster

spring of 1995 is somewhat cute, marked by the elementary school icon of the goldenrod yellow crosswalk sign, the GESO graduate students look active and united in their "walkout." This icon (sometimes called "GESO-Joe/GESO-Jane") is also the centerpiece of a GESO clothing line that was used to promote the one-week walkout. GESO-Joe is prominent on a T-shirt that reads "Our work makes Yale work" and a GESO baseball cap (fig. 20). The angular figure on the T-shirt, with a squat stance, a mortarboard, and a raised fist, offers a strong counterpoint to the undergraduate image of the GESO baby and the GESO executioner, as well as

Figure 19. GESO icon (GESO-Joe/GESO-Jane) strike poster

the lonely GESO graduate student from our early posters. Virginia's designs also have a sense of humor, demonstrating that we can laugh at ourselves. If the early images projected the lonely graduate student with a certain ironic ambivalence, this icon embraces the nerdy, mortarboard-clad graduate student with humor and pride. Furthermore, with these images we have turned the focus to the importance of our work—especially our teaching—and by extension to the positive contribution we make to the university.

Our propaganda effort has made such an impression, in fact, that the posters themselves have become the subject of parodies at Yale by undergraduates as well as graduate students. My favorite undergraduate parody is a mock version of a poster we made that listed "things graduate students do to make ends meet," such as babysitting, waitressing, mowing lawns, and so on. The undergraduate poster lists "Ways TA's [*sic*] spend time when they ought to be teaching" (fig. 21)—these include "bitching about law student 'careerism,'" "coming to terms with the scars of suburbia," "pretending to have read derrida," and "staffing for GESO." A more threatening series of parodies was generated by a group of anti-GESO graduate students who formed a group called GAG (Graduates against GESO). In GAG's mock posters, GESO-Joe wears a hard hat

Figure 20. Two strikers, Rachel Devlin and Amy Kesselman, one wearing GESO icon (GESO-Joe/GESO-Jane) T-shirt

DOES YALE MEASURE UP?

Do you think
your TA devotes enough time to his or her teaching responsibilities?

WAYS TA'S SPEND TIME WHEN THEY OUGHT TO BE TEACHING

practicing expressions of ennui in the mirror
trying to blow perfect smoke rings
bitching about law student "careerism"
finding ways to keep cool while wearing black in the summer
"suffering"
being seen reading Foucault at the Daily
practicing how to say "raison d'être" and "fin de siècle"
surreptitiously catching episodes of Doogie Howser
naming their cats
"explicating"
coming to terms with the intertextuality of the world
coming to terms with their gender
coming to terms with the scars of suburbia
coming to terms with what we've done to the earth
coping with their own racism (everyone is a racist)
coping with everyone else's racism
coping with patriarchy
undergoing therapy
getting plastered at the GPSCY
raving about truth or dare
raving about paris is burning
raving about the cappuccino at atticus
"constructing discourse"
pretending to have read derrida
embracing indigenous cultures
trying to pick up undergraduate babes without seeming desperate
drinking evian in machine city
translating into gender-neutral language
staffing for GESO

Support UGLY, Undergraduates for Graduate Labor at Yale working for academic excellence.
For more information about UGLY, call the union office at 624-5161, or stop by Machine City (we'll be waiting for our TAs to show up).

Peter Vallone says "Join UGLY!"

Sponsored by UGLY and the Committee for Liberal Reform

Figure 21. "UGLY" undergraduate parody of GESO's poster "Things We Do to Make Ends Meet"

Figure 22. Graduates against GESO (GAG) anti-GESO poster parody

instead of the mortarboard and rallies for an Indian reservation and a casino instead of for recognition — a parody that presumably was inspired by the transformation of the slogan "Be There" to "Bet Here" (fig. 22).

But the real success of GESO's images might be better measured by our organizing around teaching issues. Between 1993 and 1996, graduate students took increased ownership over the quality of education at Yale. We ran a popular TA training program, lobbied for more resources for teaching assistants, and argued for smaller section sizes. And, unlike 1992, when it was difficult to conduct a strike, let alone call a strike a strike, in 1995 and 1996 we conducted two teaching strikes — the one-week strike in April of 1995 and the five-week grade strike in December and January 1995–96. These strikes were not easy to organize, nor were they enough to win GESO formal recognition as a union. But as we have increased our focus on teaching, we have been better able to see — and use — the power we have as teachers. During the chaos of the grade strike, it became very clear that the university could not function without our teaching and grading labor — or at least could not function for very long.

On the one hand, by focusing on our role as teachers, rather than on our role as consumers, it has been harder for us to garner the soft support among undergraduates and faculty that we had during the 1991–92 school year. On the other hand, our focus on teaching has strengthened our alliance with the other employees on campus. Additionally, Yale's treatment of graduate students during the grade strike brought unprecedented national attention, as well as national sympathy, to our cause. In fact, Yale's threats of lockout, expulsion, and disciplinary hearings helped us to raise the issue of academic freedom in a new form — in terms of our role as workers rather than students. During the grade strike we argued that academic freedom should protect our right to form unions, not just our right to free speech.

To make this point as strongly as it could, GESO staged a civil disobedience protest in front of the Hall of Graduate Studies in early January 1996; 138 graduate students, workers, faculty (from Yale and elsewhere), and undergraduates were arrested. (Our signs for this event were uniform and serious: "Stop Intimidation, Start Negotiations" [fig. 23].) The protest and the administration's response revealed that the debate had shifted from one about wants (Do graduate students want a union?) to one about rights (Do graduate students have the *right* to want a union?). This one event generated more press than the grade strike itself, making us realize that academic freedom was an issue that played well in Peoria. By calling attention to ourselves as striking teachers whose unfair employer was refusing to recognize our union, we finally found a way to explain ourselves — and our jobs — to the outside world.

Figure 23. GESO protesters with "Stop Intimidation" signs

"Grad Students Fight Class Struggle"

This was the headline that appeared in *USA Today* on January 2, 1996, the day that grades were due at Yale.[25] While the classroom is not ordinarily associated with class struggle in the popular media, the grade strike at Yale — in concert with successful graduate student union elections at big state schools like the University of Kansas and the University of Iowa — had prodded the journalists who cover higher education to rethink their image of graduate students. While coverage of the national graduate student union movement has not been consistently sympathetic, recent strikes and elections have convinced a number of journalists that something is wrong with graduate education and that graduate students and administrators do not agree either on what the problem is or on how to fix it.

Out of this coverage a new image of the graduate student has emerged: the graduate student as labor organizer. This image shares some features with the graduate student as lonely misfit and crazed killer so prevalent in popular and university cultures. Like the graduate student in popular culture, the graduate student in this press coverage is still a little downtrodden and still a little out of control.

But according to these news reports, the source of the graduate students' misery is external to the graduate student, rather than internal. These accounts are more likely to blame unrest among graduate students on the university than on the graduate students' misfit-psyches.

A good example of this kind of press coverage can be found in the longest and most analytic piece on the Yale grade strike, published in *Lingua Franca*. The article draws heavily on a video documentary about GESO made by a Yale undergraduate named Laura Dunn, and, like the video, the article accepts the child/parent metaphor as the appropriate metaphor for explaining the relationship between graduate students and their advisers: "As long as graduate students hope to learn anything from their mentors, and remain dependent on them for the evaluations that lead to a job, some kind of parenting-child relationship will remain."[26] But at the same time the article admits that Yale bears a great deal of culpability for the breakdown in familial harmony, accusing Yale of being a "neglectful parent" and an "absentee father" (59–60). By offering this image of Yale as a deadbeat dad, *Lingua Franca* presents the disruption at Yale as a shared project, not simply as the product of the "aggressive, willful and demanding" GESO children (60).

Other papers that covered the grade strike, however, did not accept the breakdown-of-the-medieval-mentor model as the explanation for disruption at Yale. Papers like the *New York Times* and the *Washington Post* put the Yale grade strike in the larger context of the downsizing of the academy, as well as the downsizing of white-collar professionals. The *New York Times* published a series of probing articles about the strike, most of which put it in the context of graduate student organizing nationwide.

But perhaps the most striking feature of the *New York Times*'s coverage was an illustrated image of graduate students printed on the letters to the editor's page, drawn by the artist David Suter. It shows six graduate students walking in a circle (fig. 24). The two at the top of the circle are wearing huge mortarboard hats; the two in the middle have mortarboard hats that are sliding down in front of them, and the hat-tassels are becoming sign sticks; the last two graduate students are distinctly hatless, and their mortarboards have been transformed into picket signs, which they grasp with both hands.[27] Perhaps the mortar-board-into-picket-sign trans-

Figure 24. Illustration for the *New York Times* by David Suter

formation is not entirely coincidental, since the word "mortarboard" has two meanings: (1) graduation hat; and (2) a square board with a handle for the purpose of carrying brick mortar, used by brick craftsmen. If the job market gets any worse, graduate students may indeed be exchanging one mortarboard for the other. But whether or not Suter was aware of the double meaning of the mortarboard, his image suggests that there could be an easy slippage between graduate student and labor agitator.

In a similar vein, the *Washington Post* editorial about the Yale grade strike suggests that the downsizing of the academy has helped graduate students make the transition from medieval apprentice to union member. This editorial points out that as fewer and fewer Ph.D. graduates get jobs in the academy, the wait between graduations becomes longer and less worthwhile:

> The imbalance between PhD recipients and tenured jobs is getting out of whack again, as it did in the 1970s, but the universities are, if anything, on even leaner terms now than they were then. The

> expense of hiring lifetime employees and giving them, say, health coverage, has driven more and more schools to hire young "gypsy" professors who, years after they get their degrees, are still shuttling between two or more ill-paid, no-track positions.[28]

The grade strike at Yale, according to this *Washington Post* editorial, made the human costs of the downsizing academy visible in new ways. The *Post* argues that the grade strike was a sign that these human costs would have to be figured into the bottom line: gritting teeth, raising prices, and cutting at the margin would not be enough.

While the *Post* and *Times* stories are not terribly upbeat in tone, seeing the grade strike as a grisly bellwether of things to come in the downsizing academy, a more hopeful image of the grade strike emerged on the West Coast. The *Los Angeles Times* published a comprehensive editorial about graduate student unionizing that was written less from the perspective of the academy and more from the perspective of the labor movement. The author of this editorial, which is titled "Labor Movement Finds New Home — Universities," is a graduate student himself, active in the TA union drive at UCLA and hopeful that universities will be a growth area for the labor movement: "In these days of renewed vigor for U.S. labor, a new activism is spreading across campuses. Students who work as teachers, researchers, and tutors are mobilizing to demand the right to bargain collectively with administrations."[29] From this perspective graduate students are neither the blessed of the earth nor the wretched of the earth, but instead are young activists on the front line of a new wave of unionism: the next generation of union organizers.

At Yale there is good evidence to support the implications of this *Los Angeles Times* editorial. Not only is graduate student union organizing spreading to campuses like the University of Illinois, Cornell, and Duke, but a substantial number of GESO leaders have exchanged their Yale mortarboards for professional careers in the labor movement — landing jobs in such diverse unions as Hotel Employees and Restaurant Employees International Union (HEREIU), UNITE (the new amalgamated clothing and textile workers' union), and graduate student unions such as GEO Michigan. As the academy is downsizing, the AFL-CIO is upsizing, especially at the level of new organizing. And thus without realizing it, Yale is giving its graduate students access to a whole new set of marketable skills: the skills of labor organizing. If we do not use them within the university to change the academic profession, we may use them outside the academy, perhaps to change much more.

The Last Supper

Outside the academy, and even outside the mainstream press, the popular image of the graduate student has not yet been transformed into that of a sign-waving proletariat crusader. Graduate students in popular culture are still losers and killers, misfits and maniacs. Yet as losers and killers go, the most recent pop-culture graduate students are more interesting and, for the most part, more likable than their counterparts from previous decades. There has been some movement toward representing graduate students more realistically, as complex and interesting main characters. Recent movies such as *The Last Supper* and *How to Make an American Quilt,* as well as the NBC comedy *Boston Common,* are signs that the representation of graduate students may be changing.

The Last Supper features the graduate student as maniac killer, but there are no otherworldly monsters to do the killing, as in *Candyman.*[30] *The Last Supper* is political satire, not horror. The movie ridicules the central characters — five liberal graduate students who attend a large, midwestern university and who share a house. But it also ridicules their archconservative dinner guests, whom the graduate students decide to kill one-by-one, with glasses of arsenic-laced red wine. The viewers are supposed to identify with the graduate students in their hatred for conservatives, but they are also supposed to laugh at the graduate students for their political intolerance and ineffectualness.

Though it may hardly seem like a redeeming portrait, *The Last Supper* may be the most significant representation of graduate students to reach the pop-culture register to date. To have an entire plot revolve around five graduate students in an ordinary setting, even if it turns out bloody, is a significant breakthrough. First, it suggests that popular audiences might be able to see graduate students as familiar, normal folks. Second, the fact that these graduate students are assigned the irritating liberal qualities of the much-defamed "politically correct" university professors suggests that their power as ideology-reproducers is genuinely feared. In their increasingly visible role as teachers of undergraduates, graduate students are becoming the primary social reproducers on most university campuses.

The Last Supper was given somewhat favorable reviews, but it was not a box-office smash. *How to Make an American Quilt,* in contrast, was a successful "chick film," starring Winona Ryder as a Berkeley graduate student named "Finn." She studies African folklore and travels to her grandmother's house in northern California to finish her master's thesis. She leaves her fiancé behind for the summer and enters the world of her grandmother's quilting bee, which is made up of older women who tell their own stories of love and marriage as they sew the squares of Finn's wedding quilt.

In some ways Finn fits the convention of the nerdy graduate student. She is a misfit, shunning modern technology for an old typewriter and burying her nose in her work. On the she-devil side, she does have a brief affair with the mysterious son of a local orchard owner. He promises flesh and passion, but little else, since he barely speaks a word the entire film. Her fiancé, in contrast, is an architect and is designing their wedding house. At the end of the movie they are reunited, and they ride off into the sunset in his 1960s VW bus: thesis finished, culture understood, and the potential for lifelong friendship affirmed over raw passion. What makes this film an evolutionary breakthrough in the representation of graduate students is that it portrays Finn as a woman, not a vampire, a graduate student, not a creep. Finn is tough and vulnerable, likable and irritating, determined and emotional. She is not likely to kill anyone, and she poses no sexual (and little ideological) danger to the children of the university-attending middle class.

I might not be inclined to make much of this representational breakthrough, but it has been reinforced by the representation of a graduate student on the NBC comedy *Boston Common*. This series is set in the common room of a small Boston university, and the graduate student in question is young and female, studies folklore, and is named Joy. Even though her name is probably intended as an ironic parody, she is rather joyful as the love object of the series's main character, a trickster figure from the South named

Boyd, who drives his sister to school and stays on as the college handyman.

The first time I watched the show I was stunned in disbelief. Here was a graduate student on prime-time television, using the acronym TA as a verb. She was wearing the short, bobbed, graduate student haircut, funky earrings, and an outfit with a hint of Salvation Army chic. She was grading papers, setting up field interviews, and leading classes. She was doing the things that I do every day, and she was getting a 15.6 ratings share. Finally, after years of struggle, we had made it to prime time — not as monsters, creeps, vampires, killers, seducers, or supergeeks, but as ourselves.

Joy

I don't want to celebrate these representations *too* much, since most critics have found *The Last Supper* graduate students as intolerable as their political views, Finn of the *American Quilt* a little pathetic, and Joy of *Boston Common* a little ditzy. But it may not be entirely a coincidence that representations of graduate students are improving in popular culture, even if only slightly, at the same time graduate students are unionizing. For one thing, the producers of popular culture — from journalism to television — are increasingly recent graduates of universities, if not recent graduate students themselves. The economic downturn of the university has affected these graduates in two ways: (1) they are more likely to have had graduate students, perhaps even unionizing graduate students, as their primary teachers in college; and (2) graduate students themselves are moving into the culture industry. These days, getting a job in Hollywood might be easier than getting tenure. In a celebrated example of this phenomenon, the actor David Duchovny, who stars on the hit television series *The X-Files,* was a graduate student in the English department at Yale in the 1980s. Though he never submitted a dissertation, rumor has it he was quite a TA.[31]

There may be another connection. Perhaps graduate students, with the help of journalists and other purveyors of popular culture, have finally found a way to explain our usefulness to the general public. By organizing teaching assistant unions we call attention to our role as teachers and as workers. We advertise the fact that we, in conjunction with professors, are teaching the kids of the middle class how to write, argue, and think critically. When we explain our role in the university as teachers, rather than as subsidized consumers, we generate more sympathy and understanding. Moreover, by framing our union drives in the larger context of academic downsizing, we link our issues to the issues of the average working American — in almost any profession. These days, everyone is getting downsized. But not everyone is organizing to fight it.

My quick scan of pop-culture representations shows that there are some tentative connections between graduate students and archetypal members of the working class. In *The Last Supper,* a truck-driving hick played by Bill Paxton is the first conservative character to be killed by the graduate student housemates. On the positive side, in *How to Make an American Quilt,* Finn's affair with the orchard hand is clearly a cross-class alliance. He may be the boss's son, but he drives a big truck and has big muscles, in contrast to her pale and skinny architect fiancé. More overtly, the graduate student character, Joy, gets together with southern handyman Boyd in the final episode of the spring season pilot of *Boston Common.* She shuns her hoity-toity professor boyfriend for Boyd's down-home anti-intellectualism. Will Joy's love affair with the handyman last? Stay tuned for next season. We can only hope that it will.

Meanwhile, the more important battle over representation for graduate students is still on university campuses. In time, maybe one of us will write that novel about graduate student life. For now I am content to hold a picket sign — while I finish my dissertation and look for an academic job. The most important lessons I have learned at Yale have been outside the classroom. Through organizing I have found a voice, as well as a life. And I have the union to thank for that.

NOTES

I thank Michael Denning, Cara Hood, Trip McCrossin, Robert Perkinson, Corey Robin, Eve Weinbaum, and the Seattle chapter of "The Last Supper Club" for their many contributory insights, for helping me to find graduate students in popular culture, and for proving that graduate students don't have to be lonely and unhappy — even at Yale.

1. John E. Kramer, *The American College Novel: An Annotated Bibliography* (New York: Garland Publishers, 1981).

2. The Fox series *Class of '96* had at least two former Yale undergraduates on its writing team. Though the series was filmed in Toronto, the university in the series was called Havenhurst — a pun on New Haven — and certain aspects of Yale were reproduced in great detail, including Yale's undergraduate radio station.

3. Dolores H. Thurgood and Julie E. Clarke, *Summary Report 1993: Doctorate Recipients from United States Universities* (Washington, D.C.: National Academy Press, 1995), 12. The figure "half-million" is a rough estimate. In 1993 there were nearly 40,000 Ph.D.'s awarded in the arts and sciences. If this figure is multiplied by the number of years to degree (8), the result is 320,000. If the number of masters students and dropouts is added in, the totals should approach 500,000.

4. William Goldman, *Marathon Man* (New York: Delacorte Press, 1974), 41. This quote is from the novel, but the professor gives a very similar speech in the film.

5. For an excellent account of university restructuring in the 1970s, see Paul Lauter, "Retrenchment — What the Managers Are Doing," in *Canons and Contexts* (New York: Oxford University Press, 1991), 175–97.

6. Clarke, *Summary Report 1993,* 20.

7. Richard B. Freeman, *The Overeducated American* (New York: Academic Press, 1976).

8. *Kansas City Star,* October 19, 1994.

9. There are recognized graduate student unions on the following campuses: University of California–Berkeley, University of Florida, University of South Florida, University of Kansas, University of Iowa, University of Massachusetts–Amherst, University of Massachusetts–Lowell, University of Michigan, Rutgers University, State University of New York (SUNY), University of Oregon–Eugene, University of Wisconsin–Milwaukee, and University of Wisconsin–Madison. There are recognition drives in progress at Yale, the University of Illinois at Champaign-Urbana, the University of California at San Diego, and UCLA, as well as other campuses.

10. Mia Bay, "Too Much, Too Soon," *New Journal* (February 1, 1991): 25–27.

11. I recently visited the Yale undergraduate admissions office with a friend of mine who is thinking about applying to Yale College. The admissions officer, upon learning that I was a graduate student at Yale, asked me if I felt like a second-class citizen at Yale. I was so taken aback I almost couldn't answer. "Second-class citizen" is a term graduate students use discreetly, so as not to make people think we our claiming an oppression out of proportion with reality. But this admissions officer made me feel as if Yale really does see us as second-class citizens, especially relative to the undergraduates.

12. President Levin and Dean Brodhead made a similar suggestion at an alumni fund-raiser in Chicago in March of 1996, which I attended.

13. When I arrived at Yale in the fall of 1990, the health care fee was $345 per year. For the 1996–97 school year, it will be $717 plus $120 for supplemental coverage. While this may not seem too expensive, $837 is close to 10 percent of a TA's salary for one year. Worse still, family health care is almost $4,000 per year, which is close to 40 percent of an annual TA salary.

14. Noah Kotch, "Officials Say TA's Claims Are Not True," *Yale Daily News,* April 5, 1996, 1, 7.

15. GESO, *True Blue: An Investigation into Teaching at Yale* (October 1995), 2.

16. See Cary Nelson, *Manifesto of a Tenured Radical* (New York: New York University Press, 1997).

17. This illustration by Jon Lucas accompanied an undergraduate opinion column: Neomi Rao, "Grad Power," *Yale Herald,* April 7, 1995, 7. This column appeared on the last day of our one-week strike.

18. David A. Moore, "Slap-Happy," *Yale Herald,* December 8, 1995, 4.

19. "Students Deserve Grades: GESO Threatens Undergraduates," *Yale Daily News,* December 7, 1995, masthead editorial.

20. Rebecca Smullin, "Yale Officials Will Retaliate against TAs," *Yale Daily News,* December 13, 1995, 1, 8; Alice Dembner, "Union Drive Erupts at Yale: Graduate Students Could Be Expelled," *Boston Globe,* January 10, 1996; George Judson, "Yale and Unions Reach Tense Phase," *New York Times,* January 11, 1996, B1, B7; Professor Dennis Hollier, chair, Yale French department, memo, "To: All Graduate Students with a Current or Eventual Teaching Assignment in the Department of French" (December 15, 1995).

21. Emily Eakin, "Walking the Line," *Lingua Franca,* March/April 1996, 56; Davidson Goldin, "Yale Teaching Assistants Vote for a Grade Strike," *New York Times,* December 13, 1995, B7.

22. These posters were designed by Juliette Guilbert, a graduate student in American studies.

23. This poster was designed by Kathleen Clark and Faulkner Fox, also graduate students in American Studies.

24. This poster was designed by Juliette Guilbert.

25. Dennis Kelly, "Grad Students Fight Class Struggle," *USA Today,* January 2, 1996, D1.

26. Emily Eakin, "Walking the Line," *Lingua Franca,* March/April 1996, 59.

27. This illustration accompanied letters to the editor about the grade strike at Yale (see *New York Times,* December 19, 1995, sec. A, p. 24, col. 5).

28. "Strike at Yale," *Washington Post,* January 22, 1996, editorial, A18.

29. John Medearis, "Labor Movement Finds New Home — Universities," *Los Angeles Times,* April 21, 1996, pt. M, p. 3.

30. This transformation of the graduate student into a monster is the fate of Lily Taylor in the horror flick *The Addiction,* in which Taylor is turned into a vampire.

31. In a *Playboy* interview, Duchovny tried to explain the Kierkegaardian essence of his *X-file* character: "I probably got it from Yale — this horrible, all-leveling relativism," he explains (Jack Hitt, "Sucker for the Occult? David Duchovny Has Just the Show for You," *Playboy* [November 1995]). In keeping with the Yale legacy, in the film *Kalifornia,* Duchovny plays a graduate student who goes on the road to do the research that will allow him to expand his dissertation on serial killers into a book.

Chapter 4
Why Provoke This Strike? Yale and the U.S. Economy

Rick Wolff

How can we make sense of the 1996 strike at Yale? It is the fourth richest university in the United States and the largest employer in the fourth poorest large city in the United States. Now it wants to lower what it pays its nonfaculty staff and cut back on their benefits to "save money." Yet, in 1995, when the U.S. stock market rose in value by 30 percent, Yale's vast stock and bond holdings *rose* by between $500 million and $1 billion: *this in the year preceding the strike.* In addition, Yale's holdings in land, buildings, art collections, antiques, books, and equipment *rose* by hundreds of millions more. Its annual budget is approaching $1 billion, and—as in previous years—its incomes exceed expenses by millions, which the university adds to its endowment and other funds.[1] Yale University is floating in money as its income and wealth reach historically unprecedented levels.

Yale claims that it "needs" to save money by gaining the contractual right to replace current unionized workers by outsourcing, hiring temporary labor, or otherwise obtaining lower-paid employees. A Yale victory will do more than damage the replaced workers, their families, and their neighborhoods; it will also lower regional pay standards (set by Yale as the area's largest employer) and thereby further depress the already deeply broken economy of greater New Haven.

A few moments of economic calculation will quickly show that the regional economy's losses would likely far outweigh Yale's gains. Another few calculations will quickly confirm that whatever Yale managed to save would make no significant contribution to Yale's wealth or income. So why, then, did Yale provoke the strike?

The answer lies in the broader relation of Yale to the U.S. economic system and to the set of economic theories that rationalize its operations. Most of the members of the university's top governing body — the aptly named Yale Corporation — are themselves managers and directors of other top U.S. industrial and commercial corporations. Their mentality — the set of theories with which they understand and act in the economy — is to do all the market allows them to do to make money. Those theories guarantee that if every entity in the market maximizes its own self-interest, the result will be the greatest advantage not only for that entity but also — as if by Adam Smith's invisible hand — for everyone in the economy. Free markets, being the best of all possible economic systems, make everyone best off. Such theories — themselves taught and celebrated at Yale — legitimate the university's charging as high prices as it thinks it can get away with and paying as little for its laborers as it can get away with.[2] The recession in the early 1990s, the last recession to hit the U.S. economy, lasted longer and bit more deeply in New England than elsewhere. Unemployment, shaky job security, sharp cutbacks in government supports, and high taxes have been terrorizing workers. These conditions present a good market moment for corporate leaders to try to lower workers' pay.

As Yale's leaders know, the university's existence has been shaped in basic ways by how it took advantage of other "market opportunities" in the past. During the Great Depression of the 1930s, for example, Yale saw and grasped the chance to rebuild its campus on the cheap. By hiring desperate unemployed laborers, it could afford to build the neo-Gothic structures of downtown New Haven that tourists have admired ever since (often imagining them to be ancient originals rather than modern copies). The current New Haven depression, while less severe than the 1930s, nonetheless presents Yale with another historic opportunity to "solve" its "problems" by market maneuvers not possible under less dire economic conditions.

The strike thus forms but one aspect of what I now suspect may be Yale's broader market strategy. That strategy entails taking full advantage of hard economic times, not merely by lowering workers' wages but by taking full advantage of Yale's economic and political power in the community while remaining indifferent to any damage these maneuvers create. For example, the reduced wages Yale seeks to achieve through the 1996 strike will further collapse the economy of New Haven. This will worsen an already extremely tense and often violent environment, one that has placed Yale in the position of being known as the most dangerous Ivy League venue today. At the same time, Yale continues to refuse to make tax payments or otherwise compensate New Haven for the vast properties it takes off the tax rolls.[3] This leaves New Haven with the highest property taxes of all 169 towns in the state of Connecticut. Businesses leave for the suburbs, where tax rates are much lower; upper-income residents follow; and commercial malls complete the escape panorama. New Haven is left with mostly the people who cannot afford to join the exodus. Its tax revenues crumble while the population left behind has the greatest needs for government support. New Haven becomes, to an ever-increasing extent, the disaster zone that is creeping across the geographies of so many contemporary U.S. cities.

Enter Yale to take advantage of the urban collapse its own policies—including the 1996 strike—do so much to foster. Piecemeal it buys up local properties whose depressed values make them especially cheap. It offers to rescue strapped local politicians by supplementing inadequate local tax revenues by buying city property (Yale recently purchased an entire street, dug up the pavement, and converted it into a walkway internal to a campus increasingly cut off from the surrounding urban disaster). A pattern emerges that promises to solve many of Yale's problems as it faces the new century.

Its contours, so far as an outside observer can discern them, include completing a systematic transformation of New Haven. The decline of a northeastern industrial city is to become the birth of a college town. The mass of the poor will be made to leave as jobs, decent public education, government supports, and affordable housing disappear. The remaining portions of downtown not already owned by Yale will be bought or converted into a colony of businesses catering to Yale students, employees, and one another (banks, architects, accountants, lawyers, restaurants and bars, boutiques, etc.). The residential neighborhoods will be "renewed" to house the workers who staff Yale, local government, the utilities, and the colonized businesses listed above.

The reduced size and changed composition of the population — especially the emigration of the poor — will permit a reduction in the crime, violence, and general social decay that have characterized New Haven for decades. In Yale planning offices, this presents a pretty picture. "Progress" will be the label Yale attaches to the collapse of New Haven as an industrial city and its reconfiguration as a college town. The transformation, disastrous for so many, will be rechristened as "economic development" that is part natural and part the product of Yale's benevolent market activities.

To achieve this ambitious goal — especially without such a pattern being seen as a deliberate affair — Yale will likely continue to refuse to pay taxes that might enable the city to pursue other futures (on grounds of Yale's "difficult economic circumstances"). It will likewise probably try to deplete and further undermine the local economy by squeezing its workers through strikes such as the one in 1996, by buying more local properties and removing them from the tax rolls, by further downsizing of employees, and so forth.

So the questions for unions and others aware of the context of the strike at Yale are these: Will Yale be able to get away with it? Will workers and students permit their strikes to be defeated and Yale's broader strategy to succeed? Or will Yale find strong, solid worker opposition and, beyond that, sustained and effective political criticism? When you push workers and communities as far as Yale is prepared to do, will they realize their strength in numbers and fight back? Did the 1996 strike mark a turning of the tide at Yale, in Connecticut, and indeed nationally? Was the strike the beginning of a revolt against the free-market ideology of corporations laying waste to an economy while they repeat endlessly how efficient, natural, and progressive this all is?

The stakes in the Yale strike are great for the future of the university, its employees, and its communities; but they are also great for the future of the entire United States. As the U.S. economy marches resolutely backward toward economic and social conditions of the nineteenth century — extreme inequalities of income, wealth, and hope — will the mass of Americans see and reverse the process?

Winning the strike at Yale would make a major move toward just that reversal.

NOTES

1. As has been repeatedly documented, for almost all of the last twenty-five years Yale annually received income in excess of its expenses. This excess was usually added to its endowment portfolio. However, it counts such additions to its endowment as "expenses" (provisions for the future). By then adding these latter sorts of "expenses" to all its other expenses, it can and does regularly announce that its books are "barely balanced." This act of "creative accounting" serves nicely to legitimate rising tuitions for students, appeals to donors, refusals to pay taxes to local government, and refusals to entertain wage demands of employees.

2. While a graduate student at Yale, I learned these theories well enough to obtain a Ph.D. in economics.

3. In this behavior, Yale parts company with Harvard, Princeton, and most other Ivy League schools, which have been willing or have been politically pressured to make such payments. Why Yale should be different is what the text seeks to explain.

Chapter 5
Boola!

Duncan Kennedy

I don't feel like an outsider in writing about Yale because I went to the Yale Law School, and thinking back on my time there is full of all sorts of images of the late 1960s for me. A very powerful image that's stayed with me all these years is one that could be from a *Life* magazine special edition of news photos of 1970: a young man and a young woman, Yale undergraduates, handing roses to young men in a row in uniform, National Guardsmen called up to line Broadway to protect the Co-op and the other shops against looting or just plain civil disobedience at the time of the trial of the New Haven chapter of the Black Panthers.

The National Guard guys were at first terrifying in their uniforms, with their rifles, but then as one's eyes focused there were some upper-middle-class college kid faces among them, not managing to look stony, just embarrassed, averting their eyes as the flower-bearers approached them along the sidewalk. A girl asked, "Hey, Joe, what are you doing here?" But in the line there were also working-class faces; some angry, classless, "you assholes" faces; and black faces. The flowers were not innocent.

In a sense they were the equivalent of weapons, an aggression against the other kids in their uniforms, as well as against the grown-ups' surreal school play in which they were the "forces of order," we the insane disrupters. It wasn't just a play, though, not only because the guns seemed to be loaded but because all kinds of ignored and suppressed and feared relationships among us, strollers, boys and girls, Guardsmen, were briefly flushed like birds.

That was a long time ago, and the thread that binds oppositionists down the generations has stretched taut and thin. What does it mean today to join the labor movement if you're a graduate student at an elite university, thinking of yourself as part of the tradition of humanistic or social-scientific culture? One thing it means is conversations with your professors, maybe not many, maybe not long, but highly charged, like the conversations of those earlier days. Both law and the psychology of professionalism figure here: professors say you have no right to form a union because you are students or that it's inappropriate because you are apprentices, not workers.

Even if the professor who says this to you is wearing a beautiful suit and tie, even if you've read his book and would stake your life on his ability to distinguish two manuscripts of *Beowulf,* even if you would feel honored to be chosen to do research for him, his statement is still wrong. You do have a "right" to form a union. It is not illegal for you to form a union or to strike or to bargain collectively with Yale. Everyone in the United States (prisoners and soldiers maybe excepted) has the right to form a union; it's not illegal; it doesn't matter whether you're a student.

The only valid legal point is that federal labor law, namely, the National Labor Relations Act (NLRA), the charter of organized labor in this country, may not apply to you, and I say "may not" advisedly, if you are a graduate student. If, a big if, it doesn't apply to you, then your employer can use a lot of union-busting tactics on you that would be illegal if you were covered by the act. Under the act, it is an unfair labor practice to discipline workers for union activity; if you are not covered, and there is no state statute that applies to you either, then the employer isn't breaking the law if it fires you for organizing or striking.

It's no disgrace to be in one of the categories of workers not covered by the federal protective act. The categories not covered include, for example, farmworkers, who are not covered because the forces that lived off farm laborers were strong enough to make sure that the act wouldn't get through Congress unless those workers were excluded. The act doesn't include domestic workers for the very same reason. Not being covered doesn't mean that Big Daddy Law decided that you shouldn't unionize. Not at all. It means that you have to get your union without Big Daddy's help, that you are, as the saying goes, "unprotected."

After "you have no right to form a union," a second important phrase is "you're unprotected." Repeated a few times, "you're unprotected" picks up some modern sexual connotations. It means: "We can do anything we want to you, and we might, and the consequences could be terrible. Don't forget it for a minute: *you're unprotected*." But when a faculty member says that because you're a student you're unprotected, he or she is indulging in legal speculation. As I said above, whether graduate students are covered is an open question. The NLRA doesn't say students aren't or can't be covered. It says that "employees" *are* covered. No court and no administrative agency has decided a case under the NLRA involving students who have the kind of relationship to a university that the typical Yale graduate student teaching a section has to his or her university employer.

My own opinion, speaking as a law professor, is this: since the National Labor Relations Board will probably remain a liberal board (now that it is under the control of a Democratic president) through the end of the 1990s, it is probable that graduate students employed as they are at Yale will win recognition. Student employees of that type will be held to be covered. And all the people who are saying that TAs are not protected because they are not employees will turn out to be just wrong. The November 1996 opinion by the NLRB legal staff reinforces the likelihood that the full board will recognize teaching assistants as employees. On the other hand, if the issue is not settled in the next few years and if the Republicans regain control of the White House in a future election, things may be different. So when TAs' teachers deploy the law against them, TAs should laugh: the teachers don't know what they're talking about.

Thinking about these matters as a set of bizarre legal questions is sometimes reassuring, I think, as a way to keep a certain ambivalence at bay. People, teachers and students, who are against the union or unsure about it are sometimes responding to an image of Big Labor, of industrial unionism, one that might be reinforced if it turned out that graduate students can be employees for purposes of the NLRA. These people seem to fear that if graduate students unionize, they'll put on hard hats, carry metal lunch pails, and punch the clock; when they can get a cup of coffee will be a question of union work rules, inflexibly set by top management negotiation with top labor bureaucrats. Also, many of those involved seem to fear that graduate students will be declassed by unionizing, which is a fear we need to just get over.

It's not true, however, that the alternative to the status quo is bureaucratic union organization confronting the university at the top, destroying all the one-on-one, decentralized, emotionally charged relationships that graduate students have with faculty. That idea comes partly from what I can only call employer propaganda about unions and partly from the realities of organizing production workers in large factories, but it misconceives what unionization is like when people manage to do self-organization and to create, especially in this kind of context, something like a living labor movement for our own moment, for large and small workplaces, blue-collar and white-collar jobs, workplaces with very different atmospheres.

American labor law is facilitative; it encourages worker self-organization in any form the workers want to adopt. The American labor movement as an organized institution, Big Labor, doesn't, indeed couldn't, impose on newly organizing workers any of the stultifying forms employers warn against. There's no legal, social, or institutional reason why a graduate student union shouldn't nurture and further good relations between graduate students and faculty members, relations based on one-on-one contact, completely flexible relations between individual faculty and individual students. If there is an issue, it's not what unionization "means" in the abstract but what forms of self-government graduate students would choose and how they would feel, not all good for sure, about having to fight and haggle and compromise among themselves about this kind of thing, rather than leaving it to the authorities.

No one should forget that no matter how many times the administrators say the word "apprenticeship" (which implies a kind of decentralization), the university acts as a single, unitary organization with respect to many issues that affect its own interests, and it doesn't do this in a decentralized way. It sets rates; it decides how many graduate students to employ; it frames the basic conditions of their lives as workers from the center, using all the power that comes from its own centralized, unitary organization. And it exploits the weakness that comes from the fact that graduate students deal with the center as individuals, with just about zero bargaining power.

There's something a little crazy in this part of the antiunion rhetoric. Professors tend to be happy and proud that they, as pure thinkers, have left the dirty work of setting the terms for the administration. They say it's not their fault if graduate students are exploited, because they have no control; then they turn around and say those students shouldn't organize to deal with the center because it will chill or kill their warm relations with them as individuals. But why should graduate students have to act as individuals when dealing with the administration when it acts as a unit in dealing with them? And why should organization at that level interfere with graduate students cultivating loving, individual, idiosyncratic relations with their teachers and supervisors?

The real issues for professors are hard to figure, but maybe they know that they are competing with graduate students, for resources and compensation vis-à-vis the administration, and doing very well at it, a little better than they'd do if TAs were organized. And then there is the idea of apprenticeship. This is an idea that I think has real pull, real emotional meaning for many professors and for many graduate students. But like most images or "figures" with that kind of power, it has its dark side, its neo-Gothic, hierarchical side, fitting the architecture of schools like Yale.

What was apprenticeship legally? (We don't have apprenticeship anymore, but we can still look at it legally.) It was contractual, and you were bound by it. If you were a minor, the contract might be made on your behalf by your father or the local overseers of the poor. It was also a status, because once you entered it you were bound by its rules. When you were an apprentice, your master was legally obligated to provide you room and board in his house and training in his art or craft, an art or craft you couldn't be employed at except through him and the other members of his guild. In exchange, you agreed to work for him and, don't forget, to subject yourself to discipline of two different kinds. First, if you left, you could be brought back by force — the local justice of the peace would return you to the master's household. Second, within the house you had a duty to obey his commands, and he could send you to the local authorities for punishment if you disobeyed or misbehaved. In the 1950s, millions of schoolchildren read a turgid novel called *Johnny Tremain*, about an apprentice in the time of Paul Revere. I remember a horrifying scene in which liquid silver flowed across Johnny's hand. . . . things could go badly wrong.

Of course, apprenticeship isn't all bad; it has positive connotations as well. It evokes the truth of filiation, the emotional nexus that sometimes does exist between graduate students in Ph.D. programs and their professors, the element of vulnerability and of self-surrender of the student, the element of good patriarchal and matriarchal emotion and responsibility in the professors.

One of the things that was repeatedly most powerful for me as a student at Yale Law School from 1967 to 1970 was the experience of the disappointment of my expectations as an apprentice. I was a strongly anticommunist, left-liberal who wanted to join the progressive part of the ruling class, to make good policy. I identified, easily, quickly, with the leading scholar-activist professors who were liberals and seemed to have exactly that agenda, as well as access to the power through which one might realize it.

I didn't like radicals in the beginning. I was not a radical. I was radicalized by law school, by my interactions with my teachers rather than by experience in the movement. It wasn't just one event, but there was an event that summed all this up. Alexander Bickel, a brilliant, complicated, left-liberal professor and intellectual leader, briefly a Bobby Kennedy speech writer, was freaked out by the emerging, sometimes threatening, rudeness of student activists, particularly of the first generation of black students in the Yale Law School, there because of an admirably progressive outreach program. He was the quintessential liberal-against-loyalty-oaths, but in the spring of 1970 he felt, in utter good faith but absurdly, it seemed to me, that there was a parallel between, on the one hand, black radical and white radical activism and, on the other hand, Brownshirt activism in the late Weimar Republic. He proposed that every student should sign an oath of loyalty to the "academic enterprise" on admission, with no enforcement mechanism, but just as a symbolic act.

It wasn't the proposal that freaked us out in turn, but our civilized discussion with him. He seemed terrifyingly different than I had thought him. He seemed to think we, his students, in a sense his followers, were terrifyingly different, too. There were others like him. At first we'd be having a cool exchange with them, and then there would be a moment in which they, a whole generation really, just flipped. You could see in their body language, in their eyes, that it was revulsion; it was fear; it was shame that we were jamming them from the left; and it was more anger than we could account for.

There was more anger than we could account for because our demands seemed just the extension of what they had taught us, demands around the war in Vietnam, race, gender, demands for more student power in administering the school. In the moment of seeing ourselves in their eyes, we thought (just as grad students might think today): "Maybe we are criminals; maybe we are destroying the academic community." Then we'd think, "Nah."

The upshot was that they withdrew from us and we from them, a withdrawal that was hurtful but never complete, because we were bound to them willy-nilly, even when we were maddest at them. I think we were right to be mad as well as hurt. As it got more intense, the mean ones among them got meaner and meaner, and the timid ones got more and more timid. Those among the junior faculty who were timid but brave in spite of themselves, or just plain brave, got hurt, sometimes seriously, denied tenure, because they tried to protect us in one way or another, and that's still not forgotten. It sometimes seemed the meanest ones (Or was it just the ones whose meanness hurt the most?) were the ones who had had the most unself-conscious confidence that they *were* enlightened American progressivism.

They were the ones who'd say, "Who do you think you are? Bolivian peasants? You are Yale law students." It was tricky, the feeling of being shamed for one's privilege by a person who was unbelievably more privileged, a person saying to you, "Because you are privileged, you have to do everything I say."

We didn't do what they said, but in spite of that, in spite of what we thought we learned in our tense, disappointing conversations with them, now we, my generation, are them. We are the faculty that in one school after another bristle — shamed, trapped, cornered, self-righteous, and to my mind often pathetically confused in argument — when graduate students say to us the kind of things we said to the "them" of our own day.

One of graduate students' most basic functions is to revive the moral sense of their faculty interlocutors by keeping on and pressing them and not even for a minute letting themselves be carried back into the feeling that maybe they're the bad children and maybe they were wrong from the beginning. In this, today's graduate student union activists are more like the militants of the early American labor movement than at first appears. A lot of the fight, all along, is against the part of us that responds with fear and passivity not just to material threats but to the felt legitimacy of the boss, the master of apprentices. Overcoming that, through the kind of brave stuff GESO members have been doing, is what is redeeming in the moment of joining organized labor, no less today than a hundred years ago.

Chapter 6
The Labor behind the Cult of Work

Andrew Ross

I participated in the strike moratorium in February 1996 as only one of thousands of non-Yale faculty who have been saddened and angered by the university's responses to the current labor disputes. No doubt, many of the unsympathetic Yale faculty and administrators viewed our presence and our remarks there as further evidence of the outsider's unfamiliarity with the fragile web of affinities and obligations that binds together a vibrant college community with an Ivy League pedigree. And yet this insider perception is one of the reasons why we were there. From the outside, the Yale strikes of 1996 exposed a sharp contradiction — between Yale's select academic ethos of intellectual largesse and entitlement and its cruel neocorporate appetite for trimming labor costs to the bone. To varying degrees, this disparity affects all of our institutions, public as well as private, because it is intrinsic to the political economy of prestige that underpins higher education. The Yale strikes attracted so much attention because they came at a time when many consider it no longer possible to ignore such contradictions. Needless to say, the strikes were an affront to that part of the academic mentality that considers it bad taste to view our campuses as sites of wage labor and union organizing. While it has become rote to bemoan the impact on liberal education of the tendency toward market rationalization and technocratic planning, few within academe are in the habit of making links between the corporatization of the modern university and corresponding shifts in its labor infrastructure. The Yale strikes have changed all of that, and now mark a turning point.

On the face of it, Yale's responses to Locals 34 and 35 and to GESO appear to reflect its status as the largest employer in town. An uncommonly wealthy institution (fiscally constituted as a corporation) is exploiting its near-monopoly position within the labor market of a severely depressed city and region. Taking advantage of the hard times, Yale has manipulated (or manufactured) its own fiscal "crisis" to accelerate a low-wage revolution among its clerical, service, and maintenance workers, demanding wage cuts of up to four dollars per hour, laying off workers for up to twenty weeks out of every year, slashing benefits, and reserving the unlimited right to fill any openings with outside subcontractors. These are by now familiar hallmarks of an aggressive corporate strategy to win a nonunion workplace through casual contracting. In addition, Yale's ability to drive down regional wage levels may have a substantial impact on the local economy. New Haven, once a proud industrial town, will more and more resemble an Ivy League theme park for tourists to gawk at and for upper-income Connecticut to colonize.

In many respects, then, Yale's labor strategies are little different — though this hardly excuses them — from any other local corporation operating within a pro-scarcity climate. Books are cooked for PR effect; fiscal shortfalls are announced; and an "unavoidable" solution is pursued through wage and benefit reduction. And yet any economist will tell you (as Rick Wolff does in these pages) that in the short term Yale stands to benefit only sparingly from these concessions. The real story here is the long-term elimination of organized labor, which is a principle of faith among the corporate executives who sit on the board of the Yale Corporation and whose advocacy of such a policy is therefore as natural as breathing the boardroom air. Union-busting law firms, high-priced PR operatives, and beefed-up security and surveillance staff provide the heavy rhetoric and muscle, while the university's vast riches allow it to starve out striking workers.

It is hardly news that universities more and more resemble corporate entities, whether in their investment strategies, their budgetary priorities, their industrial contracting of research, or their servicing of elite needs in sectors of the state, business, and the military. The sharp expansion of administrative strata has devolved all forms of decision making away from faculty, while it has facilitated the absorption into academe of many of the rituals and values of corporate life. At Princeton, where I used to teach, one department chair I knew read a handful of textbooks on corporate management to prepare for the job of handling faculty and students — though not a resounding success, this was a sign of the times. The proliferation of divisional and subdivisional deans has strengthened the power of administrators to reorganize the map of departments and disciplines in accord with often ephemeral institutional needs. Budget directors often now make decisions of an academic nature. University presidents increasingly take their cue from the much-lionized CEOs of the day, while their PR image-doctors try to maintain the soft-focus ideal of higher education as it should be: a composite of the liberalism of the British undergraduate ethos, the professionalism of German postgraduate research, and the public orientation of U.S. pragmatism.

The impact of these developments varies from college to college. Currently, I work at New York University, which, unlike blue-chip Yale, has a relatively small fixed capital in its endowment but which has been using the proceeds of its successful fund-raising to purchase faculty and students in a nouveau riche bid for prestige all the more noticeable in a time of hiring freezes up and down the country. One little joke I have heard is that Lawrence Tisch, who is chair of the trustee board, will one day sell off NYU the same way he sold off CBS. Such quips are part of the sick humor of academics, who for a long time have been used to responding to the neoindustrial demand for "productivity" but who now face the injunctions of downsizing, casualization, and the erosion of tenure as a potential contractual guarantee. Add this economic pressure to the acute political siege of sectors of the humanities and social sciences via the Right's media-oriented campaign against the political correctness of tenured radicals: the result is an extensive backlash against the generational revolt of the 1960s that declared that universities could no longer be seen as reliable sources of legitimation for the values and actions of the corporate-military state. The New Right's extracurricular response to the "long march" of the Left through the institutions has been the lavish creation of a made-to-order neoconservative intelligentsia in the heritage foundations and policy institutes of the last two decades. But the abdication, in state capitals and in Congress, of the political will to fund education is hardly disconnected from the efforts to squeeze the academic Left.

To academics who subscribe passionately to the liberal ideals of disinterested scholarship, academic mentorship, and collegial autonomy, all of this economic and political turbulence is highly distasteful. Consequently, a psychology of denial has set in and is now entrenched within the comfortably tenured strata of academe. This has taken its toll. The possessive investment in the privileges of tenured seniority is not only a prominent obstacle in the path of solutions to the crisis of academic labor; its resistance to change has become one of the causes of the crisis itself.

It is still a novelty to speak of academic labor. In the academy, the employment of teachers is only revealed as "labor" when a severe job shortage occurs, leaving a vast portion of teaching needs to be met by graduate students, adjuncts, or part-time employees with few prospects of a permanent appointment. When these needs are seen in the context of the large-scale economic patterns that are rapidly changing the character of universities, then the commonality of the interests of teachers and nonteaching staff becomes more evident. Consequently, academic work becomes labor only when the morality of employment is called into question, as has been the case with the casualization of teaching in recent years. Academic business as usual depends on concealing or mystifying these labor conditions. This is a considerable achievement, given the huge numbers employed within the U.S. higher education sector and given the crucial role played by its institutions in training a professional and technical workforce. How does labor come to be so mystified in the academy? This question goes to the heart of the issues faced by graduate students active today in the business of organizing. What graduate students confront daily, after all, is a *cult of work,* sustained by a high degree of discipline, most formal when it involves the suspension of funding or accreditation. As a practical art form, teaching is viewed as an organic extension of this cult. To partake fully of the cult — imbued by its apostles with Arnoldian sweetness and light — is to desire, naturally, to initiate other, younger adepts. This mystique is partly responsible for obscuring institutional reliance on graduate student labor and for sustaining the belief that such teaching is a form of apprenticeship and not a mode of employment. But if it conceals and obscures, the mystique also honors the most vital tradition of the academy—that of intellectual freedom. Beneath the often baroque decor of university culture are monuments to academic freedom that must be protected and preserved.

Nothing is written in stone, however. Indeed, the loose collection of rights affiliated with the concept of academic freedom is often only informally acknowledged. In the case of the right to form unions, it is actively discouraged; indeed, ever since the *Yeshiva* decision (which declared faculty to be managerial employees), it has become impossible for faculty in private institutions to form unions under NLRB auspices. With the new interest in graduate student unionization, the scope of academic freedom is once again put to the test. Should it encompass the right to freedom of association with others to protect interests held in common, to bargain collectively with employers, and to advance principles of fairness that are fundamental to academic life? To many of us, the answer is as clear as day. For others, such talk about labor and rights does violence to the sacred core of what Yale's president Levin has called the "pedagogical compact" between teacher and student.

I am as respectful of this compact as any educator and believe that it is quite unique among social bonds, for reasons that can be deeply satisfying for both parties. But this compact, however noble, does not exist in an institutional vacuum. For the most part, it is only as good as the current state of the profession. At best, this compact is based upon a culture of subprofessional informality that yields little protection for graduate students, other than the brittle thread of obligations and debts that is spun from the psychology of paternal benevolence. At worst, devotion to this compact creates expectations that can never be met, as witnessed by the "overproduction" of Ph.D.'s in recent years. Two generations of overspecialized graduate students have emerged bright and blinking from their library cubicles to face recruitment into the reserve army of underemployed intellectual labor. By now we are all too familiar with their cautionary tales about life in the low-wage limbo of part-time appointments. As for their professional training, for upward of five years, most will have been guided along stiflingly narrow disciplinary grooves, discouraged by mentors and gatekeepers from straying from the disciplinary path for fear they will not be perceived as bona fide scholars and thus be unemployable. In other words, they may even have been deprived of the authentic opportunities that a graduate education affords — to respond expansively to *the* field (rather than a field) of knowledge. Why were they led on in this manner? In part as a result of the precious pedagogical compact, which is a medium through which the tenured professoriat seeks to reproduce itself in its own overspecialized image. With the academic job crisis as acute as it is, it would be heartening to report that such attitudes are changing. Think again. Disciplinary retrenchment seems to be the order of the day, as the general response to pro-scarcity injunctions takes the form of preserving traditional strengths in established departments. The opportunity to use this crisis to launch innovative curricular reforms is being passed up in favor of defending existing ground. How should this impinge upon the way in which graduate students conceive and build a union?

Stereotypically, unions are seen as exclusively preoccupied with bread-and-butter issues like wages and benefits and as anti-intellectual in their attitude to broader social and political issues. Yet an important part of the labor movement has always had an active interest in education. Historically, unions have often played a leading educational role, whether in fields directly related to workers' jobs and skills or in assisting in the kind of general education that compensates for the antilabor ideology that saturates the media. A healthy labor movement has the political function of educating public consciousness and voicing opinions about salient issues of the day. In this respect, it is wrong to think of unions as antipathetic to the spirit of education. Combine the best of this history with the new activist tenor of the labor movement in its campaign against acute economic disparities — the ratio of CEO salaries to janitor wages and of corporate welfare to social welfare — and you have a potent formula for organizing within higher education and for addressing the plight of graduate students in particular.

For if there is going to be a graduate union at universities like Yale, why not aim for an expansive, utopian union with a broad intellectual role to play on and off campus? Don't settle for a technocratic bargaining unit, whose only mandate is the protection of its students' material concerns. Make sure that it also has some voice in curricular reform and in faculty recruitment and that it is set up to sponsor and broker debates about academic matters. These must include issues related to the vocational structure of graduate education. Make sure, in other words, that your union has something to say, because a union with nothing to say in the long run may be a union not worth having.

Figure 25. Poster designed by Virginia Blaisdell

Chapter 7
The Proletariat Goes to College

Robin D. G. Kelley

"So we're here in Pittsburgh: Where are the steel workers? Why aren't they here?" This question was raised at the 1995 American Studies Association (ASA) meeting during a special panel titled "Does Cultural Studies Ignore Class?" The discussion had reverted to the same old left-academic angst over whether we are capable of addressing "real people in the real world." Someone suggested that the ASA program committee invite Pittsburgh steel workers to formally participate in the conference. Next thing you know, a string of scholars in attendance started to give testimonials about their own privilege, the need to speak to broader audiences, to participate in the world as public intellectuals, ad infinitum. In the midst of this academic self-loathing, a grad student standing in the back of the room injected a dose of reality by reminding everyone that a "real" struggle was going on at Yale University to unionize teaching assistants and that, as progressive scholars, we should be doing all we can to support their efforts. In other words, don't mourn, organize.

The young woman who spoke from the floor that November morning indirectly brought home another lesson. If you're looking for the American working class, you'll do just as well to look in hospitals and universities as in the sooty industrial suburbs and smokestack districts. And these workers are more likely to be brown and female than to be the good old blue-collar white boys we're so accustomed to seeing in popular culture. The combination of immigration and the transformation of work from manufacturing to service, from decent-paying full-time work to low-wage part-time and temporary work, means that the employed working class is increasingly female, Latino, black, and Asian-American, and its main employers are hospitals, universities, food-processing plants, food-service companies, and various retail establishments. Sweatshops are making a huge comeback, particularly in the garment industry and electronics assembling plants, and homework (telephone sales, for example) is growing.

Universities (as well as hospitals) make up one of the largest sectors of the service economy. Besides employing full- and part-time faculty and researchers, universities also employ a vast army of clerical workers, food-service workers, janitors, and other employees whose job is to maintain the physical plant. In 1991, for instance, colleges and universities directly employed 2,662,085 workers — a figure that does not include employees who work for other firms contracted out by universities and colleges.[1]

Public and private universities, like the rest of corporate America, are also undergoing major restructuring. Administrators claim that cutbacks in governmental and private support, compounded by political attacks on university affirmative-action policies and multicultural curricula, have created a major financial crisis. During the past decade we've witnessed massive downsizing in staff and even faculty while enrollments have remained steady or have increased. These circumstances translate into layoffs, wage freezes, speed-ups, and the increased use of part-time and temporary labor without benefits or union protection.

Yale University officials have also declared a crisis, announcing major cuts to help reduce their $8 million deficit. Yet, just as the Fortune 500 companies are reaping some of the greatest profits in history, Yale University has earned a 15.7 percent return on its investments, bringing its endowment to almost $4 billion. Yale's proclaimed crisis is not only disingenuous but camouflages its real agenda: to bust existing unions — mainly Locals 34 and 35 of the Federation of University Employees — and nip any other organizing activity in the bud. Yale's treatment of its dining hall, custodial, and maintenance workers, represented by the predominantly black Local 35, can only be regarded as draconian. The proposed cuts would essentially create a permanent two-tier system in which Local 35 workers would be unemployed during the summer months.

The thirty-week schedule would reduce the typical full-time salary from $23,000 to about $10,000. It means that dining hall and service workers will be forced to go on welfare during the summer if they cannot find adequate full-time work during that period. Yale also proposes cutting the health benefits of retirees by 40 percent. The average New Haven retiree, after working at Yale for twenty-five years, will effectively have his or her retirement package cut from roughly $500 to $350 per month. Furthermore, Yale plans to increase subcontracting to bring in nonunion labor to perform clerical, food, and maintenance work.[2]

Clearly, the university is as much a part of the "real world" as Citibank and AT&T. Institutions of higher learning are by no means above exploitation or resistance, and the rules of the game are determined by the flow of capital. Thus unions are critical for defending university employees from corporate downsizing — a lesson few full-time faculty want to acknowledge. Beyond the obvious issues facing low-wage service workers at universities, few of my colleagues recognize that they are about to be caught in the crisis themselves, especially with the elimination of tenure just around the corner, the hiring of casual labor to teach undergrads, and the reliance on academic stardom as the first wedge in the creation of a two-tiered faculty. The only way to overturn these developments is to challenge the universities we work for and the administrators who carry out these corporate downsizing policies. We have to decide whose side we're on and realize that our base of support has already been established by the very black and brown workers who clean our offices and to whom most faculty don't even speak.

But the question of unionization is not just a pragmatic issue. What kind of unions should university employees build, especially if their work brings them in contact with students? What should be the relationship between low-wage workers, faculty, students, and the larger community? After all, despite the resemblance, universities aren't exactly banks or investment firms. They have historically been places where alternatives to exploitation and oppression have been discussed and imagined in an institutional setting. They have been the sites of historic movements for social change precisely because the ostensible function of the university is to interrogate knowledge, society, history, and so on. Students and some faculty at City College of New York participated directly in the movement on behalf of labor and the unemployed in the 1930s; African-American students at Fisk University and North Carolina A&T helped launch the civil rights movement; the free speech and subsequent student movement got its start partly at the University of California–Berkeley. And even when important social movements have emerged out of factory settings, students have often played some role: for example, students at Wayne State University played a key role in the Dodge Revolutionary Union movement in Detroit.

Not surprisingly, unions that operate in the universities not only have been at the forefront of labor conflicts on campuses but also have on occasion articulated a larger vision of social justice. Two important examples that are analogous to Local 35's struggle with Yale University took place almost three decades ago at Duke University and the University of North Carolina, Chapel Hill. Because the struggles at Duke and UNC were as much a product of the black revolution in the South as of the horrible working conditions of dining hall and maintenance workers, strikers made demands that extended far beyond basic bread-and-butter issues. On April 8, 1968, just four days after the assassination of Dr. King, students and faculty organized a massive sit-in on the quadrangle in front of Duke Chapel to demand a $1.60 an hour minimum for nonacademic employees — primarily maintenance workers and food-service employees organized in Local 77 of the American Federation of State, County, and Municipal Employees (AFSCME). They also demanded that Duke University president Douglas Knight form a grievance committee consisting of faculty, students, and employees; that he resign from the all-white Hope Valley Country Club; and that he sign a petition in support of open housing for African-Americans. Despite militant opposition from workers and students, Duke University proved more powerful. When the food and maintenance workers finally returned to work, their union was in shambles.

In Chapel Hill, black food-service workers at UNC walked off their jobs in November 1969. It was the second strike that year — the first ending successfully with the university paying $180,000 in back overtime. And their success depended on support from black students and faculty. The second UNC strike is strikingly similar to the struggles being waged by Yale's locals of the Federation of University Employees in that they, too, were fighting the practice of subcontracting work to firms that hire cheap nonunion labor. In Chapel Hill, the food-service workers, members of AFSCME, fought the university's decision to contract out the running of dining halls by Saga Food Service. Saga had pretty much ignored the earlier contract between the university and strikers and apparently fired ten workers for alleged union membership. They also cut back UNC's staff from 147 to 100, despite protestations from workers. It turned out to be an extremely violent strike, with sixteen arrests and six people injured—most of whom were students in solidarity with striking workers.[3]

These strikes at Duke and UNC anticipated the current situation university workers are facing, and they point to the need to think critically about the unique opportunities universities offer as sites of working-class struggle. First, during the last quarter-century, at least, subcontracting has been part of a larger corporate strategy to reduce wages and benefits and to bring in casualized, temporary, nonunion labor. Of course, this general trend mirrors the rest of the corporate world, but within a university it also serves to take the administration off the hook by rendering even more invisible the exploitation of labor at the university. University officials work hard to project an image of their campuses as places of free exchange and intellectual inquiry. That universities are often the biggest exploiters of labor, not to mention the biggest landlords in some cities, is a fact their PR people try to bury.

Second, the low-wage workforce at most major universities and colleges really reflects the American working class in general and the renewed labor movement in particular. Workers of color, especially women, were at the forefront of the struggles at Duke and UNC in the late 1960s. The same holds true for Local 35 as well as for similar locals across the country. Despite the fact that these workers tend to have relatively high union participation rates, they are nevertheless among the poorest paid and most exploited workers on campuses. Indeed, Yale's draconian policies toward dining hall and custodial workers is rooted precisely in the fact that these kinds of jobs have historically been associated with black labor (domestic servants, janitors, etc.). Racism and sexism largely explain the disparity in wages, as well as the labeling of these jobs as "unskilled." Clearly there is skill involved, but definitions of skill are raced, sexed, and historically determined. Hence, any union fighting for the rights of low-wage service workers, in the university or elsewhere, must make the struggle against racism and sexism fundamental.

Finally, the role of students and faculty in all of these strikes offers key lessons for future labor conflicts on college campuses. At both Duke and UNC, student and faculty support was pivotal. During the UNC strike, for example, student groups mobilized African-American students from all over the state of North Carolina to descend on campus to observe "Black Monday," the deadline set by students demanding that a settlement be reached. Fear of unrest forced Chapel Hill mayor Howard Lee to withdraw police from campus and compelled university officials to negotiate a settlement between the union and Saga Food Service. Students helped organize workers, joined picket lines, and incorporated tactics developed in the civil rights movement. Indeed, most student activists saw these campus strikes in much the same way Dr. Martin Luther King Jr. viewed strikes by the Memphis sanitation workers and Charleston's hospital workers in Local 1199: they were part and parcel of the civil rights movement. Even when the workers lost, the strikes gave birth to new movements for social justice. Several Duke University students in the college and medical school who actively supported the strike went on to be active in other labor movements, anti-Klan organizations, left-wing parties, and various Third World liberation movements. Owusu Sadaukai (Howard Fuller) became the business agent for Local 77 of AFSCME after the failed strike at Duke University. Soon thereafter, Sadaukai founded Malcolm X Liberation University in North Carolina, served as a leader in the African Liberation Support Committee, and developed a reputation as one of the leading black radicals in North Carolina.[4]

Unions at universities and elsewhere need to adopt a broad vision of social justice if they are to succeed. They cannot be business unions as usual. They need to embrace a far-reaching civil rights agenda and the struggle against class-based racism in addition to the basic bread-and-butter issues.[5] And there are a growing number of labor leaders who see their own efforts as part of a movement for social justice. This has certainly been the case in the heavily Latino and black Service Employees International Union (SEIU: from which came John Sweeney, now AFL-CIO president) and its offshoot, Justice for Janitors. In California, for example, Gilbert Cedillo, leader of Local 660 of the SEIU, has led a fight against Proposition 187 and attacks on immigrant workers. Other movements seek to push labor beyond a defensive posture, beyond acceptance of the principle that profit, competition, and productivity are more important for both labor and capital than justice. Among the groups involved in these movements are progressive labor support groups such as Black Workers for Justice, the Labor/Community Strategy Center, Collective Action, Solidarity, New Directions, Jobs with Justice, to name but a few.

Movements and groups like these contain the seeds of a new political vision. A new vision is something progressives and labor organizers are sorely lacking, especially when it comes to dealing with the problems of a predominantly nonwhite, urban working class relegated to low-wage service work, part-time work, or outright joblessness. Ironically, universities might ultimately be the source of a new radical vision, but in order to grasp that vision we would do well to pay less attention to the classroom and its attendant culture wars and more attention to the cafeteria and the workers there.

NOTES

1. U.S. Department of Education, National Center for Education Statistics, *Integrated Postsecondary Education Data System* (Washington, D.C., 1995). There are very few studies of union activity and workers at universities (aside from the issue of labor education), though much has been done on hospitals. Some key examples include Toni Gilpin et al., *On Strike for Respect: The Clerical and Technical Workers' Strike at Yale University, 1984–85* (Urbana: University of Illinois Press, 1995); Joel Denker, *Unions and Universities: The Rise of the New Labor Leader* (Montclair, N.J.: Allanheld, Osmun, 1981); Karen Sacks, *Caring by the Hour: Women, Work, and Organizing at Duke Medical Center* (Urbana: University of Illinois Press, 1988); Leon Fink and Brian Greenberg, *Upheaval in the Quiet Zone: A History of Hospital Workers' Union, Local 1199* (Urbana: University of Illinois Press, 1989); Susan Reverby, *Ordered to Care: The Dilemma of American Nursing, 1850–1945* (Cambridge: Cambridge University Press, 1987); Barbara Melosh, *The Physician's Hand: Work Culture and Conflict in American Nursing* (Philadelphia: Temple University Press, 1982); Darlene Clark Hine, *Black Women in White: Racial Conflict and Cooperation in the Nursing Profession, 1890–1950* (Bloomington: Indiana University Press, 1989).

2. See *New Haven Register,* February 8 and 9, 1996; *New Haven Advocate,* February 15, 1996.

3. *New York Times,* April 9, 1968; *New York Times,* December 7, 1969.

4. Elizabeth Wheaton, *Codename Greenkil: The 1979 Greensboro Killings* (Athens: University of Georgia Press, 1987), esp. 23–24.

5. Furthermore, students and faculty in support of campus unionism must pay more attention to corporate campaigns and boycotts. Let us not forget the incredible success of the antiapartheid divestment campaign, which required support from students, faculty, and staff.

Chapter 8
The Blessed of the Earth

Michael Bérubé

Not long after graduate students at the University of Kansas voted to unionize, affiliating themselves with the American Federation of Teachers, I was invited to speak at that university on the future of graduate study in the humanities. In the course of my talk, I not only endorsed the unionization of graduate students at the University of Kansas and elsewhere but also referred, in passing, to what I called the "bad faith" attempt of administrators and faculty at Yale University to claim that their graduate students who taught were simply students and not also "employees." As long as people are working as instructors or as teaching assistants and being paid for their work, I thought, it makes sense to consider them "employed," to consider their work "employment," and to admit, therefore, that they are in some sense "employees." And if administrators and faculty at Yale or elsewhere want to claim that their graduate students' wages are not strictly wages because their teaching is not strictly teaching and is merely part of their professional training as apprentice professors, then it makes sense to call the bluff: take graduate students out of the classrooms in which they work as graders, assistants, and instructors; maintain their stipend support at its current levels; and give them professional development and training that does not involve the direct supervision of undergraduates. *Then* we'll see how long Yale University can survive without the labor (which, it says, is not strictly labor) of its graduate student TAs.

At the time, I thought my support for graduate student unions—in a speech delivered to, among other people, unionized graduate students—amounted to endorsing candidates after they'd won their elections. To my surprise, however, I learned later that the graduate students were very pleased with my speech and that some even considered it "courageous." It seems that I had denounced as ridiculous Yale administrators' claims that graduate students were not employees in front of a number of Kansas administrators who had claimed that graduate students were not employees. (I told the students I had had no idea that my audience included actual bad-faith negotiators and that my "courage" in denouncing them was therefore attributable to simple ignorance.) I asked them what other kinds of opposition the union had met; they told me of faculty in department after department who had insisted that the unionization of graduate students would disrupt "morale" and destroy the delicate, collegial relationship so characteristic of, and necessary to, healthy interactions between graduate students and faculty. When I asked these students whether their faculty had entertained the possibility that delicate, collegial relationships don't normally involve one party dictating the other party's interests and threatening punishment if party number two failed to act in what party number one had determined those interests to be, I was met with bitter laughter. It would be one thing, I was told, if the faculty's relation to graduate students were simply paternal rather than collegial; that would be undesirable but understandable. "But Michael," said one union leader, "half the faculty who spoke to us about the importance of faculty-student collegiality didn't even know our *names*."

•

Nothing, I suggest, could make more palpable the vast differences between Yale and Kansas. If there's one good thing we can say of the faculty who broke the graduate student strike at Yale University, it is this: they knew their students' names. Indeed, had they *not* known their students' names, they would not have been able to preserve the delicate, collegial faculty-student relationship at Yale by submitting their students' names to Yale's administration for disciplinary hearings and possible expulsion. As Yale president Richard Levin put it in a November 1994 letter to the then-chair of Yale's Graduate Employees and Students Organization (GESO), unionization of graduate students would inevitably "chill, rigidify, and diminish" the relationship between graduate students and their mentors and advisers on the faculty.[1] Accordingly, from that point on, Yale graduate students who were not satisfied with their warm, flexible, and capacious relations with faculty members would have to be punished harshly and swiftly.

I will not attempt here to retell the history of graduate student organization at Yale or the Yale Corporation's long and sorry history of union busting and unfair labor practices.[2] Instead, I want to examine a more narrowly professionalist issue — the role played by Yale faculty during the events leading up to the short-lived grade strike of 1995–96 — and its implications for professional self-governance in American higher education. I believe the actions of the faculty at Yale have potentially grave consequences for the future of graduate study in the humanities and social sciences, just as they provide (less importantly but more poignantly) an object lesson in just how politically obtuse, shortsighted, and self-serving a university faculty can be.[3]

This is not to say that GESO has been always and everywhere beyond criticism or that it is impossible for a well-informed person to lodge reasonable objections to the grade strike that precipitated the faculty's collective decision to crush GESO. That grade strike did indeed pit GESO against the interests of undergraduates and faculty alike, thus isolating the union politically, and it strained the meaning of "academic freedom," a principle GESO had hoped would protect graduate students involved in job actions: to wit, GESO could claim that its members should be free from "academic reprisals, including letters of recommendation, disciplinary letters, academic probation, firing of teachers, denial of promised teaching jobs, or expulsion" (in the language of the resolution submitted by GESO to the MLA) and that any such action taken by Yale administration or faculty constituted a violation of academic freedom; but faculty could also legitimately respond that *their* academic freedom would be violated if they could not consider their students' participation in the grade strike as a factor in writing letters of recommendation or awarding teaching positions. At the very least, then, the grade strike muddied the question of whether the job actions at Yale were matters of labor relations or of academic protocol: if they were the former, then Yale was clearly involved in illegal union busting; if the latter, then striking GESO members were clearly abrogating one of their primary obligations as undergraduate instructors by failing to turn in their grades.

Of course, the grade strike made a crucial political point, a point that Yale's administration denied and incredibly *continues* to deny — namely, that a great deal of basic undergraduate instruction at Yale is carried out by graduate students. What's more, Yale students have convincingly argued that the strike was a measure of last resort; every prior attempt to meet and negotiate with Yale had been rebuffed. As Cynthia Young reports, by November 1995,

> the grade strike was the only effective action — short of a teaching strike — left to GESO. Demonstrations, petitions, a one-week strike, a union election, and corporation visits had all failed to convince the Yale administration that graduate teachers were indeed serious about winning a collective bargaining agreement. It was this bleak recognition that mobilized GESO organizers with barely three weeks left in the semester to begin organizing graduate teachers to withhold their grades. A grade strike would not only reinforce the central import of graduate teachers' labor at the university, but it would also undercut the Yale administration's attempts to depict GESO as dependent upon the other two locals to secure a contract. A grade strike barely a week before final exams had the capacity to spur undergraduates and faculty to pressure the administration to negotiate with GESO. It was certainly not intended as a strategy to harm undergraduates; in fact, striking teachers expressed their willingness to write letters to graduate and professional schools evaluating the student and explaining the reasons for the grade strike. In any case, it is unlikely that any school would have disqualified Yale candidates because of their incomplete transcripts. A grade strike is far less disruptive of undergraduate education than an indefinite teaching strike, a possibility that seemed to loom on the spring horizon. Weighing these various considerations, graduate teachers voted to withhold their fall semester grades until Yale committed to negotiating a written and binding agreement with GESO's negotiating committee. ("Strike," 188)

Even when considered in the light of these various justifications, however, the grade strike seems to have made two tactical errors in a Machiavellian sense. First, it underestimated the possibility that such an action would in fact spur undergraduates and faculty to pressure the administration to move forcefully against GESO. Second, and no less crucial, it regrettably allowed Yale faculty to pretend, after the fact, that they had been sympathetic to GESO, or generally supportive of graduate student grievances, or even opposed to GESO but in favor of collective student organization — until that deplorable grade strike came along and ruined everything.

The level of faculty vindictiveness and double-talk on this issue has been simply astounding. At various times, Yale faculty and administrators have claimed that they are opposed only to GESO and not to the idea of graduate student unionization; or that they are opposed to student unions at Yale but not other forms of collective (and nonbinding) student representation; or that they are opposed to unionization at Yale but not elsewhere, at other schools. It should not escape notice that each one of these rhetorical escape-maneuvers begs the original question concerning the sanctity of faculty-student relations. Perhaps it is plausible, for instance, that GESO would disrupt the delicate, collegial relations between graduate students and faculty, but another union would not. Or perhaps it is plausible that faculty would look kindly on graduate student representation that took some shape other than that of a union, as Peter Brooks claims.[4] Or finally, perhaps it is plausible that unionization always disrupts the faculty-student relationship but does so in ways that can be tolerated at plebeian, inferior schools like the Universities of Kansas, Oregon, Michigan, Wisconsin–Madison, Wisconsin–Milwaukee, Massachusetts–Amherst, Massachusetts–Lowell, Florida, and South Florida, or at Rutgers, SUNY, and Berkeley (all of them home to recognized graduate student unions), but not at an institution so prestigious as Yale University, where talk of "unionization" is not only harmful to morale but also, and more vexingly, *bad form.*

What's remarkable is not that different Yale faculty have appealed to these various, contradictory rationales for union busting; what's remarkable is that *individual* faculty members have frantically appealed to each of them in turn, desperately trying to justify not only their opposition to the grade strike but also their intransigence during all GESO's attempts to negotiate prior to the strike. For a vivid illustration of this brand of double-talk I need turn only to my mailbox. On January 24, 1996, Annabel Patterson, Karl Young Professor of English at Yale, wrote a letter to Phyllis Franklin, the MLA's executive director, protesting the MLA Delegate Assembly's passage of the resolution censuring Yale for its handling of GESO. Patterson's letter, together with three other letters from Yale faculty and administrators, was circulated to the entire MLA membership in February 1996. There is much to remark upon both in Patterson's letter and in the manner of its distribution, but for now I want simply to focus on one crucial paragraph — the paragraph in which Patterson addresses what she calls "the nature of the 'union' " (nowhere in Patterson's letter does she employ the terms "union" or "strike" without scare quotes). The reason the paragraph is valuable, for my purposes, is that it voices almost every single rhetorical escape-maneuver I enumerated above; when read together with Margaret Homans's equally evasive letter, also distributed by the MLA, it provides us with a useful introduction to faculty psychology at Yale.

Patterson writes:

> The university administration, whose leaders are all Yale faculty, has consistently refused to recognize [GESO] as a "union," not only because it does not believe this to be an appropriate relationship between students and faculty in a nonprofit organization, but also because GESO has always been a wing of Locals 34 and 35 of the Hotel Employees and Restaurant Employees International Union, who draw their membership from the dining workers in the colleges and other support staff. Yale is not prepared to negotiate academic policy, such as the structure of the teaching program or class size, with the Hotel Employees and Restaurant Employees International Union. Yale administrators have made it perfectly clear that they have no objections to working with an elected graduate student organization other than GESO, one that is not tied to the nonacademic unions on campus.[5]

According to Patterson, Yale has properly refused to recognize GESO because the graduate student "union" is affiliated with the smelly hotel and restaurant workers, who don't know how a university works. But wait a minute: look at the closing and opening passages of Patterson's paragraph. Apparently, Yale has no aversion to "working with an elected graduate student organization other than GESO" so long as the organization is not tied to Locals 34 and 35. Does this mean that Yale would have been happy to recognize GESO if only GESO had had the good taste to affiliate with the American Federation of Teachers (AFT)? The earlier passage had seemed to close off this possibility, declaring that Yale had refused to recognize GESO as a union because "it does not believe this to be an appropriate relationship between students and faculty in a nonprofit organization." So what is one to conclude from this? If only GESO hadn't affiliated with a nonacademic union . . . , if only GESO had been something other than a union . . . , and (by the by) if only the Yale Corporation were something other than a nonprofit institution . . . , *then,* obviously, Patterson implies, we'd have had no objection at all to dealing with these students in good faith.

Margaret Homans then adds two more "if" clauses to this already impressively obfuscatory list when she writes, in her January 14 letter to the MLA:

> Quite possibly, it would be appropriate for students to unionize at those schools where teaching loads are much higher than at Yale and where reliance on graduate teaching is much greater. Part-time and adjunct faculty with PhDs present an even more legitimate motive to unionize, although they are not part of the union movement at Yale. ("MLA," 11)

If only they were worse off, like those students at second-rate schools like Berkeley . . . , if only they were among the *truly* exploited, like part-time and adjunct faculty . . . , why, of *course* we would break bread with these students. Note here that Homans's admission that graduate student unionization is sometimes appropriate (at lesser schools) makes hash of the claim that faculty-student relations are destroyed by unions. Yet Homans's attempt to play one underpaid constituency off another — in this case, juxtaposing graduate students to adjuncts — presents an odd mixture of fuzzy thinking and bad faith: fuzzy thinking, because adjunct faculty already have the right to unionize (precisely the right denied to Yale's graduate students), and bad faith, because the nation's largest union of college faculty, the American Association of University Professors (AAUP), had already disposed of this question, when its Collective Bargaining Congress passed a resolution on December 2, 1995, strongly endorsing the right of *all* graduate teaching assistants to engage in union activities, from collective bargaining to grade strikes.

It is possible that somewhere deep in the recesses of its political unconscious, Homans's text always already acknowledges its bad faith in adjudicating and ranking the rights-claims of graduate students and adjunct faculty; for no sooner does Homans mention the exploitation of adjuncts than she moves on to threaten Yale students with the exploitation of adjuncts. "The students who introduced the resolution," she writes, referring to the MLA Delegate Assembly's resolution to censure,

> captured and capitalized on a legitimate anxiety, widespread in the profession, about the exploitation of nonladder instructors. But graduate students at Yale are "paid" more (in some cases twice as much) for running a weekly discussion section of a lecture course (often with as few as fifteen students) than PhDs are paid for teaching their own independent courses at area schools. . . . If they were paid the local rate for part-time academic work, they would receive a good deal less. ("MLA," 11)

What is the implication of this last sentence? Take *that,* you pampered, sheltered students! You people haven't yet *seen* what we could do to you if we really wanted to *exploit* you! If Patterson's letter was notable for the extent of its author's identification with the Yale administration — "Yale is not prepared to negotiate academic policy . . . with the Hotel Employees and Restaurant Employees International Union" — then Homans's is notable for its author's willingness to begin the union busting herself. For why else would Homans remind Yale graduate students (as if they needed to be reminded) that Ph.D.'s are working for even lower wages at the University of Bridgeport or Southern Connecticut State? (Though Homans does not acknowledge as much, rumor has it that the endowments and budgets of Bridgeport and Southern are somewhat smaller than Yale's.) Are GESO members, then, supposed to be grateful that their masters and overseers at Yale are at least treating them better than the freeway fliers at the college down the road? "Well," one imagines a Yale ABD replying, "we're paid two thousand dollars less than Yale's own cost-of-living estimate for New Haven, and Yale requires that we live here so that we cannot seek higher-paying part-time employment elsewhere while pursuing our degree; but golly, it's great that we're doing so well compared to the part-time schleps and losers at New Haven's own Albertus Magnus College, a nearly penniless institution. Thank goodness Professor Homans straightened us out on that one."

Despite the passages I've cited above, Homans is not unaware that unethical labor practices might in fact be unethical. Though

Homans is not shy about suggesting that graduate students be paid "the local rate" for discussion sections in which they do all the grading (so that people like Homans don't have to), she is appropriately uneasy about the charge that Yale might have had plans to hire "replacement workers" to take on the teaching responsibilities of striking graduate students when classes resumed in the spring of 1996. The aura of hiring "replacement workers" is apparently more unsavory than the aura of breaking unions and depressing wage scales, and thus Homans writes:

> The most basic standards of evidence were not adhered to in the formulation of the resolution, which complains (for example) of faculty being asked to "serve as replacement workers for striking graduate student staff." Faculty teaching lecture courses are in fact responsible for all grades; forms for reporting grades are mailed only to the faculty in charge and not to the Teaching Assistants, who are exactly that — assistants. We can't be described as replacement workers if we turn in grades for our own courses. ("MLA," 10)

One has to admire the faculty member who can write this without fear of exposure or contradiction. *Faculty are responsible for all grades:* the wording suggests that Yale faculty are actually reading the papers and evaluating the written and oral work of all their undergraduates, when, in fact, teaching assistants in lecture courses are hired precisely to release faculty from much of the labor associated with those tasks. (Hence the rationale for the grade strike.) One wonders how many MLA members, many of whom are actually college faculty themselves, are going to be fooled by Homans's reasoning here: *the grade forms are mailed to us and not to the "assistants," so obviously we're the ones doing the grading!*

Delectable also is the "we" in Homans's declaration that "we can't be described as replacement workers if we turn in grades for our own courses." For one thing, the fear at Yale was not that Professors Homans and Patterson would step in and teach extra classes; the fear was that *junior faculty* — Who you mean, "we"? — would be "asked" to teach in place of graduate students or, still more outrageously, to do the grading for the lecture courses of senior faculty (some reports indicate that this latter request was in fact made by the senior faculty of the English department). And for another thing, Homans's letter is in this respect directly contradicted by Patterson, who admits freely that "some classes had been reassigned to faculty members" ("MLA," 5). (Personally, I am glad that Yale faculty have so little practice in conducting disinformation campaigns. Were they more practiced at the art they would never have let a major slip like this get into a mass mailing.) Homans, of course, would countercharge that faculty can never be considered "replacement workers." Again, though, one wonders who might be fooled by this. Even if faculty turn in all the grades "for their own courses" (once their teaching assistants have collected them, that is), that doesn't mean that faculty are not being used as replacement workers when they are asked to turn in the grades for *other people's* courses, particularly when those other people are out on strike. A faculty member who is asked to teach a course or lead a discussion section for a striking graduate student is being asked to cross a picket line and thus to serve as a replacement worker. That should be clear enough. And when the faculty member in question is untenured, then such a request broaches serious ethical and professional issues that neither Homans nor Patterson attend to. That, too, should be clear enough.

Yet why is it *not* clear enough to most of the senior faculty most immediately involved? I want to suggest that something strange is going on here. When a professor of English begins sounding like an employer of migrant citrus workers (*at least you're being paid here — at Sunkist they give their workers only an orange a day*), or when the possessor of a named chair at one of the world's wealthiest universities insists that $9,750 is more than adequate compensation for graduate teaching assistants (see Patterson, "MLA," 6), then clearly some of the protocols of the profession have gone haywire. For the response of the Yale faculty to GESO is by no means confined to the rhetorical circumlocutions of Homans and Patterson; on the contrary, as Patterson herself notes, a special late-December meeting of Yale faculty, attended by 170 persons, indicated "*overwhelming* support for President Levin's policy of refusing to recognize GESO, with perhaps half a dozen voices against it" ("MLA," 7; emphasis in original) — and Michael Denning, one of those half-dozen voices, does not dispute the numbers. David Brion Davis, professor of history, went a good deal further than Homans or Patterson and submitted the name of one of his students, Diana Paton, to the office of the dean for disciplinary hearings, as did Sara Suleri-Goodyear, postcolonial critic extraordinaire (in the case of Cynthia Young);[6] meanwhile, Thomas Carew, chair of the psychology department, called one of his students in India during the winter break, "falsely informing her that everyone else in the department had dropped out of the grade strike."[7] Some faculty, it appears, were truly eager to go the extra mile to break the strike and punish the students they "mentor."

But the full extent of the group psychosis involved in these faculty responses to GESO doesn't begin to come clear, I think, until you step back and realize that for all their bellowing and blustering, *Yale faculty had no direct stake in the prospect of unionization.* GESO was not demanding to have student salaries augmented by stripping Annabel Patterson of the Karl Young chair; at no time did GESO demand that David Brion Davis be personally prevented from dictating university policy regarding class size and health care for graduate teaching assistants. Nevertheless, many Yale faculty insisted that graduate student unionization would take fundamental issues concerning graduate employment out of their hands, apparently oblivious to the fact that most of the issues GESO had placed on the table — from salaries to health care — were always already out of their hands. Faculty resistance to GESO, then, was almost entirely a matter of imaginary relations to real conditions, as Peter Brooks demonstrated when he claimed that "a union just seems to militate against core values" (quoted in "Walking," 58).

No commentator on the Yale strike has yet made this most obvious point: Yale faculty had nothing important to lose in recognizing GESO. By contrast, once the grade strike was underway, *then* Yale faculty most certainly had something material at stake — namely, public recognition of the fact that graduate students do more hands-on teaching and evaluating of undergraduates than faculty do.[8] One would think that any sane, calculating university faculty members who are interested in maintaining their privileges and hierarchies — and few faculties, clearly, are so interested in this as are Yale's faculty — would have foreseen the potentially explosive political ramifications of well-publicized job actions by graduate students and would have moved to palliate GESO with Band-Aid, stopgap measures while the faculty still had nothing at stake in the dispute. The fact that the faculty did not do so suggests that we should not look for "real" explanations of the Yale dispute — we should look instead to the realm of the imaginary.

By their own report, antiunion faculty at Yale were stunned by the volume of GESO's sympathetic support among faculty members at other institutions — hence their obsessive insistence on their own near-unanimity in opposing the grade strike and their willingness to accuse GESO of lying in order to manipulate public opinion. As Annabel Patterson puts it, when Yale received over three hundred letters from faculty protesting Yale's refusal to recognize GESO, "we observed that many of [the letters] were from people conscious that they were hearing only one side of the story" ("MLA," 7). In other words, GESO's external supporters were really rather tentative, because they knew they had not yet taken into account the weight (and the prestige) of the opinions of Yale's senior faculty. The arrogance here is palpable. But if you want to get a vivid sense of just how insular and blinkered Yale's senior faculty have been with regard to the broader issues at stake in the recognition of GESO, Patterson's letter is insufficient on its own; you need to hear another side of the story. You need, at the very least, to read an account of the Yale strike written by people for whom the legitimation crisis of American higher education is always foremost on the agenda:

> There can be little doubt that graduate students at Yale, like graduate students almost everywhere, are exploited as cheap labor. Teaching assistantships are notoriously poorly paid, and the rationale that they should provide a welcome "apprenticeship" for future college professors looks more and more shabby as universities increasingly rely on these cadres of relatively untrained teachers to supplement their regular professorial ranks at discount prices. In fact, Yale has been better than most institutions at requiring its "big name" professors actually to teach undergraduates. But even at Yale, *the habit of fobbing off the ever more expensive education of undergraduates on teaching assistants is a scandal waiting to be exploded*. For graduate students, teaching has more and more become simply a form of financial aid instead of a genuine apprenticeship; for universities, graduate students have become more and more like a pool of migrant workers.[9]

There isn't a false note in this passage, but you'll search in vain for this succinct, scathing analysis of American universities' labor relations in the pages of the *MLA Newsletter*. It appeared, instead, in that stalwart voice of trade unionist activism, the *New Criterion*.

Of course, the folks at the *New Criterion* have only a limited sympathy with GESO, and they go on to inveigh against the existence of *any* university-based unions, not only among graduate students but also among faculty, claiming incoherently that "the idea that students of any description should seek to organize themselves into a union is preposterous. The spectacle of graduate students doing so is only marginally less ludicrous than the prospect of undergraduates or high-school students doing so would be" (3). Somewhere between paragraphs, surely, the *New Criterion* editors forgot that graduate students teach classes whereas undergraduates and high school students generally do not; and you would think Roger Kimball, managing editor of the *New Criterion*, would have good reason not to forget this, since he himself taught undergraduates at Yale when he was a graduate student in the English department at the turn of the 1980s (this was the basis of the claim on the back of his famous book, *Tenured Radicals*, that he had once taught at Yale). But whatever the source of the *New Criterion*'s schizophrenia concerning graduate teaching assistants, one thing is indisputable: when the editors of the *New Criterion* have a vastly better sense of what's at stake at Yale than the faculty at Yale, it's time for some serious *perestroika* in the groves of academe. Yale officially insists, of course, that each of its "teaching fellows" is guided and supervised by a faculty member, but this claim is emphatically contradicted even by one of GESO's strongest critics, Camille Ibbotson, who told *Lingua Franca* not only that "no faculty member has ever visited my class or expressed an interest in what I was doing" but also that "there is no formal teacher training in my department" (quoted in "Walking," 60).

Surely, part of this debacle is attributable specifically to pathologies endemic to Yale and Yale alone. The Yale Corporation has long had a history of toxic aversion to unionization of any kind, be it among graduate students or clerical workers, and the vast majority of Yale faculty, apparently fully interpellated as members of the Corporation, seem to have such an enormous investment in their own prestige that the very idea of unionization threatens their sense of privilege, their sense of *distinction* from mere public universities like Kansas and Berkeley. The weight of "prestige" in the collective faculty imaginary should not be underestimated here. The *New Criterion* casts Yale graduate students as "exploited cheap labor"; Peter Brooks insists that "they really are among the blessed of the earth" (quoted in "Walking," 56). They are not, after all, just any garden-variety cheap labor; they are cheap labor *at Yale.* What makes Brooks's insistence all the more interesting is that Brooks is reportedly one of the few antiunion Yale faculty who freely admits that TA teaching loads (in contact hours) have risen over the past twenty years while wages (per hour, adjusted for inflation) have fallen. That profile sounds more like the plight of post-Fordist American workers in general — higher productivity, lower wages — than like a description of the blessed of the earth. Does Brooks know a secret the *New Criterion* and the AAUP do not know? Or is Brooks revealing something about the assumptions undergirding graduate instruction at Yale?

Let me propose the latter, and let me further propose that if I am right, then many Yale faculty may have been not merely offended but positively *hurt,* emotionally and professionally, by the existence — and the persistence — of GESO. When Yale graduate students point to the job market as evidence that humanities Ph.D.'s are not automatically to be classed among the blessed of the earth, what must this argument signify to Yale faculty? The very premise of the school is that there is no need to pay graduate students a "living wage" because the Yale degree assures them of lucrative academic employment at the end of their term as "apprentices." When Yale students reply to this premise by pointing out their school's abysmal placement record in the humanities, what are they saying? They're saying that Yale is not exempt from the rest of the economy in American higher education. They're saying that they're not the blessed of the earth, any more than are the graduate teaching assistants at the University of Kansas. And *that* means that Yale faculty are no longer so uniformly powerful as to grant their Ph.D. students exemption from the great depression in the academic job market.

Recall that Yale has more to lose than most schools in this matter, particularly with respect to the self-regard of its faculty in the modern languages. It was not long ago that Yale was not merely a school but a School, where protégés and epigones could be produced in the high European manner, carrying forward the work of the Yale masters in learned journals and even (sometimes) in the interior of the Continent. Back when Roger Kimball was still working away at his dissertation, Yale dominated the English charts in the manner of the early Beatles, and Paul, J. Hillis, Geoff, and Harold "Ringo" Bloom made their insights and influence felt even as they redefined "influence" and "insight." Later came the breakup, the solo efforts, the persistent rumors that Paul was dead. But all that did not matter, because the imprimatur of the Yale degree was still a sure thing, academe's version of a vintage Lennon/McCartney single. If GESO has done nothing else, the union has put Yale faculty on notice that this is no longer the case. And the revelation is so painful, it seems, that the vast majority of affected faculty can only respond by lashing out at the students who would dare to act on the recognition, *pace* Homans and Brooks, that graduate student labor at Yale is not, in the end, significantly different — even after the Ph.D. has been granted and the years of "apprenticeship" ostensibly ended — from graduate student labor at Kansas.

In one sense, then, Yale is an object lesson only for Yale. But in another, more important, sense, Yale is not a special case at all; on the contrary, the events at Yale in 1995–96 might very well signal a new day in higher education throughout the United States. Toward the end of her letter to the MLA, Margaret Homans names the problem precisely, arguing for Yale's exemption from the academic economy in terms that make clear why Yale is not exempt from the academic economy:

> I believe the delegates [who voted to censure Yale] confused legitimate problems in academic labor relations with issues quite specific to the situation at Yale, issues of which they seemed content to remain ignorant. . . . The exploitation of academic professionals — a national problem — is being trivialized for the sake of winning a small, elite group a fleeting PR victory. ("MLA," 11)

In a dazzling display of looking-glass logic, Homans has derived exactly the wrong lesson from the job actions at Yale: her argument is not only (once again) that there are real problems *elsewhere* that have no bearing on the blessed graduate students of Yale; now, her argument is that GESO, by highlighting the "national problem" of exploited academic professionals, by putting the issue in the pages of major American newspapers up and down the eastern seaboard, has somehow *trivialized* the problem. Thank goodness the *New Criterion* knows better: the exploitation of academic professionals is indeed a national problem, and Yale is but the leading edge of a national scandal.

Think of Yale this way: the university's endowment is already over $5 billion and recently has been growing faster than the national debt. According to Michael Denning, "The University's investments manager recently revealed that Yale's endowment is having its best year in a decade. In 1995–96, the endowment will earn roughly $1 billion — after accounting for all expenses, Yale is earning almost $2 million a day, every day of the year."[10] Moreover, whatever the limitations of its humanities faculty, the school remains relatively well-respected and much in demand among high school graduates (though one presumes that aspiring graduate students in the modern languages, if they have some sense of self-preservation, will want to apply elsewhere in the future). Given Yale's extremely fortunate position in American academe, then, it should not have been hard for Yale faculty to have adopted something like the following reasoning: *if Yale University can't pay graduate students a living wage, complete with free health care, then who can?*

The reason so few Yale faculty have adopted this reasoning, I suggest, is precisely that they cannot see any structural relation between Yale and the vast legions of lesser American schools. The idea, for instance, that destroying GESO at Yale might just have deleterious effects for graduate student unions elsewhere (even at schools where such things might conceivably be necessary) seems never to have occurred to Homans or to her colleagues in arms. Likewise, none of GESO's opponents on the Yale faculty seems even to have entertained the possibility that other universities might look to Yale and say, "If a school so incredibly rich can farm out so much of its undergraduate instruction to adjuncts and graduate students, surely we have all the more reason to rely on part-time labor." Nothing, I submit, could be more painfully indicative of academe's idiot-savant culture than the spectacle of dozens of bright, articulate scholars, skilled at reading mediations, overdeterminations, and cultural texts galore but incapable of understanding that their relations to graduate students at their own university might just have repercussions for labor relations at other universities.

As if this spectacle weren't depressing enough, there's the further question of GESO's relation to Locals 34 and 35 of the Hotel Employees and Restaurant Employees International Union. Here I must shed the temperate language I have used to this point and speak bluntly for a change: in late 1995 any damn fool, even a distinguished Yale professor, could have seen that the Yale administration's attempt to crush GESO was but the prelude to its full-scale attempt to crush Locals 34 and 35 in the spring of 1996. Yale faculty may have been offended that their doctoral students had chosen to consort with menial laborers, but Yale administrators had a much better reason to oppose the affiliation: recognition of GESO would have complicated — perhaps even short-circuited — their plans to devastate the working conditions of Yale employees across the board.

Here, in a nutshell, is what those plans look like. One of the world's wealthiest universities proposes to cut future workers' wages by 40 percent and redefine them as ten-month workers so as not to pay them benefits. Again, this is at a school that's clearing a cool $2 million a day. As Denning notes, "Since Yale is realizing this level of profit under the current labor contracts, it cannot be that drastic cuts are required for the university's fiscal health."[11] The Yale labor pool is (of course) overwhelmingly nonwhite and drawn from New Haven, the seventh poorest city in the United States; Yale is by far the city's biggest employer, accounting for roughly one in seven jobs in the city. According to Gordon Lafer of the Federation of University Employees, when Locals 34 and 35 went out on strike, during one of New Haven's coldest winters on record, the university tried to ban workers from keeping fires in oil cans for warmth on the grounds that the fumes would violate campus air quality standards; when a local bakery offered its day-old bread to striking workers, Yale threatened to cut off all future contracts with the bakery unless the bread was thrown out. Yale's new policies for its service staff are so draconian and mean-spirited, in fact, that I do not know whether to call them post-Fordist or pre-Fordist. So let's simply call them obscene.

Annabel Patterson's letter to the MLA, as I have noted, remarks that the leaders of the Yale administration "are all Yale faculty"; presumably Patterson made this point in order to suggest that she and her colleagues were professionally bound to stand by their men in their opposition to GESO. The question for Patterson and her colleagues, then, is this: Does that logic also dictate that Yale faculty should support their administration's Dickensian assaults on the workers in Locals 34 and 35? Financially there is absolutely no justification for Yale's latest effort at union busting: the university is rich and getting richer, an enviable position for a nonprofit institution. One would think, therefore, that Yale's senior faculty, being the humane, decent people they are, would oppose their administration's policies with regard to Locals 34 and 35. But then, one would also have thought that Yale faculty, being the smart, well-spoken people they are, would have seen the connection between their university's opposition to GESO and their university's broader plans for union busting on campus.

If ever an institutional crisis demanded the attention of professional organizations like the MLA, this is it. But the MLA's response to the strike at Yale has been somewhat less than encouraging. Six weeks after the Delegate Assembly passed the resolution censuring Yale in December 1995, the MLA conducted its mass mailing of the letters of Homans, Patterson, et al., introducing its twelve-page document with the words, "We write to initiate a new procedure" ("MLA," 1). The chief purpose of the mailing was to circulate to the MLA membership the views of Yale faculty opposed to GESO, the grade strike, and the resolution. No views sympathetic to GESO were included. In subsequent communications, the rationale for the mailing became clear: the GESO forces had had their say during the MLA convention, and, according to Margaret Homans, Yale faculty had not been able to respond sufficiently to the resolution at the time it was proposed: "[I]f the MLA sees itself as representing and honoring diversity of opinion," Homans wrote, "the process by which the resolution was pushed through gives the lie to that claim" ("MLA," 10). (Homans and Brooks were both present at the Delegate Assembly, though Homans's letter does not indicate as much.) The MLA staff dutifully investigated the charges that the resolution had been improperly introduced and found, in the words of Executive Director Phyllis Franklin, that "the assembly's action was valid" ("MLA," 1). So much for Homans's precarious sense of proper procedure. Nevertheless, the mailing itself quite clearly seems to accent Homans's charge that "diversity of opinion" was not honored at the convention; no other explanation will account for the MLA's curious decision not to seek opinions sympathetic to GESO for the purposes of the mailing. As a result, the claims of Yale faculty were allowed to stand utterly uncontested — including Homans's unsubstantiated and grossly misleading "procedural" complaints that "the most basic standards of evidence were not adhered to in the formulation of the resolution" (regarding the status of faculty as "replacement workers") and that "the resolution violates several of legal counsel's criteria for acceptable resolutions: it is factually erroneous, slanderous, and personally motivated" ("MLA," 10).

When I first read over the special MLA mailing, I was appalled — so appalled that I did not consider it worth my time to complain to the MLA directly. Instead, I considered leaving the organization altogether. A great deal of effort and deliberation had obviously gone into the production and mailing of this unprecedented and one-sided document; a portion of my MLA dues had supported it, as had a portion of the dues of every graduate student and adjunct faculty member in the MLA; and as a result, my own professional organization had clearly given its members the strong impression that the Yale resolution was ethically dubious and factually mistaken. Ironically, Homans's claim that the MLA had violated its commitment to "diversity of opinion" had been circulated to over thirty thousand faculty and graduate students without a single word of rebuttal; the claims of Yale faculty that the Yale resolution was ethically dubious were themselves circulated in an ethically dubious manner.

At the very least, the MLA mailing suggested that when confronted with a professional dispute between senior faculty and graduate students, the organization would go to extraordinary lengths, even "initiate a new procedure," to publicize the views of senior faculty *at the expense of* the views of graduate students. It is worth remembering here that the Yale resolution is the only substantive resolution the MLA has passed in many years that materially addresses the professional working conditions of MLA members; the other burning issues on the table for 1996, for instance, include a resolution expressing "appreciation of and respect for the support staffs in our departments" and another resolution recommending a "common application form" for fellowships in the humanities. It is difficult, in the wake of the MLA's February 9 mass mailing, to imagine what the professional role of the MLA — and its Delegate Assembly, to which I was recently elected — can conceivably be. For the moment, it appears that the MLA is quite efficient at passing resolutions about being nice to secretaries, treating books with extra care, condemning U.S. foreign policy, and refusing to hold the national convention in forty-six of the fifty states. But when the MLA at last confronts an issue that addresses head-on the crisis of labor relations in American universities, the entire "resolution" system is thrown into profound crisis — by, of all things, the objections of a small handful of elite faculty seeking to win a fleeting PR victory.

And yet if recent volumes of the *MLA Newsletter* are any indication of the state of the profession at its highest echelons, MLA inattention to academic labor relations may prove to be much less harmful to the profession than actual MLA *attention* to academic labor relations. In the winter of 1995, as the Yale standoff heated up and thousands of new and recent Ph.D.'s made their preparations to attend the MLA convention for yet another costly and generally fruitless exercise in job hunting, the *MLA Newsletter* featured a column by the brilliant and internationally renowned Sander Gilman, who, writing his final column as MLA president for 1995, proposed a novel solution to the job crisis in the humanities. The column was titled "Jobs: What We (Not They) Can Do," and it was written explicitly as a response to angry graduate students caught in the job crunch. Gilman opens by narrating a confrontation with such graduate students at the 1994 MLA convention, remarking that "it was clear that the candidates' anger was directed not at any amorphous 'they' but at their own professional organization, the MLA, and that they were yelling at me not because I had done anything specifically to block them from getting jobs but because I represented that force of nature, the MLA — that is, 'us.'"[12] He proceeds thence to suggest that the MLA create "postdoctoral mentored teaching fellowships — nontenured, two-year appointments with limited benefit packages" (4). These mentored postdocs, writes Gilman, will solve the profession's employment crisis by offering younger colleagues "serious, meaningful employment" (5) while also affording "the flexibility administrators demand in our fields" (4).

One can only guess at what "flexibility" might mean here (it seems to be a synonym for "fire-ability"), let alone why "flexibility" might be an employment criterion that a professional organization like the MLA would seek to embrace. Gilman notes, in a brief remark uncannily like that of Annabel Patterson's insistence that Yale's leading administrators are also Yale faculty, that his plan will be smiled upon by those above: "[W]e can create new jobs in our departments if our administrators, many of whom are also members of the MLA, see that we are serious in our desire to reallocate resources" (4). In other words, our administrations are downsizing, but *they* are really "us"; the graduate students who were once part of that "us," in an earlier paragraph, are now resources to be reallocated so that "we" can show "our" administrators how serious we are about signing on to the latest downsizing initiative. Gilman briefly suggests that his proposal is a kinder, gentler form of exploitation — "new Ph.D.'s will become better teachers," he suggests, as if they haven't already done enough teaching as graduate students, and "faculty members will have rewarding mentoring tasks" (4). But what if the senior faculty don't want to "mentor" these two-year, part-time, piecework pseudocolleagues? No problem, says Gilman — we'll just leave out the "kinder, gentler" part: "[I]f we [note the 'we' here] don't want to take on a mentoring role because of our overloaded schedules, we can create two-year lecturer positions" (5).

What follows this bizarre suggestion is a still more bizarre paragraph insisting that we should not hire undergraduates as unpaid laborers to teach "drill sections." "Nor should we listen," continues Gilman, "to the argument that this arrangement provides a perfect apprenticeship for students who plan to go to graduate school" (5). Here, I think, is an "argument" beyond human comprehension: Who, exactly, is arguing that we should staff undergraduate courses with undergraduate teachers as "apprentice" graduate students? I cannot answer this question, but I can suggest that Gilman's stern, forceful paragraph ruling out the use of undergraduate instructors serves the purpose of making his own mentored-postdoc suggestion sound "reasonable" by juxtaposing it to the truly insane option of having undergraduate classes taught by unpaid undergraduates. There's nothing wrong with creating a new tier of second-class faculty, in other words, but when it comes to charging undergraduates tuition to teach themselves in drill sections, *that* we will not countenance.

What, in the end, is Gilman really proposing, and how would it work? In his antepenultimate paragraph, he writes:

> Graduate programs that still admit masses of graduate students could temporarily amalgamate two teaching assistantships into a two-year postdoc. Institutions would receive the same amount of teaching for less money, because they would not have to pay graduate school tuition for these postdoctoral fellows. (5)

Let's parse out this suggestion carefully. Apparently, Gilman's postdocs would teach at twice the pay scale of graduate teaching assistants and teach twice the course load, thus providing their institutions with the labor of two graduate students. All right. At Illinois, that would mean that the Sander Gilman Flexible Postdoctoral Fellows would earn just over twenty-one thousand dollars a year for teaching four courses per semester. And, Gilman adds, Illinois would not have to pay their tuition. But, of course, Illinois does not "pay" the tuition of any graduate student; it *waives* graduate student tuition in return for undercompensated teaching (and even that arrangement is being contested as I write). No money changes hands in a tuition waiver; the transaction happens entirely in an executive assistant's software program, as spreadsheet numbers are fiddled and adjusted. The idea that universities "pay" their graduate students' tuition, in other words, is an especially threadbare fiction, though it seems to have been put to good use by the anti-GESO faculty at Yale, who are apt to claim that their students are "paid" almost twenty thousand dollars yearly in tuition waivers—as if the university is gallantly taking a loss by providing graduate students with twenty thousand dollars worth of valuable instruction at no charge. It is this threadbare fiction that allows Gilman to present his plan as a money-saver ("the same amount of teaching for less money"), as if universities actually gave tuition waivers in cash and could pocket the dollars themselves by hiring a Gilman Flexible Fellow.

Tuition waivers, however, are not the crucial issue for Gilman's argument. The crucial issue is that if Gilman's argument becomes widely circulated in American universities, the profession of college teaching as we know it is basically finished. "Let us generate new postdoctoral fellowships throughout the country," writes Gilman (5). Lethal as this might be to the future of tenure-track employment, in some ways it is not a bad idea: if the going rate for these Gilman Fellows is twenty-five hundred dollars per course, many of my former students, teaching at small colleges as part-time laborers, are in for a raise of anywhere from 60 to 200 percent. But I don't think that's going to happen. The colleges that now employ Ph.D.'s at the rate of eight hundred to fifteen hundred dollars per course are not likely to sign on to the Gilman Program in order to convince senior administrators of their "seriousness." (And, I should add, Ph.D.'s who teach at these rates are extremely unlikely to need further "mentoring" to hone their pedagogical skills.) For many American colleges, then, Gilman's proposal is simply irrelevant. What then of the colleges that now employ Ph.D.'s as assistant professors, at the rate of thirty thousand to forty thousand dollars? Wouldn't they do well to cut their salary and benefit costs by eliminating tenure-track faculty entirely and hiring, instead, new Gilman Fellows with limited benefit packages? For such colleges, I cannot imagine a labor relations "solution" more administration-friendly than Gilman's. If you want a flexible workforce at a discount rate, there's no need to mount difficult, costly legal challenges to the institution of tenure; just hire a gaggle of part-time Gilman Fellows at twenty thousand dollars with optional health coverage (mentoring also optional), and, presto, you've created a new stratum of part-time faculty while saving your institution untold thousands of dollars in salaries and benefits. And *that* will show you're serious in your desire to reallocate resources.

What Gilman is proposing for new Ph.D.'s, in other words, is precisely what Yale is proposing for Locals 34 and 35: a 40 percent pay cut (from thirty-five thousand to twenty-one thousand dollars, more or less), redefinition as part-time labor, and a significant rollback in benefits. For some reason I do not understand, Gilman seems to believe that university administrators will agree to create a wholly separate category of underpaid, part-time, short-term faculty *while also maintaining full-time tenure-track lines* for truly distinguished new Ph.D.'s — say, candidates from Yale or Chicago who've respected their mentors and haven't caused trouble. Yet the only difference between Gilman's proposal and Yale's attempt to eviscerate its local labor unions is this: Gilman thinks *his* proposal will be attractive to administrators, faculty, new Ph.D.'s, and undergraduates alike. "Indeed," he writes, "postdoctoral mentored teaching fellowships will provide a real model for undergraduates who may wish to enter graduate school in the humanities" (5). Thankfully, Gilman does not go into detail about what kind of undergraduates would be enthralled at the prospect of attending graduate school for seven to ten years with the hope of eventually becoming a two-year Optionally Mentored Fellow at twenty thousand dollars per year.

•

I have tried, in these pages, to analyze what I regard as the deeply destructive response of Yale faculty to the prospect of graduate student unionization, and I have taken that response as a harbinger of future labor relations in the academic professions. Further, I have tried to link that response to broader tendencies in the leadership of the MLA, an ostensibly "professional" organization that should, if it is going to serve any useful professional function, be defending professional standards for the treatment of its most impecunious and vulnerable members. But I hardly know what to make of my own analysis. When Patricia Meyer Spacks served her term as MLA president in 1994, she addressed the job crisis by candidly admitting that she had no idea how to address it;[13] Sander Gilman, by contrast, has come forward with a considered, detailed plan for redressing the crisis, and his "plan" turns out, instead, to be a blueprint for dismantling what little job security still exists in academe. I am compelled to conclude that our recent MLA presidents would do better to ignore the job crisis than to attempt to speak to it, for when they speak to it they sound strikingly like the faculty at Yale: overidentified with the budgetary priorities of university administrations, clueless about their relation to American higher education at large, and all too willing to sustain the profession's ever-dwindling positions of privilege by assigning basic undergraduate instruction to underpaid and overworked adjuncts, "teaching fellows," and graduate students.

By opposing and finally breaking GESO, Yale faculty set an awful precedent for faculty and administrators elsewhere in the country. The MLA, in turn, committed both a tactical and an ethical error by not including GESO spokespersons in its mass mailing to members of the profession with regard to the Yale resolution; and when it comes to professional leadership with regard to the job crisis, nothing could be worse than to have Sander Gilman's postdoc suggestion fall into the hands of cost-conscious administrators. But worst yet — or, perhaps, best of all — Yale faculty and the MLA leadership have now sent an unmistakable message to graduate students, adjuncts, and part-timers everywhere that their nominal spokespersons and their professional organizations are singularly ill suited to represent their interests and may in fact be best suited, on the contrary, to the desperate, misguided preservation of systems of prestige and reward that are no longer defensible in American higher education's post-Fordist economy. By the AAUP's most recent count, part-time faculty now make up approximately 45 percent of the American professoriat; and at many large American universities, graduate students teach more than half the introductory undergraduate courses in all fields. All told, adjunct faculty and graduate teaching assistants now make up the bulk of the workforce in U.S. higher education. The time has come for that heretofore silent majority to take matters into its own hands.

NOTES

1. Quoted in Cynthia Young, "On Strike at Yale," *minnesota review* 45–46 (1996): 179–95; hereafter cited as "Strike."

2. For information on those histories, see Young, "Strike," or contact Gordon Lafer, research director of the Federation of University Employees, the union with which GESO had voted to affiliate. Lafer can be reached at Glafer@aol.com. As of this writing, Yale had still not negotiated an acceptable contract with Locals 34 and 35, and contributions to the strike fund are, I believe, very welcome.

3. Here and throughout this essay, I need to exempt a handful of exemplary individuals, such as Michael Denning, Hazel Carby, David Montgomery, and Rogers Smith, among others, from my wholesale castigations of "Yale faculty." Indeed, I owe Michael Denning, in particular, a number of accumulated debts in the writing of this essay, since he has been one of my major sources of information on the Yale strike, as well as a keen editor and consultant on the various editorials and brief articles I wrote in January 1996 when it looked as if the *Nation* was going to run a story on the events at Yale.

4. Peter Brooks, quoted in Emily Eakin, "Walking the Line," *Lingua Franca* (March/April 1996): 60; hereafter cited as "Walking."

5. Annabel Patterson, letter to Phyllis Franklin, MLA packet of February 9, 1996, 6; hereafter the packet is cited as "MLA."

6. Of the disciplinary hearings of early 1996, Cynthia Young writes, "it was clearly no coincidence that all three of the strikers charged [the third was Nilanjana Dasgupta] were members of the Team Leaders' Committee, GESO's leadership council. However, Dean Appelquist insisted that we had been individually iden-

tified by our faculty supervisor, because two of the professors involved — Sara Suleri-Goodyear in my case and David Brion Davis in Diana Paton's — wrote letters requesting our grade records and then referred our cases to the Dean when we refused to submit them" ("Strike," 191).

7. Beverly Gage, "Have You No Shame?" *New Haven Advocate,* December 21, 1995, 11; quoted in Young, "Strike," 189–90.

8. No claim is more hotly contested by antiunion faculty than this one. Yale president Richard Levin insists, for instance, that graduate students teach only 3 percent of the courses above the freshman level; but that figure relies on Yale's insistence that teaching assistants are not to be counted as "teachers" for the purposes of calculating figures on "contact hours." However, according to a comprehensive report compiled by Yale graduate students, *True Blue: An Investigation into Teaching at Yale,* graduate teaching assistants in the humanities and social sciences spent 864 hours in the classroom each week whereas full-time faculty spent 756.5 hours.

9. Editorial, *New Criterion* (February 1996): 3.

10. Michael Denning, Internet bulletin to the Faculty Committee to Support Striking Yale Workers, May 13, 1996.

11. Ibid.

12. Sander Gilman, "Jobs: What We (Not They) Can Do," *MLA Newsletter* 27, no. 4 (1995): 4; hereafter cited as "Jobs."

13. Patricia Meyer Spacks, "The Academic Marketplace: Who Pays Its Costs?" *MLA Newsletter* 26, no. 2 (1994): 3.

Part II

Academic Workers Face the New Millennium

Figure 26. Jenny Schmid's cover design for a publication issued by the graduate employees at the University of Michigan

Chapter 9
Academic Unionism and the Future of Higher Education

Stanley Aronowitz

In spring 1969 I was asked to come to Madison to meet with the leadership of a new Teaching Assistants Association (TAA) at the University of Wisconsin and address a meeting of its membership. I suppose the invitation had to do with two of my preoccupations at the time. Throughout the 1960s I had been a full-time union official, first for the Amalgamated Clothing Workers (now UNITE) and then for the Oil, Chemical, and Atomic Workers, where I directed organizing for the northeast district.

My other credential was in the antiwar movement. I was a columnist for the *Guardian,* then the preeminent newspaper of the New Left, and, as a leader of the movement (in 1965 I had co-organized the first national coordinating committee against the war) (see Aronowitz 1984, 1996), during the previous year I had been asked to debate the assistant secretary of state for Southeast Asia affairs, Roger Hilsman, on the occasion of the centennial of the University of Wisconsin. Maybe five thousand students and faculty, most of them war opponents, heard me rail against the war. Hilsman, a very nice person, had to carry the water for the Johnson administration's unpopular policy in one of the strongholds of the opposition. I did not have to be particularly effective to win the day.

The two thousand or so graduate teaching assistants wanted help from a quarter other than the official labor movement, which, in 1969, was riven over the war question as well as many other issues. As a known independent labor radical with strong ties to the student movement, I could be trusted, even though I was over thirty.

What I had to say was far less important than the fact of the close connection between a new social movement and trade unionism, a connection that accounts, in my opinion, for the startling and largely unexpected rise of unionism among public employees and professionals — doctors, attorneys, as well as professors and other teachers — in the same period. Among the forgotten stories of the much-celebrated and excoriated 1960s was the explosive growth of public employee unionism and the birth of a new era of professional unionism as well. By 1975 about four million public and service employees had joined unions, the same number as the far more heralded movement of industrial workers in the late 1930s (Aronowitz and DiFazio 1994). While the thirty years since the mid-1960s was a period of decline for the independent professional and, for professors, a period of steady proletarianization, it was also a moment that witnessed the explosive power of the feminist, civil rights, and antiwar movements to change the culture of American life. Nearly all of the new union leaders associated with this "white-collar" movement were sympathizers with, when not active participants in, these social movements. This is true of the teachers even though the New York local — then more than now the heart of the national organization — was led by staunch defenders of the administration and its foreign policy (those union members in New York were largely indifferent to feminism but were actively engaged in mainstream civil rights struggles).

The modern labor movement was born in the turmoil of mass immigration, much of which was destined to fill the industrial plants of the Northeast and the Midwest. From 1880 to 1920, organized workers — skilled and unskilled — fought for a measure of industrial democracy and social justice *both* as newly arrived immigrants and as laborers. While the post–Civil War labor movement had been dominated by native-born craftsmen, the AFL (American Federation of Labor), still a craft-dominated movement, was led by Irish and German immigrants who were acutely aware of ethnic discrimination as much as class exploitation. The great (defeated) Homestead Strike (1892) is exemplary of the combination of efforts by traditional craftspeople to protect their gains in the wake of encroaching industrialism and the yearning of unskilled Eastern European immigrant workers for social justice. The turn of the century was marked by the rise of the Jewish Labor Movement and the struggles of Italian and Polish textile workers, miners, and steelworkers for a union (Krause 1992).

Seen in the perspective of the unfulfilled promise of immigration, even the industrial uprisings of the 1930s cannot be viewed as a pure class movement. While the auto industry was, together with electrical production and oil refining, among the first industries in which the workforce was mainly native-born, steel, mining, textiles, and the needle trades were still bastions of foreign-born labor and, in the case of steel, blacks.

W. E. B. Du Bois declared the color line to be the defining social question of the twentieth century (Du Bois 1903). Indeed, from the standpoint of black labor, even the CIO (Congress of Industrial Organizations) drive with its pledge of complete equality did not erase the exclusionary practices of the postreconstruction industrial era. The period between 1935 and 1955, when industrial unionism was at its peak, was filled with struggles against discrimination within the unions as well as the companies. To this day, blacks have not been fully integrated into industrial crafts such as those practiced by tool and die workers, machinists, and electricians. The color line persists, and it is virtually impossible to write a history of the labor movement in this century without placing the race question at the center (Lichtenstein 1996, 374 and passim).

Although the emergence of the feminist movement in the 1960s may be ascribed, in the main, to a cultural rebellion against the traditional woman's role as wife, homemaker, and exclusive child-rearer, one of its notable consequences was that when women marched out of the kitchen and into the paid workforce, they discovered that "women's" jobs paid less than those of men in union as well as nonunion workplaces and that women suffered poor working conditions and little job protection in the factory and clerical workplace. To protest these conditions without collective action invited harassment and discharge.

One may conjecture that these injustices, long festering in public employment, health care, teaching, and social work, suddenly came to the surface in hospitals, social welfare agencies, and schools, just as the U.S. post office, where blacks were able to get jobs because much of the work was underpaid, became a hotbed of unionism in part because of the emergence of race politics in the 1960s. Even as most unions in production industries were beginning to witness membership erosion due to technological change and "runaway" shops in the late 1960s, public employees unions were flourishing.

Of course, union growth in the public and nonprofit workplaces was spurred by relatively prolabor national administrations in the 1960s; in 1962, President Kennedy signed a landmark executive order introducing collective bargaining for federal employees. But, although state and local governments outside southern and other blatantly antiunion states followed with similar laws and administrative edicts, these prolabor gestures did not result in automatic success. New York social service employees conducted two major strikes during this period; teachers' strikes spread from the groundbreaking New York 1964 walkout to other parts of the country, and many of the movement's leaders went to prison for their defiance of state statutes barring public employee strikes; hospital worker strikes were a commonplace of the decade, especially among the lowest paid workers (those in the patient care, dietary, and housekeeping categories), most of whom were women — and in the big cities, they were largely black and Latino (Fink and Greenberg 1989).

The turn-of-the-century battles of garment workers for decent wages and working conditions coincided with the first wave of feminism — the struggle for the vote and for birth control. Thus, needle-trades unions, once dominated by craftsmen, were obliged and able to address the needs of a growing female workforce as most other male-dominated unions were not. The famous "uprising of the twenty thousand," marking the emergence of mass needle-trades unionism following the Triangle Shirtwaist fire, was a movement of women against sweatshop conditions suffered largely by women. Similarly, more than fifty years later Hospital Workers Local 1199 and the American Federation of State, County, and Municipal Employees (AFSCME) translated the struggle for equality into a fight for women's and blacks' equality on the job. In contrast to the usual economistic appeals of industrial and craft unions, public and health care unionism wrapped themselves in the iconography of the feminist and civil rights movements.

Martin Luther King Jr. became the willing patron saint of the hospital workers' campaign, and many AFSCME affiliates established women's committees, promoted women to middle and high union positions, and developed strategies for dealing with wage inequality between women and men. One of these strategies was to reevaluate "women's" jobs upward by introducing the concept of "comparable worth," which analyzed male and female jobs according to the same criteria and which struck terror into the hearts of politicians and public sector bureaucrats until a series of court decisions slowed and ultimately defeated the movement.

The concept of comparable worth stems from the widely accepted tenet of "equal pay for equal work." Because few women have the same jobs as men, however, this popular principle does little to advance women's interests. Comparable worth advocates argue that the principle should be extended, as objective measures show that women's jobs are underpaid compared to the equivalent male jobs (Blum 1991).

At the time of the TAA fight for recognition at the University of Wisconsin, academic unionism, among faculty as much as among students, was a relatively rare phenomenon. Although the American Federation of Teachers (AFT) had a number of small locals of college and university teachers, almost none of them had yet won collective bargaining in matters pertaining to salaries, workloads, and benefits. Academic unionism, like teacher unionism generally, was still at the lobbying stage; state legislatures and city councils were the main arena for winning more money for teacher salaries. TA unionism was virtually unheard of.

Indeed, when I arrived at Madison, the TAA officers were still unsure of their ground. They had managed to recruit the vast majority of the TAs, but they were not at all confident that the university administration would recognize them as bargaining agents. The administration made now-familiar arguments against TA unionism: the TAs' teaching duties were part of their academic program as *students;* in effect they were professors "in training," not employees. They received grants, not salaries.

The TAs were concerned with workload as well as income issues; from their point of view, they were part of the instructional staff of the institution and enjoyed few of the perks of privileged graduate students in the natural sciences. Far from being apprentices, many handled classes with almost no supervision: they prepared lessons, provided undergraduates with academic counseling, and, in the aggregate, accounted for a considerable portion of undergraduate teaching. When not delivering lectures to large assemblages, the professoriat was busy performing the research activities for which they were rewarded. For the typical tenured professor at such a university, undergraduate teaching was a nuisance when not an actual impediment to professional advancement.

By 1969, it was already clear to most English, philosophy, and history graduate students that the job market had tightened, and, except for economists, whose job prospects did not really dim until the great downsizing of the 1990s, social scientists, if not natural scientists, were beginning to feel the pinch as well. While jobs in research universities were available for some, perhaps a majority of those trained in the humanities could look forward to teaching in a small state school or a community college or, worse, becoming part of the academic proletariat of temporary, part-time, and contingent adjunct instructors. A few years later, the full-time job had all but disappeared in history and philosophy; English was making its long march from literary to composition studies, and only those attached to well-known national figures in their respective fields could expect to obtain a research university job — and even then they were often hired not to teach literature but to direct composition programs.

At the same time, university administrations were solving the problem of expanding undergraduate enrollments not primarily by hiring new full-time faculty but by increasing class size in lower-division courses and pressing TAs to teach sections of fifty students or more. My son, who entered Rutgers University in 1971, told of attending three-hundred-student lower-division courses addressed weekly by a professor who was never available for office hours. His main contact with the university was the semiweekly section with a TA. In fact, when I began teaching at Staten Island Community College in 1972, I was surprised to discover that the City University of New York (CUNY) did not have such practices. My classes and those of my colleagues were relatively small. Today, things are different: my own CUNY graduate students now report they are entirely responsible for introductory sociology classes enrolling some eighty students at the Queens College and Hunter campuses of CUNY. At both campuses they receive no official — or, for that matter, unofficial — guidance, since the faculty is busy dealing with its own work overload.

So, the formation of the TAA at the University of Wisconsin (UW) prefigured a growing feeling of unease and even anger shared by many graduate students, then and now, a feeling that the encroaching multiversity concept — according to which only the research professor deserves the time to perform the work of knowledge production — had reached graduate education. From the perspective of the UW administration, graduate students were ready sources of teaching labor. But UW provided fertile ground for a militant response. As veterans of a mass antiwar struggle and of the southern civil rights summer projects, many students at UW had become near-professional organizers; they had experienced dealing with the administration and, perhaps equally important, knew how to deal with press and television. Moreover, the union idea was not foreign to these students, many of whom were influenced by Marxism or the radicalism of C. Wright Mills and local luminaries such as labor sociologist Maurice Zeitlin and especially William Appleman Williams, the great figure of burgeoning American revisionist history.

My advice was incidental to the course of events. After a strike, the administration recognized the TAA, negotiated a union contract, and promptly started a campaign to decertify it as bargaining agent. Briefly defeated, the TAA came back. For many of the same reasons that prompted the pioneer TA battle for unionization at UW, in the 1970s and 1980s TA unions emerged at the University of Michigan, at the University of California–Berkeley, and, in the 1990s, at Iowa and — most famously — Yale.

Since 1970, academic unionism has been far more successful among faculty, especially at the community college and state university levels. While there are some faculty unions in private colleges and universities, further unionization has been stymied by the U.S. Supreme Court's *Yeshiva* decision declaring faculty in private colleges and universities may not enjoy the protection of the labor relations law because the court considers them to be "management." The AFT is the largest faculty union, but the American Association of University Professors (AAUP) and the National Education Association (NEA) have organized thousands of college teachers, some, like AFT, in major universities.

In fact, during the dismal 1980s, when, for the first time since the early years of the depression, unions as a whole recorded a net loss of membership, faculty and academic unionism became one of the few growth fields in the labor movement. Before discussing the problems and possibilities of academic unionism, I want to address the context within which it has developed: the American university and its post–World War II transformations.

I

It is by now a commonplace that far from being a community of scholars dedicated to disinterested inquiry and intense intellectual dialogue, contemporary institutions of higher education are knowledge factories, substantial employers in many towns and cities that contribute significantly to the local economy, and, perhaps most of all, aging vats for a considerable fraction of the labor force. Needless to say, universities and colleges are by no means identical in their functions. Since the vast expansion of colleges and universities after World War II, higher education institutions have arranged themselves along a loose, hierarchically constructed grid.

At the top are two tiers of research universities, which are dedicated to the production of knowledge for the socioeconomic system. Their products are destined for use in economic and social domains, chiefly corporations and the state — especially, but not exclusively, the military. The third tier consists of nearly all liberal arts and technical colleges. Whether intended to train elite or plebeian students, these colleges *transmit* the knowledge produced in research universities and, conventionally, have a major responsibility in the elite schools to impart the Western intellectual and moral tradition to students.

Since the 1960s, when the welfare state embarked upon its brief period of dramatic growth, and consumer society reached its maturity, women have massively entered the labor force, notably the professions. Spurred by feminism as much as by economic incentives since 1970, most female graduates of small, four-year private colleges and a relatively large proportion of state school graduates enter professional programs — in law and medical schools but also in institutions that prepare them for postsecondary teaching, social and private services, and research. The technical colleges, once the preferred site for producing middle-level computer specialists, are engaged preeminently in *training* students to take their (diminishing) places as computer programmers and technologists in the medical, engineering, chemical, biotechnology, and other industries.

The fourth tier includes the community colleges and two-year technical schools; their main job is to provide technicians to business and industry. A declining group of students use these schools as a stepping-stone to four-year programs, and in recent years the two-year degree has increasingly become terminal for the majority of community college students. And, given the shrinking demand for technical workers of all kinds, the community college is increasingly important as an *ideological* institution insofar as it fulfills, but only in the bureaucratic sense, the promise of higher education for all (Brint and Karabel 1989; Aronowitz and DiFazio 1984, chap. 8).

Since World War II, universities have mobilized — nearly monopolized — the preponderance of natural- and social-scientific knowledge production in proportion as knowledge has become the key productive force (Kenney 1986, 199). While major corporations retain considerable scientific and technical staffs who produce *practical* applications of theoretical and applied sciences, the responsibility for generating "new" knowledge is, despite draconian cuts in research budgets, still the domain of leading research universities. In effect, the state socializes the costs of research intended for use in privately held production and services through contracts let by the Pentagon, National Science Foundation, and the National Institutes of Health to "private" as well as public universities. The federal Departments of Agriculture, Labor, Commerce, Interior, Transportation, and Justice remain important sources of research funds, despite Congress's recent cost-cutting binge.

Before the 1980s, much of this knowledge had little or no immediate use; in effect, the largest government contractor, the Pentagon, subsidized much basic research because national science policy recognized the importance of *failure* as a vital ingredient of eventual success. But the tendency over the past two decades has been to punish the failures that inevitably accompany theoretical and experimental reflection. Congress and the Clinton administration now require that government grants be more dedicated, that is, be earmarked for practical, especially commodity, applications. This policy has tended to discourage pure or useless research.

America's leading magazine of the natural-science profession, *Science,* chronicles on a weekly basis both the reconfiguration of research toward industrial uses and the fears of scientists that, because of the precipitous decline of funding, the scientific enterprise is itself in jeopardy. In view of the enormous role that expensive machine technology plays in everyday research in physics and biology, the virtual end of funding for nondedicated work, especially theory, threatens to cripple U.S. science.

For example, funds are rapidly drying up for research not only in theoretical physics, especially in high-energy particle physics, but also in astronomy, cosmology, and other more esoteric endeavors. To be sure, solid-state physics has a ready source of research money in communications and information corporations. And the vast majority of funds for biological studies are devoted to producing new organisms for bioengineering. In this respect, private pharmaceutical corporations have entered into patent arrangements with relevant academic departments; in return for patent ownership, the corporations have donated substantial sums to the departments to offset losses of government funds.

II

Of the many "revolutions" of the post–World War II era — the dominance of technoscience over most aspects of everyday life, the second coming of consumer society, in many ways closely linked to technoscience's emergence — the veritable explosion of enrollments, of new colleges and universities, and of faculty in higher education may be the most important cultural event. While there can be no doubt that higher education has become a major industry in most regions of the country, it has also been one of the salient features of the doctrine according to which individuals may transcend the conditions of their birth, a hallmark of American ideology.

The aspiration for class mobility and the widespread faith that through credentials and hard work anyone can "make it" to a relatively lucrative career define our culture; and the doctrine that we make and remake ourselves through schooling has played an important part in discouraging collective action and expressions of social solidarity in favor of individual achievement. "Going to college" has become since the 1960s perhaps the main repository of the hopes and dreams of working-class blacks and Latinos for a brighter future for themselves and their children; some women have gone to college to avoid the trap of domesticity while others — in a historical moment of single parenthood — have seen a postsecondary degree as representing some expectation that they can find a job to support their families; and a growing proportion of white, working-class males who have suffered the incredible disappearance of good working-class jobs due to globalization, technological change, and the decline of the crafts have looked (reluctantly) to higher education to constitute the economic equivalent of what was once provided by the unionized workplace.

To a large extent, the claim that class origin was, in advanced industrial society, no longer destiny for those who kept their noses to the educational grindstone was richly fulfilled by the circumstances of the postwar era. The United States dominated the global economy for the quarter-century that ended about 1970. Its liberal credit system spurred production of a cornucopia of consumer goods available to anyone able to qualify for some deferred payment plan, and most of those goods were produced in the United States. And, as we have seen, from modest beginnings in the New Deal, the main features of the welfare state — mass education, social security, unemployment insurance, medical care for the aged and the poor, and federal housing subsidies for the "working middle class" as well as the poor — became a stabilizing force in our social and cultural system, legitimating the permanent war economy as well as persistent inequalities in wealth and income. After all, who cares about the rich getting richer as long as a substantial fraction of everybody else is getting theirs?

Faced with the return of eleven million members of the armed forces — about a sixth of the labor force — and an uncertain transition from wartime to peacetime economy, Congress enacted one of the most far-reaching measures in the history of welfare capitalism, the Servicemen's Readjustment Act (the GI Bill of Rights), which gave returning veterans free medical care, housing subsidies, and the right to return to school. About three million veterans availed themselves of their newly won educational opportunity, completing high school and filling a large number of seats in college classrooms. In 1945, private colleges and universities were more numerous than the relatively undeveloped public sector. Some states such as New York, California, and the major midwestern states had small public systems. The infusion of vast sums into higher education spurred an unprecedented building program in colleges and universities that, together with the postwar housing and auto boom, provided millions of jobs for construction and manufacturing workers.

By 1990, the number of colleges and universities had grown from about eighteen hundred in 1947 to thirty-two hundred, and student enrollments had increased from 2.3 million to 12.5 million (Lucas 1994). The beginnings of budget austerity in higher education in the early 1970s failed to deter the steady stream of students to higher education. In 1947, only 10 percent of high school graduates entered college; in 1960, 40 percent were accepted into two- and four-year colleges; by 1980, half of all graduates went on to higher education. Today, the number stands at 62 percent. Since 80 percent of those entering high school graduate, almost half of all youth enter college (Lucas 1994).

One of the less-noticed functions of U.S. and Canadian universities in the postwar period, during which the size of the young adult labor force has chronically outpaced job creation, is the degree to which they keep a considerable fraction of the labor force off the market. In 1994, 14.2 million students were enrolled in U.S. universities and colleges (the equivalent of 9 million full-time students). While many of these students are full- or part-time workers as well, it may be assumed that more than half of them would seek full-time employment if they were not in school. The United States leads all advanced industrial countries in postsecondary enrollments. Of about 150 million adults under age sixty-five, more than 9 percent attend some kind of higher education program. In contrast, no European country enrolls more than 3 percent of its adults in these institutions, and most hover around 2 percent. In the 1960s, the British Higher Education Reform program began to emulate the U.S. model of high university enrollments, and France followed suit, largely after the May 1968 student-led revolt.

American universities are much more than training grounds for qualified or intellectual labor. They are aging vats for a considerable proportion of the labor force that would be otherwise unemployed.

In many regions of the country, they are *the* major employer and the source of community income; even in some large cities such as New York and Chicago, colleges and universities are significant factors in the local and regional economies. And, culturally, universities embody the hopes, the aspirations, even the dreams of millions for a better future. Their fate is tied to the promise that here no rigid class system will stand in the way of substantial economic and social gain.

In Britain, Germany, and the United States, the New Left began, among other things, as a movement for university reform. In the United States, alongside the outpouring of students to participate in the southern civil rights movement and community organizing among the white and black poor in some northern cities, the question of what the university should be dominated the early years of the student movement. In Berkeley, the free speech movement emerged out of student protests against the House Un-American Activities Committee's foray into the Bay Area and the discontent with the perspective of the great theorist of the corporate university, UC–Berkeley chancellor Clark Kerr. According to Kerr, higher education is best defined in modern America in terms of the word "multiversity." In his report to the California governor and the legislature, Kerr generated a taxonomy according to which a legitimated three-tier system would prevail: at the pinnacle the research university, where professors would be, as much as possible, unburdened with heavy teaching loads in order to carry on the work of knowledge production; in the second tier, a panoply of four- and six-year institutions that would transmit knowledge to a technically credentialed student body; and, finally, a system of community colleges to provide *training* for lower-level technicians (Kerr 1972).

This system was to be geared to the segmented market for intellectual labor that emerged after the war with the establishment of a permanent war economy, the growing role of scientific knowledge in the form of computer and other automation processes in goods production, and the explosion of the tertiary (service) sector. Retail and wholesale services expanded rapidly; with the maturation of the welfare state, employment in state and local governments more than quadrupled and, by 1970, accounted for one of six jobs in the labor market. Many newly created professional, managerial, and administrative jobs required postsecondary credentials.

Under these conditions, the academic system of American society became an important industry. In addition to its ideological role as purveyor and disseminator of "American" values and its task of *training* for the new knowledge-based industrial and service economy, it became a leading producer of knowledge. Kerr's program for a three-tier university system was oriented to these new tasks.

Kerr was brilliantly clear: any intellectual culture would be concentrated at the top; the other tiers were to represent the requirement of the economy for new strata of professional and technical *personnel*. But, for Kerr and his colleagues in this emerging corporate culture, the *main task* of the university was to become a knowledge factory; its scientific culture was to be directed toward the means and the ends of economic growth and of public policy. The university was to become an instrument of state policy. Of course, there would be room for artistic and intellectual culture, but not everywhere. The main task of the public four-year and community colleges was to transmit technical knowledge to the second- and third-tier employees required by the labor market.

In the interest of this technocratic program for higher education, the UC–Berkeley administration declared students were barred from conducting political activity in behalf of "outside" interests on campus. This edict was directed at the civil rights movement as much as at radical parties and groups. But, when combined with Kerr's highly publicized multiversity taxonomy, the free speech movement's purview, which began with issues of political speech, rapidly extended to a critique of the corporate university and addressed itself to the poverty of student life in the age of the knowledge factory as well. At Michigan, Harvard, and many other leading campuses, students demanded a voice in the "decisions that affected their lives" and, in the words of Jerry Farber, likened the position of students to that of the "nigger." Far from a self-perception, fostered by administration and by the media, of the elite universities as places of truly "higher" learning, many students increasingly saw themselves as powerless objects of the knowledge machine. Some eagerly devoured the writings of Paul Goodman, C. Wright Mills, Herbert Marcuse, and even Thorstein Veblen, whose *Higher Learning in America* (1918) could have been published today. Each had argued that the whole idea of education as a force for cultural renewal had been subverted by the mobilization of higher learning for instrumental ends, chiefly for the strengthening of increasingly concentrated economic, political, and cultural power (Goodman 1959; Marcuse 1964; Mills 1956).

The movement for student participation in all aspects of university governance, which entailed representation in key decision-making bodies as well as speech rights for "outside" organizations and individual dissenters, shook American universities precisely at the moment when the notion of students as a *market* or as *consumers* began to dominate administrative thinking. Consistent with the growing view of higher education as an industry, the older notion that colleges and universities were essentially decommodified institutions gave way to one in which what the universities produced was for sale. Thus, before World War II, universities were already accepting defense contracts to produce science and technology, a practice that sustained much of the research agendas of American universities for the next half-century. Under pressure caused by reduced government funding, some universities negotiated agreements with private corporations to cede the rights over bioengineering and solid-state physics "products" in return for sustained funding for research. In the context of the galloping commodification of scientific knowledge, the student as market became a logical next step.

Neoclassical economics construes consumer choice as the foundation of economic power. When a product fails in the market, it must be replaced. Thus, ultimate sovereignty in the market belongs to the consumer. On this model, universities must maintain high quality in order to attract students to buy their services. But how to measure the quality of educational services? In econometric models, Harvard, Yale, and other Ivy League schools are the best because they have a surfeit of student applicants who are willing to pay a premium price for their product. Accordingly, if the quality of the *credential,* measured in the number of jobs and the salaries offered to graduates by employers, declines, the consumer would cease to come. *That,* and not principally the various standards of academic evaluation, becomes the crucial criterion of the worth and standing of a university.

To the traditional academic mind, this account may seem somewhat crude. But the crudeness is the result of the selling of American universities as sources of cultural capital, which, as Pierre

Bourdieu has correctly noted, is literally analogous to money capital. As universities have blatantly marketed themselves to business as knowledge- and human-capital producers and to students as cultural-capital providers, hardly anybody but the most devoted supplicant of the idea of the university as an independent community of scholars can doubt that the academic system corresponds more to the above description than to any other.

By the early 1960s, the new model was fairly well developed. The major problem remained the faculty. Except for some branches of the natural and social sciences that were well aware of the degree to which research had become subordinated to practical ends, most of the liberal arts faculty remained committed to the precepts of the older model and, for at least two decades, fought a rearguard battle to preserve the humanistic disciplines against encroachments such as administration efforts to transform English and philosophy in all but a few schools into service departments for a largely technicized curriculum. The humanities as concept survive only in the first tier of elite universities comprising, in addition to the Ivy League schools, some small, private, four-year liberal arts colleges, the University of Chicago, Duke, Emory, and a few other private institutions, along with some of the leading state universities, especially the UC system, some Big Ten schools, and selected campuses of the New York State and City University systems.

But it was in these places that the students mounted their attack on the complicity of the universities with the military and corporations. It was in these elite universities that students faced the hostility of a liberal arts faculty still committed to an academic community that, even if it was not entirely dismantled, had already suffered considerably from the practical effects of the Kerr doctrine. At Berkeley, faculty opposition emanated from former socialists and communists such as sociologist Seymour Martin Lipset, for whom student protest was an invitation to the Right to intervene and was, for this reason, more dangerous to academic freedom than merely irresponsible. Like his colleague Lewis Feuer, a philosopher who saw in the student movement a *generational* revolt directed not only at liberal authority but at the Oedipal figure of the Father, Lipset discerned a definite authoritarian strain in the shrill demand for democratizing the campus. Steeped in Cold War fears, much of the liberal professoriat was skeptical of the incipient doctrine of participatory democracy within the universities. Already buffeted by new winds emanating from on high that they were not yet fully prepared to acknowledge, let alone accept, they were surely inhospitable to the idea of student academic citizenship (Feuer 1969).

Clearly, Lipset and Feuer understood student life neither as part of the emerging consumerist and corporatist culture (an analysis they ascribed to paranoia) nor as a democratic public sphere. The community of scholars, however diminished, needed defending—not against creeping commercialism but against the callow mob of violent, deformed, radicalized, middle-class brats. The free speech movement succeeded not only in winning the right to engage in political activity but also, in many places around the country, in securing a measure of academic citizenship. Token student representatives were elected to boards of trustees and, in the departments, to various committees. Needless to say, faculty were not pleased, but the strength of the movement imposed, putatively, a new regime upon them, as administrations hastened to accommodate to the new political reality that students, through protest and press visibility, constituted, for a time, a new power on campus, one that reappeared in the 1980s under the sign of political correctness.

Yet, despite its reservations, the liberal arts faculty became some of the chief beneficiaries of the university reform movement. Conservative to the core, dormant faculty senates and councils bestirred themselves to debate the future of the university, organized unions, formed women's and black and Latino studies programs and departments, and, under the impetus of the radicalized student movement, engaged in educational innovation manifested most visibly in the development of ethnic, women's, American, and cultural studies on many campuses.

Seen in this context, the fiscal crisis of public education became an occasion for the recentralization of universities and may, perhaps unintentionally, mark the end of the brief period of academic innovation begun by junior faculty, especially women and African-Americans, in the 1970s. Thirty years after the emergence of student power, as we reach the end of the New Deal, Fair Deal, and Great Society era in which public goods enjoyed a position of some privilege, governmentality is itself in question. In the 1990s, under a centrist Democratic national administration and equally conservative local governments, the state's repressive functions overpower and mediate its diminishing social functions. For the Clinton administration, defending a provision of the welfare state may be undertaken only on condition that it be combined with a new manifestation of social conservatism. Police now routinely patrol public schools and universities as if they were identical with the mean streets of the central cities. The concern with educational parsimony in the face of legislative budget cutting eclipses the concern with democratization that accompanied the rise of the black freedom and women's movements in the late 1960s.

III

Since the late 1980s, the academic system of American society has undergone another process of profound transformation. But the logic was already established during the "golden age" of the immediate post–World War II era. Having adopted the framework and the ideology of the large corporation, universities and colleges — private as well as public — are "downsizing" in the name of rising costs compared to declining or stagnant revenues, but they also have used budget cuts to effect a decisive power shift from faculty to administration. In multicampus universities such New York's state and City University systems, the California state university system, and many others, the slogan "academic planning" has been used to remove authority over curricular decisions from the local campus community to the central administration. As the institutions have become more bureaucratized in the past twenty years, presidents and chancellors resemble CEOs rather than academic leaders. Their central functions are fund-raising, lobbying, and diplomacy, which, increasingly, are the same thing. For the most part, their grasp of the mission of the university has been articulated in terms of (*a*) the job market and (*b*) the stock market. The intellectual mission of the academic system now exists as *ornament,* that is, as a legitimating mechanism for a host of other functions, primarily the production and transmission of useful knowledge.

The priority of knowledge as *instrument* over *substance* places scholars and critics in an ambiguous position. Unless their writing and teaching can be situated within the corporate university's ongoing functions, except for the most prominent consensus intellectuals among them, they are regarded by funders and administrators as redundant except as purveyors of "critical thinking" in the elite undergraduate curriculum. There they enjoy a relatively comfortable existence, but one that is progressively marginal and anxiety-ridden precisely because the self-perception of the humanities is that they have lost considerable status in the newly restructured academic system.

Both in their methods and in their self-understanding of their role, the social sciences in this system have modeled themselves on the natural sciences. Theory no longer has a guiding role in the disciplines; it is relegated to a not very important subdiscipline. The crucial branches are those having to do with *policy,* those that can be considered state social science. In sociology, criminology has once more emerged as the leading field; those interested in academic and research jobs are advised to build a sufficient claim to this field. This transformation is entirely complete in economics and political science, is hegemonic in sociology but still contested, and has not (yet) dominated anthropology, which, in any case, may prove moot because of the crisis created by the loss of (Third World) domain in the postcolonial age.

Public universities — most typically the State University of New York (SUNY), the City University of New York (CUNY), and the California State University (CSU) — have received a clear signal from their respective governors and state legislatures either that the moment of *mass* public higher education is over or, if it is not technically ended, that the faculty must reconcile itself to becoming *managers* of ever-larger classes typical of Kerr's vision of the multiversity. In a recent decision of its board of trustees — a body of outside appointees, consisting mostly of corporate executives, lawyers, ex-politicians, and "civic" leaders recruited from the philanthropic upper crust and the black and Latino middle class — CUNY has sharply curtailed its open admissions policy by, among other "reforms," reducing to one year its commitment to provide so-called remedial courses for academically unprepared students, many of whom are immigrants requiring language training before or concurrent with entering the ordinary academic curriculum. "What the City University and other public systems have done," according to *New York Times* reporter Joseph Berger, "is to shift remediation from four year colleges to two year community colleges. The community colleges are cheaper places for remedial courses because professors are required to teach more hours, classes are larger, and in New York, a greater proportion of tuition payments can be used to pay for remedial classes" (*New York Times,* June 27, 1995).

In sum, the university's restructuring means that community colleges have been designated as *the* solution for a broad range of students requiring an extra boost on the way to credentials. The only problem is that the process has been designed on the basis of the celebrated Joseph Heller narrative: "We want to help you, but we will set impossible conditions for our helpers." Like the roach motel, students can still get in, but they can't get out except as intellectual corpses.

But, following the trend of the private corporate sector, where literally tens of thousands of professional and technical employees have been shed since the stock market crash of 1987, state and local governments, suffering declining tax revenues because of sinking real income, have followed suit by cutting their own workforces. And, in step with the steady march of Congress to dismantle key elements of the welfare state, especially federal aid to education, health care, and social services, the proprietors of state governments have begun to argue that if there are fewer jobs in these service delivery systems, as well as in banks and insurance companies whose clerical and professional workforces are increasingly subject to mergers and acquisitions and technological displacement, then maintaining expanded professional and technical education will only flood the market with credentialed, but unneeded, workers. Hence, the drive to raise admission standards in order to restrict enrollments to academically qualified students. The new public university systems' slogan might be, "Give me your qualified and deserving poor."

These broad changes are already taking their toll on graduate programs. Facing draconian cuts in student aid, many programs limit the number of students they admit to only those who can be supported by the money available. Since many schools are raising teacher workloads, and faculty are required to teach more undergraduate, particularly lower-division, courses, many have no time to teach graduate courses. As the number of graduate courses declines, seminars turn into lecture courses, and lecture courses become experiments in mass postgraduate education. The core of traditional graduate education, the one-to-one relation between mentor and mentee, is eroding as graduate school more resembles undergraduate college.

IV

The idea of the university has, like much of our moral and intellectual culture, religious roots. In medieval and Renaissance Europe, the *collegium* was formed first in the monastery or, among Jews, in the "school" as a community of scholars who together studied the sacred texts and wrote commentaries on them. Their readings became the basis of religious teaching to the underlying population. In this regime, the college was *primarily* constituted as a space for the search for knowledge of God, but it also evolved into more secular areas such as science and art.

The early "secular" colleges were similarly constituted. They remained church-sponsored, and church officials assumed the task of maintaining the institution—primarily its buildings and finance. But faculty retained authority over the curriculum and pedagogy. That did not eliminate conflicts between the two governance structures of the college, but lines of authority were far more clearly delineated than now.

Nowadays, our concept of academic freedom in the university is one-dimensional. We understand and generally support the right of individual faculty members to speak and write according to the dictates of their own consciences and remain free of legal or administrative sanction. It has become an aspect of speech protected by the spirit and the letter of the First Amendment. The many violations of this meaning of academic freedom, especially denial of tenure to the unconventional and dismissal and administrative intimidation of dissenters, have been vigorously opposed by the aggrieved, by professional associations, by faculty unions, and by civil liberties organizations.

We associate the institution of tenure with the need to protect dissenting faculty from sanction imposed by the public, the administration of the university, and colleagues who might be prone to punish apostates. Before World War II, however, tenure was rarely awarded to the garden-variety instructor. No less a figure than critic Lionel Trilling held the rank of an untenured instructor at Columbia throughout the 1930s; in 1936 he almost lost his English department job because he was a Marxist, held Freudian beliefs, and was a Jew; he achieved real job security only after the war. In fact, as a practice, tenure is barely a half-century old. In 1940 the AAUP issued a statement saying that the only way to secure academic freedom was through tenure, and tenure was gradually instituted by most universities after World War II. But the AAUP's widely discussed 1940 proposal, which had first been enunciated in 1915, is once again under attack (Lucas 1994, 197–200). The president of the University of Minnesota recently floated a proposal to abolish tenure; the president of Bennington College actually got rid of it along with a number of tenured faculty; and prominent colleges such as the New School, Eugene Lang, and Hampshire, among many others, do not offer anything more than multiyear contracts.

Further, the second dimension of academic freedom, the rights of the faculty as a *collectivity* to retain sovereignty over the educational process, has been buried with the restructuring. Questions such as whether a department or program should be established, expanded, retained, or eliminated; hiring and dismissal of faculty; assignment of positions to programs and departments; workloads and classroom sizes — these are only a few of the crucial decisions affecting schools that have gradually been assumed by administrations and by boards of trustees.

In the midst of these changes, nearly all higher education institutions have maintained the formal apparatus of faculty sovereignty and have made only tentative gestures, so far, toward challenging institutions such as tenure and faculty-based academic review. Promotion and tenure committees still deliberate on individual cases; faculty-administration retrenchment committees decide on how to reduce staff in times of budget crisis (within parameters established by the administration and, where applicable, the union contract); curriculum committees continue to approve or refuse new courses or programs; and student affairs committees, now reduced to an aspect of the policing function of administration, monitor and make disciplinary decisions on academic and extra-academic student performance.

But in both the public and the private university sectors, power has slowly but surely shifted to administrators, who retain final determination of nearly all university issues. Faculty senates and academic committees are really advisory bodies whose recommendations are no longer routinely approved by higher authorities. Everywhere, departmental and divisional recommendations for tenure (or its refusal) are subject to reversal by deans and presidents. And curriculum issues are now subordinated to budget considerations.

It should be evident to all but the most myopic observer that the worst abuses of the *collegium* have been in the abrogation of faculty sovereignty by the corporate university, even as cases of individual academic-freedom violations are the most visible. The disparity between reality and public awareness may not be ascribed to conspiracy or entirely to evil intent. The centralization of the academic system is a product of what Alan Trachtenberg has called "the incorporation of America" (Trachtenberg 1988). Just as the family-owned firm and the craft union or guild has been *relegated* to a subordinate existence in the U.S. political economy, so the *collegium* occupies a purgatory between the heaven of the corporate university boardroom and the hell of the huge lecture halls that dominate public universities. It has a voice with little authority; its crafts — reading, writing, speaking — suffer a wizened existence; its minions, embattled and dispirited, have mounted resistance in the last five years, but these efforts are sporadic, disorganized, and only partially effective.

Thus, we can see the steamroller at work. For example, during the last budget crisis, many CUNY presidents and the chancellor's office exempted professional administrators from the retrenchment plan and planted the burden of the layoffs or thinly disguised force-outs on low-level administrative and clerical staff. The corporate culture was firmly in place. At many public universities in the past two decades, faculty hiring was virtually frozen at most campuses while, at the same time, administrative hiring experienced a veritable boom. This fact is a measure of the power shift during this period. The question that must be addressed is why and how the faculty lost its sovereignty. Before dealing with this issue, however, one other question must be discussed: Does the *collegium* include students? Is the power shift a violation of their academic freedom?

Symptomatically, we now speak of a corporate "culture," which in the academy signifies a *displacement* of the old intellectual culture of the sciences, humanities, and the arts. Research and writing go on, but they become increasingly instrumental to the overarching goals of individual survival (or, in some cases, to advancement in the academic hierarchy) and, more to the point, a means to enhance the coffers and, secondarily, the prestige of the institution. The individual who pursues knowledge for its own sake or for human betterment may still perform this work on her/his own time. In contrast, faculty are, more than ever, urged, cajoled, and even threatened to direct their scholarship and research to the ever-decreasing pots of grants gold on penalty of losing promotions, tenure, and resources such as computer time, assistants, and equipment.

In the process, it is no wonder faculty feel like employees rather than a series of communities devoted to common intellectual concerns. In consideration of their new, proletarianized status, many have joined unions and converted their faculty senates into bodies that are adversarial to administration and legislatures that, in their perception, are bosses just like any other. Increasingly, the institutions of faculty control are losing their status and, from the perspective of administration, are, at best, viewed as a nuisance whose utility for purposes of legitimation may have (over)reached its limit. While faculty, including adjuncts and teaching assistants, have reevaluated their traditional antipathy to collective action as a means to adjudicate their grievances, they view unions as the unions see themselves — that is, as economic bargaining agents concerned chiefly with salaries, workload, and job security issues.

Today, approximately one-quarter of full-time faculty and non-supervisory administrative staff are organized in three unions: the AFT, with about eighty-five thousand members; the AAUP, with about twenty-two thousand members under contract, although its total membership is about forty-four thousand; and the NEA, with about twenty thousand members. The unions bargain for faculty at some leading universities: the AAUP has organized Rutgers and Wayne State and has dual affiliation at CUNY with AFT and at Cal State, the nation's largest public college system, with NEA, the primary bargaining agency. The AFT is the primary union at SUNY, where its affiliate has twenty-two thousand in the bargaining unit, the largest academic union in the country; at CUNY, with about thirteen thousand; and at Temple and the Pennsylvania State University system of former teachers colleges (not Penn State); and at Illinois and California community colleges. The union has won collective bargaining at the University of California (U Cal) for teaching assistants and lab workers, but not for faculty, although it has locals in most of the U Cal campuses. Some private colleges and universities, notably Long Island (AFT) and Saint John's (AAUP), are unionized. TAs are affiliated with unions ranging from the AFT to the United Electrical, Radio, and Machine Workers of America (Iowa) and the Hotel Employees and Restaurant Employees International Union (Yale). Clerical and maintenance workers in universities are organized into many unions, notably the American Federation of State, County, and Municipal Employees, the United Auto Workers (UAW), and the Service Employees International Union. These employees are not included in the exemption provided by the notorious *Yeshiva* decision, and so clerical and maintenance unions have made significant inroads in private universities such as Harvard, Columbia, Yale, and Boston University. Their strength is characteristically concentrated in the Northeast, still the largest bastion of unionism in services.

Apart from the private colleges, which faculty unions believe are, for the time being, outside the realm of possible unionization, the glaring weakness remains the public research universities where faculty enjoy considerably higher salaries than in the third- and fourth-tier institutions and where many faculty earn significant outside income as consultants. With their long-term job prospects ever more grim, TAs increasingly seek union organization. Apart from the exceptions already noted, faculty at research institutions such as U Cal, Texas, Penn State, Virginia, and the Big Ten universities generally view themselves as exempt from the imperative of collective action since they are convinced that their professional fate is, for all intents and purposes, a function of their individual talents and achievements. U Cal and many other public universities reward faculty according to merit, which is gained primarily by publishing articles in certain journals, publishing academically respectable books, and engaging in funded research.

Even when resources and pay have been cut by state legislatures, most of these faculty remain indifferent, if not antagonistic, to unionism because, I suspect, they fear to admit that their own position, in absolute terms, has deteriorated even if their relative status and working conditions are princely compared to colleagues at state and most private two- and four-year colleges. In fact, in proportion as public colleges and universities suffer vocationalization, faculty and staff reductions, and deteriorating working conditions, the cultural, as opposed to the economic, position of the elite university professoriat increases. Salary stagnation notwithstanding, the status gap between the various tiers of the academic system is widening.

Like teachers in the primary and secondary schools, professors organized unions when they understood that their diminished cultural capital would not sustain their economic and professional positions, especially in absolute terms; that regardless of the pedigree of their graduate and undergraduate degrees, they were being ground down by increasingly arbitrary administrations and vindictive legislatures, especially after the Vietnam War era; that as salaried employees they needed the advantages of collective action. More to point, they had to surrender, to a certain degree, professional illusions, especially the pernicious doctrine of genius and talent inherited from the nineteenth century.

Professors' first move as trade unionists was to frame their organizations in the images of conventional business or economistic unionism. Understandably, the more trade unionist the faculty, the more antiprofessional. Of course, although unions of professionals were never able to entirely avoid dealing with professional issues, their first responsibility was to assert, against the prevailing wisdom, that professors' interests were closer to those of the labor movement than to management. In this respect, CUNY is an example of an ideologically moderate leadership, which nonetheless steadfastly resisted the concept of merit as the basis of salary determinations. To be sure, promotions and tenure were and remain the last bastion of the merit system, but salary increases within academic rank are awarded on the basis of length of service. In contrast, many other union contracts retain management's right to distribute academic rewards subject only to the grievance procedure.

There is still much convincing to be done with perhaps a majority of the professoriat, in and out of the unions. Trained within professional ideology, most professors in research universities see themselves neither as intellectuals nor as teachers, which, in either case, would result in a politicizing reflexivity. Consequently, many union members share with other professors a primary identity with their professional associations and seek approval from colleagues within their discipline and, ultimately, from the university administration that retains the purse strings, rather than from the class of intellectuals to which they putatively belong.

The research university faculty may do better, but they are not doing particularly well. With diminished funds for research, many are teaching more than ever. Many have been forced to live primarily on their salaries, a change that, in some cases, reduced their incomes by as much as half. Austerity in research funding has been matched by legislative parsimony. Faculty salaries at leading universities have barely kept pace with inflation and are, absent a few thousand chair holders and academic stars (whose incomes nevertheless rarely exceed $125,000 a year), modest in comparison to medicine and corporate law, with which, by education at least, they are on par. Still, when they look down at their colleagues in nonresearch universities, where a full professor earns an average of $58,000 a year, somewhat in excess of $20,000 more than a beginning assistant professor, their $70,000 to $75,000 salaries look good if not sumptuous.

There can be little doubt of past union effectiveness in vastly improving faculty and staff salaries, working conditions, and benefits. Until recently, CUNY salaries compared favorably with nearly all major private and public universities and, for a time, were the highest, on average, in the country. But the fiscal crisis of 1975–76 and parallel legislative cutbacks of funds for public universities in many states combined with faculty reticence to strike (except in some community colleges, the dramatic TA strike at Yale, and the faculty strike at Temple) and otherwise take direct action to win their demands are decisively shifting the balance between public and private universities. Faculty unions still make a difference, but, like unions in manufacturing and many services, recently their advantage may be that they provide a grievance procedure and a broad range of benefits rather than increases in salaries.

What is less clear is whether unions see themselves as agents in the wider university life. Until now, the fundamental power grab by university administrations has not elicited a strong response by campus unions. Some, like CUNY's Professional Staff Congress (PSC) and SUNY's United University Professions (UUP), have addressed issues of academic planning. UUP thwarted an administration proposal to privatize the two SUNY medical schools and medical centers; PSC played an important role in helping to remove several college presidents who were acting against the interests of faculty and students. The union recently joined in a successful suit against the CUNY board of trustees for its premature declaration of financial exigency before the state budget was completed, declaring that the action was a ploy to force retrenchments and most importantly organizational changes not warranted by the budget situation. Yet, beyond these and some other instances, faculty unions have seen themselves in a severely restricted compass; for understandable reasons they have made the sphere of economic bargaining, including job security, their special province. Issues such as the creation of new programs, the elimination of old departments, and major curricular changes are, in a rough division of labor, understood to be the province of the faculty senates and the administration.

PSC's active participation in the creation of City College's Center for Worker Education and its collaboration with a major literacy center in New York City, the Consortium for Worker Education, may be exceptions to the rule of noninvolvement in educational innovation. Yet if recent bipartisan assaults on higher education persist, faculty unions may be obliged to consider whether to become leading vehicles for counterplanning if faculty senates — which are frequently dominated by the most senior professors, who shuttle back and forth from faculty to administration — lack the political will to oppose downsizing/reorganization programs aimed at vocationalization.

V

What has been the response of faculty and students to the new regime of educational disaccumulation? Where there *is* an organized response, it has been confined to resistance. I want to offer CUNY's experience in the 1990s as a case study of what is possible and of what faculty and students have perceived to be the limits of their power. In spring 1995, faculty and student organizations, including PSC, effectively mobilized to oppose the new Republican governor's proposal to cut the university's budget by more than 15 percent and Mayor Rudolf Guiliani's threat to cut off $20 million from community colleges. Thousands demonstrated, called public meetings, and lobbied legislators on behalf of blocking the budget cuts. At the campus level, some faculty fought administration-sponsored "retrenchment plans" that proposed to eliminate entire departments and programs rather than anticipate across-the-board cuts. In the end, the cuts *did* result in some departmental closings and layoffs, but early expectations that some state campuses would be discontinued and the two state university medical centers would be privatized never became reality because of adroit efforts of the UUP and the state's teachers' federation, which led an intense legislative lobby.

Even as the coalition opposing the cuts celebrated its partial victory, the governor's budget proposals for SUNY and CUNY in 1996–97 and beyond stepped up the pressure for reorganization and downsizing. While denouncing the proposed cuts, administrations at both universities used the occasion to begin a process of academic planning from above aimed at sharply reducing the liberal arts to service departments for enhanced professional and technical programs. Accelerating tendencies built into both systems, administration plans called for the overt establishment of a few research-oriented campuses while relegating most to vocational roles.

While resistance is necessary, it is hardly sufficient to address the systematic dismantling of the democratic mission of the university. On the whole, the educational imaginary of faculty and students has been limited to preserving the existing state of affairs — especially the much-maligned open admissions policy — rather than being devoted to generating ideas for a different kind of restructuring of the university that would not diminish access but would radically improve the curriculum, pedagogy, and school governance. Even the most progressive have hesitated to propose anything innovative or even different, fearing that any change could only enhance the administration's drive to further centralization.

Like so many other struggles in this corporate "downsizing" era, the Right has all the ideas and the opposition finds itself backed into a corner: the liberals have become the conservatives, the most staunch defenders of the status quo. For example, in the fight to prevent the dismantling of the archaic welfare system, the "Left" seems to have forgotten its own critique of the cynicism of the welfare bureaucracy; it has now become the most fervent defenders of a system it once excoriated. Similarly, whereas educational radicals (not to be confused with the traditional left liberals) once condemned the disciplinary basis of school knowledge as an outmoded, repressive regime, many now resist any hint of educational reform, since such proposals rarely signify the enlargement of resources but are used by administration to facilitate consolidation.

On the run, the liberals have steadfastly refused to enter a serious dialogue with their adversaries. For example, critics howled when CUNY Chancellor W. Anne Reynolds announced the College Preparatory Initiative (CPI) in 1993, a program that would force high schools to raise graduation standards by offering serious language, science, and math courses; the stated goal of the program was to relieve the university of some of the obligations of providing remedial programs, obligations that would then be taken care of by secondary school curricula. The critics simply refused to believe that CPI was more than a thinly veiled effort to phase out open admissions. Perhaps they were correct.

Yet who can deny urban high schools need significant reform? Those concerned with preserving open admissions might have explored the possibility of joining the chancellor in fighting to upgrade the curricula of many of New York's high schools. It would have entailed finding new money for laboratories, hiring math and language teachers, and, perhaps equally significant, reforming administrative structures in secondary education. Specifically, educational reformers in the schools have successfully argued that the factory-like, monolithic high schools containing two to four thousand students are inimical to learning. In New York City, some two dozen smaller schools, each enrolling about five hundred students, have been established in the last twenty years, most of them since the late 1980s. School districts have extended their alternative intermediate schools to high schools, introducing a 7–12 concept for secondary school. And the board of education has approved breaking up some existing big high schools that are not working into smaller houses. So far, the results have been encouraging, if inconclusive.

The higher educational Democrats are, with exceptions, not part of this movement. Rather they are stuck in a sniping, marginal position, refusing to acknowledge that many New York high schools aren't working. Or, even if they agree that students come to CUNY and other large urban university systems without sufficient academic preparation, their deep suspicion of the administration's *motives* for undertaking reform produces a state of paralysis.

The paranoid style of politics is entirely understandable in this environment. Bereft of ideas, the university administration demands of the campuses "academic planning," which almost everyone knows is a euphemism for adapting to the new downsizing programs mandated by the bond holders, who are, at least symbolically, represented on the board of trustees. Still, we must ask whether it makes sense to deny everything and construct the fight entirely in terms of resistance.

In August 1993, the CUNY administration, at a moment when their plan for top-down academic planning had been almost universally rejected by faculty and students, asked me what would be an alternative. I suggested that a faculty-controlled committee award small grants to groups who would propose and attempt to implement domain-based, rather than disciplinary-based, curricula. Each proposal, I suggested, would have to involve faculty from different disciplines and even different campuses. Working with Dean Ronald Berkman of the chancellor's staff, we procured from the Aaron Diamond Foundation enough funds for awarding some fifteen grants over a three-year period.

As I developed the program, some faculty warned me of the risks: working with the administration at a time of severe budget crisis would invite the perception that what we called "New Visions in Undergraduate Education" was simply a backdoor through which the "Goldstein Report," the main incarnation of the administration's own proposal, would sneak through. Neither participating faculty — those on the committee and the applicants — nor the administration understood "New Visions" to be other than what it purported to be: an alternative approach to academic planning. We were not being co-opted. We were aggressively intervening in the crisis, in this case not with protest but with affirmative alternatives.

Tacitly rejecting the either/or of protest and collaboration, members of the committee have protested the governor's and mayor's assault on the City University. We have, as individual faculty members, testified, lobbied legislators, and marched before City Hall. Some of us have given press and television interviews expressing complete opposition to the prevailing program to gut the institution. Yet we saw the virtue of entering the planning process; that a dialogue has not genuinely ensued is a function both of our own inability to broaden the approach in the context of the debate and of the way in which the discourse of crisis has hardened positions on both sides.

Needless to say, the great battle for higher education did not end when, in the face of massive protests, the legislature and the governor scaled back the cuts and the university's shortfall was closed by raising tuition by $750 for senior college students and $400 for community colleges. More than a dozen programs were shut down in 1995, and we can expect new stages in the crisis: once again, facing reduced revenues (a reduction produced, fundamentally, by the legacy of bipartisan tax concessions to business and the wealthy, the governor's own tax cut, and the recession in the state's economy), the governor will try to radically reduce the budgets for public education — both the lower and higher institutions. Heaving a sigh of regret, the university administration will be forced by these new budgetary calumnies to consider closing several colleges, retrenching faculty, and closing thousands of courses. Once again, faculty and students will face the choice of protest or alternative.

A small but dedicated group has joined in sustaining the CUNY coalition that has consistently fought the budget cuts; some of these activists have formed a new caucus within the union to provide more determined and imaginative leadership to the faculty. And the groups working on new curricula have not surrendered hope; in some cases, their plans have been realized in new undergraduate programs. But the obstacles are formidable. Many are deeply committed to their own disciplines and to professional and technical education. They are willing to resist reductions that hurt their own programs but are unwilling to entertain new approaches that might entail radically rethinking their own professional status. Some, indeed, are in state of deep denial. They hope for renewal on the basis of a new liberal state government, economic growth, or a surge of political support for public education (which, in spring 1996, seemed to have emerged somewhat). And a considerable portion of the most thoughtful and experienced faculty have already left for other universities or have retired rather than suffer the humiliation of standing on the deck of a sinking ship.

The deep issue is, of course, power. Have the faculty and student communities effectively surrendered the vision of the community of scholars and now accepted their already institutionalized status as employees and consumers? Or is there still hope that *in addition* to the rituals of resistance (which, it must be admitted, can slow the steamroller down but not stop it), these communities, recognizing they are in the same boat, will abandon the moralistic, ritualized, paranoid style for a more nuanced, and ultimately strategic, effort to fight for a democratic university? Although a democratic university would include some of the elements of the hard-won open admissions policy, it would go beyond it to ask the fundamental question: What is the mission of the university in a postwork society? Can we disengage the orientation to jobs, jobs, jobs and to a corporate culture to found our own?

The answers to these questions are ineluctably linked to other issues: What is political will? Who are the agents? What is the program? Beyond rage lurks a new approach. Whether we will stumble on it before we have been locked into antagonistic and ultimately futile positions remains to be seen.

For academic unions there can be no question of reversing the tendency toward the de facto end of mass public higher education through collective bargaining. Having successfully shown that the professoriat in some academic precincts can act like traditional trade unionists without seriously damaging their academic integrity or standing, the unions are now faced with the awesome task of becoming institutions of alternative as well as resistance. In short, they are challenged to accept responsibility for the academic system rather than remaining representatives of specific interests of faculty and staff within its technocratically defined boundaries. The challenge is to become agents of a new educational imagination — that is, to join with others in counterplanning that aims *both* to retain mass higher education as a *right* and to suggest what education is in the new, postregulation, postwork era.

Works Cited

Aronowitz, Stanley. 1984. "When the New Left Was New." In *60s without Apology*. Ed. by Sonhya Sayres et al. Minneapolis: University of Minnesota Press.

———. 1996. *Death and Rebirth of American Radicalism*. New York: Routledge.

Aronowitz, Stanley, and William DiFazio. 1994. *The Jobless Future*. Minneapolis: University of Minnesota Press.

Blum, Linda. 1991. *Between Feminism and Labor: The Significance of Comparable Worth*. Berkeley: University of California Press.

Brint, Steven, and Jerome Karabel. 1989. *The Diverted Dream: Community Colleges and the Promise of Educational Opportunity in America*. New York: Oxford University Press, 1989.

Du Bois, William Edward Burkhardt. 1903. *Souls of Black Folk*. Chicago: A. C. McClung.

Feuer, Lewis. 1969. *The Conflict of Generations: The Character and Significance of Student Movements*. New York: Basic Books.

Fink, Leon, and Brian Greenberg. 1989. *Upheaval in the Quiet Zone: A History of Local 1199*. Urbana: University of Illinois Press.

Goodman, Paul. 1959. *Growing Up Absurd*. New York: Random House.

Kenney, Martin. 1986. *The University/Industrial Complex*. New Haven: Yale University Press.

Kerr, Clark. 1972. *The Use of the University*. New York: Harper and Row.

Krause, Paul. 1992. *The Battle for Homestead*. Pittsburgh: University of Pittsburgh Press.

Lichtenstein, Nelson. 1996. *The Most Dangerous Man in Detroit: Walter Reuther and the Fate of American Labor*. New York: Basic Books.

Lucas, Christopher J. 1994. *American Higher Education: A History*. New York: Saint Martin's Press.

Marcuse, Herbert. 1964. *One-Dimensional Man*. Boston: Beacon Press.

Mills, C. Wright. 1956, *The Power Elite*. New York: Oxford University Press.

Trachtenberg, Alan. 1988. *The Incorporation of America*. New York: Hill and Wang.

Figure 27. An April 1, 1976, TAA work-stoppage rally at the University of Wisconsin. Photograph by Daniel Czitrom, taken just before he mounted the platform to address the audience

Chapter 10
Reeling in the Years: Looking Back on the TAA

Daniel Czitrom

After a recent conversation comparing the arc of our work lives, my father, a retired steamfitter and lifelong union militant, summarized the differences this way: "Everything I ever got on the job was won through collective action; everything you'll ever get will be through individual achievement." He expressed what sounded like a simple truth about class difference with a combination of wistfulness and pride, the mix of family emotions that accompanied my upward mobility. For years he has tried vicariously to unravel the mysteries of the academic job hunt, the long march to tenure, and the dialectics of promotion. Although I recall thinking it was a good line, his comment didn't tell the whole story. But it made me think about my personal efforts to reconcile individual career and trade unionism and how these in turn connect with the fundamental political problem facing all teachers unions: how to resolve the contradictions that emerge amid competing claims for professionalism, material gain, and a more democratic and effective educational system.

From 1973 to 1976 I served as history department shop steward for the Teaching Assistants Association (TAA) at the University of Wisconsin (UW), the oldest such union in the country and the first to bargain collectively and obtain a contract. What follows is a part history/part memoir of my experiences in the TAA, with no claim to being a comprehensive account of the organization. Rather, what I hope to do here is review some of the achievements of the TAA; stimulate thinking about which strategies and tactics from those days might still prove fruitful for organizing today; and open up dialogue about the too-often undiscussed contradictions faced by teachers unions.[1]

When I arrived in Madison in 1971 to pursue a Ph.D. in American history, the TAA already had a tumultuous history. Its political and economic successes had made it an important presence on the UW campus. It began in the spring of 1966 when several dozen TAs held a series of meetings to discuss campus antidraft protests. Many of these TAs were antiwar activists themselves, and they were especially concerned that, under the draft laws of the day, giving a failing grade to a male student was equivalent to sending him off to fight in Vietnam. In the fall of 1967, the TAA went on a four-day strike to protest police brutality against antiwar students who had sat-in to protest Dow Chemical recruitment on campus. In these years the TAA also joined with undergraduates in a variety of educational reform efforts and teaching innovations at UW, including improvement of course syllabi and participation in departmental curriculum committees.

The early political experience gained in the antiwar and student movements helped TAs to organize into a labor union when, in early 1969, they found themselves under economic attack. The Wisconsin state legislature introduced a bill to rescind out-of-state tuition remission for all TAs. This would have cost most TAs about $450 more per semester, or one and one-half month's salary for the highest paid TAs. Although still an ad hoc organization, the TAA took a strike vote and announced publicly that, in accordance with the vote, there would be a strike if the bill passed. The bill was withdrawn both because of the TAA threat and because the university administration worried that the bill might hurt recruitment of new graduate students.

The drive to create a labor union for TAs emerged during this battle. TAA leaders sent cards to all nineteen hundred TAs on the Madison campus, asking if they would agree to authorize the organization to serve as their exclusive bargaining agent. About eleven hundred TAs responded positively, motivated by a combination of three issues: the realization that, as university employees, TAs had to work collectively to improve their lot; a desire to end the isolation and inequities between TAs of various departments; and the goal of creating a new power bloc that could act as a force for democratizing the university as an institution. UW administrators at first rejected the demand for collective bargaining. But continued political agitation, the implied threat of a strike, and the possibility of attack from the state's organized labor movement forced the university to give in. It agreed to abide by the results of an election supervised by the Wisconsin Employment Relations Commission, and in May 1969 the TAA won 77 percent of that vote. A majority of teaching assistants in fifty-two of eighty-one departments chose the TAA as their exclusive bargaining agent.

At the time, conditions under which TAs worked were quite arbitrary. TA appointments were given for one year or one semester at a time. Renewals were often made on the basis of departmental politics rather than teaching ability, and there were firings for political activity. Workloads and pay varied widely by department; TAs in the humanities were the lowest paid and did the most work for the money they received. There was no grievance procedure. There was no health plan for TAs, even though every other university employee had one.

To address these problems, the TAA defined eight basic demands in its bargaining with the university. Six of these explicitly addressed economic and workplace issues:

1. establishment of a grievance procedure that would include neutral arbitrators
2. uniform workloads for TAs
3. a guarantee of appointment for the duration of a TA's graduate career, up to ten years
4. fair procedures for discipline and discharge of TAs and fair procedure for teaching evaluation
5. open files for all TA evaluations
6. health insurance covering TAs and their families

Two other proposals grew from the TAA's radical critique of the university, which connected the university's internal hierarchical power relations to inequality in the larger society. Arguing that "much of the structure and content of University education reflects and perpetuates an inequitable society through forms of explicit and de facto discrimination," the TAA proposed that the university and the union work to develop programs to end discrimination "through hiring, admission, and education policies." Finally, the union put forth an "educational planning" proposal, calling for each department to bargain with its TAA affiliate to establish mechanisms by which undergraduates and their TAs could participate with faculty in planning and structuring courses in which TAs were involved.

The landmark strike of March 1970 came after eleven months of fruitless bargaining, during which administration negotiators constantly invoked a "management right" to run the university as they saw fit. Over two-thirds of the TAA membership voted to walk out. The strike lasted twenty-four days and revealed some of the key fault lines in university life. Undergraduate activists called a boycott of classes to support the TAA demands, both economic and educational, and class attendance in the College of Letters and Science dropped to about 25 percent of enrollment. Significantly, Madison Teamsters Local 695 lined up behind the TAA. Campus bus service stopped, and truck drivers delivering everything from liquid nitrogen to office supplies refused to cross TAA picket lines.

Buoyed by the support from students and organized labor, the TAA also faced enormous pressures to settle. UW faculty called on the administration to resist the educational planning proposal, viewing it as a threat to their own professional identity and sense of autonomy. At a special meeting called during the last week of the strike, faculty overwhelmingly reaffirmed their view that all educational issues were solely their prerogative. Only a handful of faculty argued in favor of the TAA educational planning demand. The university threatened mass firings, and it secured a state court injunction declaring the strike illegal. Although the union voted to ignore the injunction, the court order had a chilling effect on more moderate members. Undergraduate support also weakened with the approaching end of the semester.

By early April the strike had thus reached a stalemate. The contract that the membership voted to accept on April 8 made virtually no concessions on the educational planning issue, save for a vaguely worded statement urging collaboration between students, teachers, and faculty in course planning. But the TAA did win establishment of an impartial grievance procedure, a guarantee of four-year appointments for TAs, health insurance coverage, limits on the size of class sections (an average of nineteen students per section figured on a course-by-course basis), and fair procedures for discipline and discharge. The 1970 strike demonstrated the effectiveness of united action with other student and labor groups. And it established the TAA as a new economic and political formation, one that combined traditional collective bargaining on behalf of its members with serious efforts to challenge the university's — and larger society's — power structure. As one union broadside of the day put it:

> Ultimately, our union exists because in our community of the knowledge industry, like in all other aspects of the American economy, wealth and power are concentrated in the hands of a few nonworkers. The Administration is a management which has manipulated the University not for the well being of teaching assistants, or students, or secretaries, or janitors, but rather for the commercial interests of a capitalistic state. . . . We do right by opposing through our contract demands, union education, and direct action the racism and imperialism which drain our natural resources as they divide our working class.

It was precisely this commitment to joining traditional trade unionism to a broader, radical critique of higher education and society that attracted many of us to the TAA orbit. The TAA was an exciting, and sometimes maddening, site for serious political activity. This became clear to me at the very first TAA meeting I attended, in the fall of 1973, as a newly minted TA and newly elected shop steward for the history department affiliate. My main memory of that first meeting is the long, contentious, and ultimately satisfying discussion of a new health plan just going into effect. After a timid-looking university or insurance company bureaucrat (I can't recall which) offered the basic outlines of the new plan, the floor opened up for questions. Members pressed the speaker politely but forcefully for specifics pertaining to coverage for abortion and gynecological services, pregnancy, and parental leave. I soon learned that most of these questions came from a very active reproductive rights caucus, feeling its oats in the wake of the recent *Roe v. Wade* decision.

Every Sunday night I attended the weekly stewards council meetings, where stewards from the departmental affiliates acted as a kind of union steering committee responsible for the everyday functioning of the TAA. The affiliate structure had been crucial for organizing the TAA and for ensuring democracy in union affairs. Although the membership also elected an executive board of officers, the powers vested in the stewards council reflected a deep distrust of autocratic leadership and a (sometimes naive) faith in decentralized power. Affiliates were the most effective site for drawing in new members, addressing specific concerns unique to individual departments, and, crucially, reproducing leadership.

The stewards council also embodied the most explicitly political side of the TAA, and the stewards tended to be more committed and more ideological than the rank and file. Indeed, a large fraction of stewards (and many other TAA activists in those years) were active in political sects, especially the International Socialists (IS), the Progressive Labor Party (PL), the Young Socialists of America (YSA), and even the Communist Party (CP). Stewards council meetings often veered wildly between discussions of nuts-and-bolts union business and more cosmic debates over how to build the *real* worker-student alliance. We allowed (even encouraged) all manner of campus and noncampus political groups to speak to us, propose alliances, offer analysis, and cosponsor actions. The downside of this policy only became apparent the night we suffered through the harangue of two men from the Larouche-ite National Caucus of Labor Committees (NCLC), earnestly urging us to disband the TAA in favor of "class-wide organizing."

Because of the revolving-door nature of the membership, union activists had to spend an enormous amount of time and energy on educating our TA colleagues. There were, of course, many times when we felt dragged down by it all, especially the "false consciousness" exhibited by TAs who could never see beyond the political dead end of professionalism. Yet these ongoing efforts provided a foundation for TAA's unique internal political culture in at least two ways. First, the union developed a conscious, thoughtfully articulated, sometimes contested collective memory that we all felt responsible for keeping alive and passing on. One rarely heard a speech, wrote a pamphlet, signed up a new member, or debated a policy without invoking the union's own history, especially its concrete gains. Those of us engaged in organizing work learned an invaluable lesson: you have to give people reasons to join and victories they can see. Second, the TAA also operated as an incubator for political activists. For a lot of UW graduate students, the TAA served as an introduction not just to unionism but to politics in the broadest sense and to the radical critique of American education and society in particular. An awful lot of people who got their political feet wet in the TAA — probably thousands over the years — took their experiences and analyses to schools, trade unions, women's groups, and grassroots political formations all over the country and around the world.

TAA involvement with the larger labor movement was a central goal during the early 1970s. Within the University the TAA helped many employees organize. Student part-time workers formed the Memorial Union Labor Organization (MULO) and the Resident Halls Student Labor Organization (RHSLO), both of which successfully negotiated contracts after striking. Efforts to help organize secretaries and research technicians proved less successful. During my first year, the stewards council devoted most of its time to the question of affiliation: should the TAA forgo its independent status and become part of the larger labor movement? In early 1974, after sustained, sometimes tiresome, debate, we voted to affiliate with the American Federation of Teachers (part of the AFL-CIO), and the TAA became Local 3220 of the AFT. Like many, I was able to swallow the idea of paying part of Albert Shanker's salary on behalf of a the greater good: AFT affiliation offered new strength in unity with the labor movement, as well as the possibility of helping to democratize that labor movement. In the years since, a number of TAA members have become leading figures in the Madison Federation of Labor, the Wisconsin Federation of Teachers, and the Wisconsin AFL-CIO. Others have become activists and staffers in Teamsters locals and teachers unions around the country.

Anyone who has ever worked under the terms of a collective bargaining agreement understands that contracts are only as effective as their enforcement. Internally, the TAA in the early and mid-1970s focused on consolidating our gains by aggressively running grievances, continual organizing among new TAs, and what seemed like endless bargaining sessions with university administrators for new contracts. With no paid staffers, TAA stewards and officers performed the bulk of this often technical and always time-consuming work on a volunteer basis.

The university's shrewd manipulation of our ambiguous legal

status made the job that much more difficult. The 1969 "Structure Agreement" recognized the TAA as the legal bargaining agent for all TAs and established the framework for negotiating. When the university resisted union efforts to bargain for wages and bring unfair labor practice charges (legal rights for all other state employees), the TAA appealed to the Wisconsin Employment Relations Commission. But the WERC refused to support the TAA on the grounds that TAs were "unclassified" state employees and not within their jurisdiction. This lack of a clear legal status always loomed over TAA bargaining strategy in the 1970s and early 1980s. Not until 1985 did the Wisconsin legislature pass a law guaranteeing TAs the same bargaining rights enjoyed by other state employees.

A great deal of union work in those years took the form of defensive struggles against university efforts to take back what had been won in 1970. The defensive nature of our struggle, as well as the problematic gap between leadership and membership, became much clearer to me in 1975–76 when I served as a member of the TAA bargaining committee for the union's fourth contract. Working with the more experienced TAA negotiators and going head-to-head with UW administrators was an empowering experience, and it gave me a valuable political education into the inner workings of the modern American university. It was also fun. Veteran TAA negotiators like Henry Haslach often made our administration counterparts squirm by calmly articulating contract proposals that directly challenged their most cherished assumptions about how UW ought to be run.

We focused on four major issues that year: maintaining limits on class-section size and pressing for meaningful educational planning by TAs and students; a cost-of-living wage escalator; enforcing the right to arbitrate all grievances; and public access to university budget and instructional reports. But in each case we were responding to university "take backs" or its failure to abide by contract provisions. That fall the university had unilaterally raised the class-size average from nineteen to twenty-one students per section, to be averaged departmentally rather than by course. Consequently, some courses were overloaded to twenty-five or more students per section. To resist the drift toward larger classes, we also proposed that undergraduates in a lecture course presently taught without small-group discussion sections have the right to evaluate that course and determine whether discussion sections ought to be integrated into it. On wages, we looked to recover the nearly 20 percent drop in our real wages over the previous three years. But as always, the university insisted it had no authority to bargain over salary. We reiterated our belief that any matter bearing on TAA-university relationships, whether explicitly covered in the contract or not, should be subject to the grievance procedure, including final arbitration by a neutral third party. Finally, since accurate economic and enrollment data were crucial to formulating our positions, we demanded access to university budget and instructional report computer tapes at cost.

Our strategy that year reflected a perhaps inevitable gulf between union activists and large parts of the rank and file. We sometimes felt we were fighting a two-front war, one with the university and one with our own members. A strike vote held in October 1975, designed to give the bargaining committee more leverage, failed. As negotiations dragged into the spring semester, the TAA adopted a new strategy — a plan for a two-day work stoppage in early April, followed by a week of negotiations and a full-scale strike if UW remained intransigent. We conducted a quiet but extensive organizing campaign, and the combination work stoppage/strike vote passed. We began to make extensive preparations for the work stoppage: planning picketing sites, setting up picket squads, and designating captains; doing liaison work with other unions on and off campus; getting our message out to the media. Undergraduates formed their own support group, Students for Quality Education, which attracted hundreds to our cause.

The afternoon before the work stoppage was to begin, the university agreed to restore the old class-size limits — but only if no work stoppage occurred. This last-minute tactic created a big problem for the union in that TAA leadership could now expect to be sharply criticized no matter what decision we made. We decided to hold a rush general membership meeting to let the rank and file decide, and after hundreds of phone calls, an overflow crowd of TAs met that night and voted by well over two-thirds to go ahead with the work stoppage. This was partly a protest against UW bargaining tactics and partly a reminder that wages, a strong grievance procedure, and educational quality remained important concerns to many TAs.

The two-day work stoppage itself went off very smoothly, and it helped politicize TAs and undergraduate students. Our picket lines kept many thousands of students (though few faculty) out of classes. TAA leaflets, media coverage, and two large noonday rallies in front of Memorial Library made our specific issues, as well as our larger critique of how the university operated, more public than ever. As one of several speakers who addressed these spirited demonstrations, I tried to emphasize how TAA contract demands were part of larger efforts being waged on behalf of improved education, a fairer shake for all UW employees, and a more open university. In retrospect, the variety of non-TAA support speakers reflected our commitment to coalition building. These included Peter Camejo, Socialist Workers Party candidate for president, Finley C. Campbell, a professor of Afro-American Studies recently denied tenure, and an official from the Wisconsin AFL-CIO.

At first, the university responded to the work stoppage by refusing to bargain. TAs received various threats — some in writing — from supervising professors, department chairs, and deans. The night before the scheduled strike, university negotiators made some concessions. Their last offer on class size was nineteen per section, but averaged by department rather than by course. This was a significant retreat from the 1970 contract because most departments had upper-level courses with small enrollments. At an intense, sometimes raucous, Sunday night membership meeting, TAs vigorously debated whether or not to proceed with the strike or to accept the final offer. Finally, at 1:30 a.m., the TAA accepted the university's contract offer by a vote of 212 to 162.

At the time, many of us felt that the week's delay before the strike gave the administration the opportunity to intimidate TAs effectively. But in retrospect the close vote reflected real divisions within the union. Most of the officers, shop stewards, and other TAA activists felt the membership had sold out the leadership. Yet when most TAs faced the choice of risking their professional futures with what promised to be a long and nasty strike, they pulled back. Despite some demoralization and bitterness over the failure to strike for the old class-size language, the year's activities revitalized the TAA. The next fall several TAA affiliates sponsored union seminars to discuss effective teaching methods. The TAA strongly supported strikes by the Memorial Union Labor Organization and the Canteen Vending Machine workers. A group of women TAs organized a feminist caucus and held a forum on problems facing women at UW. Many grievances were filed and the majority were won, including several cases taken to arbitration.

In a yellowing copy of the April 13, 1976, *Daily Cardinal,* I find myself quoted in the aftermath. "The TAA is now split down the middle in terms of what a union is and should do. Half of the members have a primary goal of improving quality education, but half are committed to becoming professionals and fitting into the system as it is now." Twenty years later I now recognize that I was describing a split within myself. I was lucky enough to survive the academic job crisis that has been more or less permanent since 1970. I left Madison in 1976, and after several years of scuffling, I completed my doctorate in history in 1979. There followed a stint driving a taxi in New York City, a brief (though not brief enough) time at a Wall Street investment banking house, and a research job in public television. I landed on my feet in a tenure-track job at Mount Holyoke College, where I have taught American history since 1981.

But I have continued to draw on my TAA experiences to improve and make sense of my situation. In the mid-1980s I was part of a group of Mount Holyoke faculty who revived a long-dormant chapter of the American Association of University Professors, and I served as president of our local chapter. Like most AAUP chapters, ours does not engage in collective bargaining, nor is it ever likely to. And, to be sure, the structural differences between large state universities and small, private, liberal arts colleges are enormous. Yet our success in revitalizing the AAUP owed a great deal to our commitment to balancing bread-and-butter faculty needs with the goals of quality education and making our college more socially responsible. We were able to get well over half the faculty to join AAUP by insisting that improving our material lot didn't mean abandoning our students or other college employees.

In lieu of collective bargaining, our AAUP chapter has had to rely on a kind of unofficial negotiating posture, playing the "bad cop" in college politics. We have won significant improvements in salary, sabbatical pay, parental leave, and day care. We have challenged the spiraling growth of administrative salaries and positions that drain more money from the instructional budget, along with the creeping reliance on corporate consultants and "management speak" in the college's public life. We have pursued alliances with campus blue-collar and clerical employees. We have tried to honestly address the disturbing connection between our improved sabbaticals and the college's increasing reliance upon temporary and part-time faculty. In 1989, when three hundred striking NYNEX workers visited Mount Holyoke to picket our president, a member of the NYNEX board of directors, many of us joined them and engaged in other support work as well. Perhaps most importantly, we have tried to make AAUP an alternative space for the kind of free and open discussion that is largely impossible in the paternalistic atmosphere of faculty meetings and college committees.

The recent upsurge in TA organizing at schools like Yale and Michigan has brought renewed attention to one of the dirty little secrets of the modern American university: it cannot function without the exploitation of cheap graduate student labor. Graduate students have always constituted a permanently transient workforce — they are people on their way somewhere else. It is now clear that this description fits a steadily growing number of Ph.D.'s and faculty as well. As Cary Nelson has forcefully argued, "The problem with graduate study now — in a long term environment where jobs for new Ph.D.'s are the exception rather than the rule — is that apprenticeship has turned into exploitation."[2] Ironically, the steadily worsening academic job crisis, especially in the humanities and social sciences, and the larger employment insecurity faced by white-collar professionals, has made adherence to the ideology of professionalism even stronger. Stubborn faith that one can make it through becomes an emotional lifeboat amid the shipwrecks of careers and lives dashed on the rocks of a job market that shows little sign of improving.

TA unions — and faculty unions — offer alternatives to the political dead end of individualism. Unions alone, of course, cannot solve the job crisis. But they do offer one important avenue for graduate students — and faculty — to improve their material situations and working conditions, to fight for a more democratic university, to pursue educational innovation, and to combat the isolation and alienation that can paralyze us. They also create concrete opportunities for connecting to larger political struggles both within and outside universities and for collectively addressing the worsening conditions that mark American higher education. The prospect of a permanently oversupplied academic job market may open new opportunities for faculty organizing as well. Now more than ever, teachers unions of all kinds have a special obligation to combine traditional bread-and-butter concerns with attention to the political and moral crises facing higher education and the larger society. That special obligation was the source of the TAA's success, and it remains its most enduring legacy.

NOTES

1. My deep thanks to my old comrade and ex-TAA president Dexter Arnold for talking through TAA history with me and for making available a number of old TAA pamphlets and documents from his files. In the meantime, I have cobbled together parts of the TAA's history from several published articles and TAA pamphlets. The most important of these are: Andrew Hamilton, "Wisconsin: Teaching Assistants' Strike Ends in Contract Signing," *Science* 168 (April 17, 1970): 345–49; Steven Zorn, "Unions on Campus," in *Academic Supermarkets,* ed. Philip Altbach et al. (San Francisco, 1971), 288–302; TAA, *Handbook* (Madison, Wis., 1974); TAA, "Shut It Down" (Madison, Wis., 1975); TAA, "Strike and Work Stoppage" (Madison, Wis., 1976); TAA, "Early History of the TAA" (Madison, Wis., n.d.).

2. Cary Nelson, "Lessons from the Job Wars: What Is to Be Done?" *Academe* 81 (November–December 1995): 18. In the same issue see also Michael Bérubé, "Standard Deviation: Skyrocketing Job Requirements Inflame Political Tensions," and Stephen Watt, "The Human Costs of Graduate Education; or, The Need to Get Practical." Nelson's essay has since been revised and expanded in his *Manifesto of a Tenured Radical* (New York: New York University Press, 1997). Together, these pieces offer the most illuminating and radical analysis of the current academic job crisis that I have seen anywhere.

Chapter 11
On Apprentices and Company Towns

Stephen Watt

> *Yale's 721 teaching assistants are already part of the Information Age's new aristocracy. . . . At Yale, they will begin building lifelong networks of other influential people, meet brilliant scholars of the opposite sex, marry, have brilliant children and generally live the life of Riley. Talk about the haves and the have-nots: Yale's teaching assistants are among the most pampered people in America.*

Rhetoricians have long advised writers not to exert their discursive muscles on puny "straw men"; in the macho world of argumentation, so the notion goes, it is advisable either to take on the "big boys" or to employ another strategy. My only defense for ignoring this sound counsel is that the language of the above editorial from the *Omaha World-Herald* (January 13, 1996) was simply too irresistible. Of course, one need not be a Cornhusker to read such deprecations of the Yale GESO members who participated in the grade strike. Peter Brooks's now infamous designation of Yale graduate students as "among the blessed of the earth" has graced the pages of both the *New York Times* and the April 1996 issue of *Lingua Franca,* among other places; and caricatures of graduate students as, alternatively, puling infants and unprincipled hipsters — all berets, sunglasses, and attitudes — have been splayed across the pages of the university's undergraduate newspaper, the *Yale Herald* (see figs. 28 and 29). As several editorialists at the *Herald* emphasized, many undergraduates viewed themselves as victims of selfish TAs who not only "betrayed" them but

Figure 28. Cartoon by Eleanor Kung, *Yale Herald,* January 19, 1996

also, at the "height of their extremism and arrogance," perpetrated acts of sheer "academic terrorism."[1]

In both Omaha and New Haven, as these brief passages suggest, graduate student efforts to ameliorate their working conditions are frequently contextualized with broader ideological issues — or contained within larger ideological fantasies. The sappy heterosexist narrative in the editorial in the *Omaha World-Herald,* for example, with its Hollywood ending of happy marriage and prodigious offspring, *almost* implies a parodic intention; its author's more malignant politics, however, surface shortly after the silliness I have already quoted. For near the end of this polemic, he (mis)identifies a "nervous and scared" Nilanjana Dasgupta, an In-

Figure 29. Cartoon by Vaughan Greer, *Yale Herald*, January 19, 1996

dian graduate student who, making $9,940 a year (*and* getting summers "off"!), deserves whatever punishment is meted out for refusing to submit final grades. After all, this editorialist notes, a salary of nearly $10,000 is "probably" some "25 times the average annual income in India"; she should be more grateful, and the Yale administration should reconsider whether such graduate student employees are "capable of thinking clearly enough to be entrusted to teach."[2] Having suffered vaguely defined "run-ins" with "postmodernist concerns about race and sex in humanities programs," Patrick Stephenson, a columnist in the *Yale Herald,* reached a similar conclusion about the targeting of certain GESO members of color for disciplinary action. The allegation that "sexism, racism, and xenophobia are tools for union-busting" seems "ludicrous," Stephenson observes, "to anyone familiar with Yale's desperate sensibilities about sex and race." "Enough is enough," and this means enough of the grade strike, the "propaganda" it produced, and what Stephenson regards as its ill-conceived "rhetoric of class."[3]

Even those Yale faculty *un*sympathetic to the GESO strike must agree that this sort of discourse, laden with misconceptions about the economics of higher education and, in the latter case, marked by an inability to distinguish acts of anonymous terrorism from the quite public tactics of a labor strike, is outrageous — and rather frightening. Yet the letters addressed in January 1996 by a cadre of Yale faculty and administrators to the Modern Language Association (MLA) in response to its resolution of censure, albeit less xenophobic and paranoid, seem at times only slightly more civil.[4] Striking TAs, "in training, after all, to occupy professional positions," are, among other evils, "unprofessional," "unethical," and "dishonest" (Margaret Homans); they are abusive of the "privilege" of teaching at Yale, and some may even engage in "far-fetched and questionable personal behavior" (Annabel Patterson), whatever that might be. But terrorists or crybabies? Hardly. In a coauthored letter to the MLA, Yale administrators Richard C. Levin, Alison Richard, Thomas Appelquist, and Richard Brodhead, several of whom have authored their own deprecations of graduate students who participated in the strike, "freely acknowledge that there are issues of legitimate concern to graduate students" and promise their commitment to engage them seriously.[5]

Other than these unseemly character assassinations of students by Yale's faculty, which ought to concern *someone,* what are the "issues of legitimate concern" adverted to in this letter? This isn't made clear, but by now most everyone following this story is aware of GESO "demands," a term that in her letter Patterson finds particularly objectionable: a two-thousand-dollar raise (which would bring the salaries of most TAs in the humanities to between $11,500 and $12,000), affordable health insurance, tuition waivers for all TAs, smaller section sizes, more formal teacher training, a more diverse university, and so on.[6] After reading this list and talking to graduate students at Yale, Indiana, Iowa, Florida, UCLA, Tennessee, and other campuses, I realized what by now must be obvious to most people (writers at the *Omaha World-Herald* and George Will wanna-bees at the *Yale Herald* excluded):[7] whatever local differences obtain, graduate employees across the country are concerned about both their economic survival and their physical and psychical well-being (and, in some cases, that of their children).[8] And, contrary to Stephenson's complaint, such concerns are *precisely about class,* for while the average full professor at Yale earns some ninety thousand dollars a year (*New York Times,* January 17, 1996, B6), many graduate students are struggling to make ends meet and accruing unprecedented levels of debt in the process. Given the uncertainty of the job market, hence the uncertainty of any ability to repay the loans they are taking, most graduate employees want to earn enough to pay the bills and to purchase adequate medical coverage. Period. That Yale TAs teach less than many of their peers at other institutions is as true as it is irrelevant, as many of them are borrowing upward of twenty thousand dollars to complete their degrees (the national average of debt carried by those graduate students who borrow presently exceeds thirty thousand dollars).[9] No one could lead the "life of Riley," at least as I imagine it, on a minimum-wage salary and the prospect of ten years of loan repayment upon graduation, job or not.

I might also point out that at least insofar as the history of mass culture is concerned, *The Life of Riley* exercised an appeal to class mobility in post–World War II America that is disappearing in today's post-Fordist economy. That is to say, in the 1950s, when William Bendix revived his former radio role as the bumbling, blue-collar, slightly Neolithic Chester Riley for television audiences, he also embodied one fundamental element of the American dream: the possibility of moving up the socioeconomic scale, in Riley's case to the security of the middle-class suburbs where life, in spite of its endless supply of minor crises, was generally quite comfortable.[10] Perhaps it is the potency of such a fantasy that induces graduate students to go into debt for what Patterson terms the "privilege" of teaching at Yale — and of pursuing the fantasy into the halls of an academy that increasingly has little room for them. The professoriat, after all, offers students a kind of cultural capital that the lovable, if insipid, Riley never enjoyed, but of course today's economic conditions are vastly different than those of the 1950s, a fact to which editorialists in Omaha and some humanities faculty in New Haven seem equally oblivious or indifferent. In today's transnational economy, as Bill Readings has recently stated, universities are being reconceptualized as "relatively autonomous consumer-oriented" corporations in which the salaries of "regular joes" (or "marys") like Riley are losing ground to inflation.[11] I shall have more to say about this latter topic in a moment.

That GESO members at Yale want more in terms of professional training and greater diversity of both student body and faculty, however, testifies to the fact that organizing efforts there and on other campuses are also the result of more than material exigency. Rather, the strike at Yale and ongoing unionization efforts at such schools as the University of Iowa illuminate the complete inadequacy or, perhaps, chicanery of institutional representations of graduate student labor (many of which are no more accurate than the sterling examples of editorial prose cited above). In this instance, the distinction between public and private institutions is more or less moot, as university administrators, eager to find terms other than "employee" to apply to TAs, attempt to essentialize through their metaphors the "as if," plural, and almost nomadic or migratory identities of graduate students.[12] Depending upon the institutional context in which they are positioned — and essentialized — graduate students are expected to perform "as if" they were students, "as if" they were faculty, "as if" they were professionals.

Worse, the indifference of many faculty to this condition helps perpetrate an institutional reality that, like the social reality Slavoj Žižek theorizes, is "in the last resort an ethical construction" comprised of largely inadequate "as if" depictions of graduate teachers as apprentices, trainees, and so on.[13] Administrators, of course, want to view graduate students as if they were apprentices to justify the meager wages they are paid; and many faculty *need* to regard TAs as apprentices to avoid acknowledging their own complicity in the exploitative calculus of graduate student employment. Until faculty can agree about this inadequacy, very little is likely to change, and the economic status of graduate employees will continue to resemble that of migrant workers, budding "freeway faculty" engaged in the seasonal labors of higher education. And if this is so, if this analogy holds, what does this suggest about the universities in which we labor? In my view, before any intervention in this economy can be effected, we must gain a clearer purchase of the language used to describe it, not allowing ourselves to be co-opted by terminologies that are contrived for the benefit of corporate managers, not of faculty or graduate students. I want to suggest that we begin with the concept of apprenticeship, a favorite of Yale's president Levin, regarding it as one of several invidious "metaphors we live by" and were better rid of.[14] Like most metaphors, "apprenticeship" provides a "systematicity that allows us to comprehend one aspect of a concept in terms of another," in this case inviting us to perceive graduate students either as "professionals in training," something like beginning workers in today's skilled trades, or the "prentyses" trained by masters in medieval guilds.[15] But will either comparison hold up? And at what conceptual cost?

If administrators really thought through the concept of apprenticeship, of its frequently riotous and turbulent history, they would rush to disclaim it. In a January 1996 letter to "Friends and Graduates of Yale," for example, after outlining the "immediate challenges" of negotiating with clerical and technical employees — the grade strike effectively quashed, graduate employment presumably was rendered "less immediate" — Levin turns to the matter of graduate funding:

> Although our financial support for graduate students is generous, graduate student life could be improved. . . . But we remain convinced that collective bargaining would fundamentally alter the teacher-student relationship, during the course of which a graduate student develops into a professional colleague. We believe that graduate students are apprentice teachers and scholars, and the teaching they perform is part of their training.

Levin's counterparts at such institutions as UCLA make similar assertions but typically fail to delineate precisely what "part" teaching plays in a doctoral student's training. *The Ohio State University Graduate School 1995–1996 Handbook* unintentionally advances at least one possible answer:

> A graduate student's principal objective is to earn a graduate degree. Appointment as a GA [Graduate Associate] contributes to that objective by providing an apprenticeship. This apprenticeship complements formal instruction and gives the student practical, personal experience that can be gained only by performing instructional, research, or administrative activities.[16]

In this formulation, teaching merely supplements a graduate student's formal course of study; it is something added to it to bring it to perfection or completion. Indeed, only in the past two decades or so have beginning faculty been expected to bring a diverse repertoire of teaching experiences or, for that matter, completed doctoral degrees, to their first jobs. In fine, and regardless of the quality of mentoring and pedagogical instruction a graduate student receives, the Ohio State handbook clarifies the secondary role teaching plays in the graduate curriculum, begging the question of exactly how long a TA profits by the experience. When does teaching simply become a job?

Since the early Middle Ages, "apprenticeship" has meant various things, but an engagement in activities secondary or subordinate to another enterprise is not one of them. This history is by no means irrelevant, as it is frequently invoked in discussions of the labors of faculty and graduate students in the contemporary university. In her detailed account both of the recent grade strike and of previous labor actions at Yale, for example, Cynthia Young alleges that faculty and administrators maintain the "fallacy of an antiquated guild system" to defend the idea that "graduate students function as apprentices whose primary compensation is the on-site training they receive."[17] In their critique of the concept, Cary Nelson and Michael Bérubé make a similar indictment, linking its failure to the present job crisis:

> For many years graduate students served not only as colleagues of lesser status but also as apprentices. The economic tradition in which "apprentices" are underpaid is older than capitalism itself; but throughout its historical transformations, the apprentice tradition typically held out eventual full-time employment with better working conditions as its delayed compensation.[18]

Apprenticeship, though, assumes — or, rather, once *assumed* — the existence of a beneficent guild that "stood like a loving mother, providing and . . . car[ing] for her children even after death."[19] Although many would bridle at this familial metaphor, which in Lucy Toulmin Smith's account was rendered obsolete by the middle of the fourteenth century, a guild of scholars seems preferable to businesses like the Yale Corporation, the phrase typically used when earnings on Yale's vast endowment are announced.[20]

But as Smith and, more recently, Paul Strohm have shown, such visions of a guild of scholars are largely utopian (in the most uncritical and nostalgic sense), for the "harmonious relations" enjoyed by early craft guilds in England had almost certainly dissipated by the plague year of 1348 when the "consequent depopulation" brought "the opposition between the interests of the working-class and the employers for the first time . . . to a crisis."[21] Much the same is true of the relationship between apprentices and "maisters," as readers of Chaucer's "The Cook's Tale" might recall — according to the story, Perkyn Revelour, a "prentys" in the "craft of vitaillers," was given "his leve" when "he were ny out of his prentishood." Strohm regards Perkyn's name as significant, as "the imagery of revelry carried a heavy symbolic freight in the later fourteenth century." In this reading, Strohm argues that by the 1381 peasant rising, apprentices constituted a "volatile grouping," one more subversive of authority than the "disport" (singing and dancing) for which the Cook's Perkyn is famous: "Apprentices, together with journeymen and others," Strohm contends, "may be assumed to have been on the Westminster chronicler's mind when he suggested that the London officials were paralyzed" with the fear that they might join rebels and, hence, the city "would be lost."[22]

It is important to recognize, I think, that in this chapter in the chronicle of apprenticeship, "journeymen" joined their younger colleagues in revolt, presumably because they enjoyed more interests in common with them than with their "masters" or "employers." Such, quite obviously, was not the case between striking graduate student employees and faculty at Yale during the grade strike, nor has it been in recent court rulings.[23] In *N.L.R.B. v. Yeshiva University* (U.S. 1980), for example, the Supreme Court denied a National Labor Relations Board petition to enforce its order giving faculty the right to bargain collectively at Yeshiva. Justice Lewis Powell, speaking for the 5–4 majority, argued that because faculty "exercised supervisory and managerial functions," they were excluded from "the category of employees" and thus not entitled to the benefits of collective bargaining. Writing the dissenting opinion, Justice William Brennan distinguished between medieval and modern institutions:

> The Court's conclusion that the faculty's professional interests are indistinguishable from those of the administration is bottomed on an idealized model of collegial space that is the vestige of the great medieval university. But the university of today bears little resemblance to the "community of scholars" of yesteryear. Education has become "big business," and the task of administering the university enterprise has been transferred from the faculty to an autonomous administration. (100 S.Ct. 856 [1980]: 872–73)

This ruling defines faculty not as professional employees, a designation made available by the National Labor Relations Act, and not as mentors or journeymen, but as supervisors so "aligned with management" as to be indistinguishable from it. This is hardly surprising given the terms of this discussion: if universities are now corporations, not communities of scholars, and if graduate students really aren't apprentices in any meaningful sense, how do faculty function as journeymen? This question would seem particularly difficult for the growing ranks of part-time faculty and those assistant professors at schools like Yale with little or no expectation of tenure. Are these fully enfranchised members of the profession, or do they share more in common with graduate student "apprentices"? *N.L.R.B. v. Yeshiva* depicts a faculty qua manager that wields supervisory authority over students and all "academic matters" pertinent to them, and maybe this portrayal is closer to the everyday realities of today's (and tomorrow's) academy than many faculty might wish to acknowledge.

Just as there is little comparison between the compensation academic "apprentices" and faculty earn, there is scarcely any similarity between the salaries of graduate student employees and those of apprentices in the skilled trades. As I have mentioned, the ratio at Yale between the average salaries of full professors and those of advanced graduate employees in the humanities approaches nine to one ($90,000 to $9,940); the ratio between graduate associates in English and full professors at Indiana University is around seven to one; and that of graduate associates to humanities faculty of all ranks at such schools as the University of Illinois is closer to five to one.[24] Such disparities are rare in most unions with which I am familiar; moreover, the carefully calibrated systems of salary increases in most apprenticeship programs confirm one premise absent from the payment schedules of many graduate employees: namely, that as one acquires more sophisticated skills, his or her salary rises sufficiently to distinguish experienced practitioners from beginners.

In the skilled trades, an apprentice's salary typically rises in the final year of training to between 90 and 100 percent of a journeyman's salary, as is the case with both the Central Indiana Carpenters Joint Apprenticeship Training Committee in Indianapolis, which operates on behalf of several locals, and the apprentice program of UA Local #136 Plumbers and Pipefitters in Bloomington, Indiana, where I live (see table 1).

Table 1
Percentage of Full Salary Received in Each Year of Apprenticeship

	Central Indiana Carpenters	*Local 136 Plumbers*
Year 1:	45% (of $19.70/hr.=$8.86)	40% ($21.68/hr.=$8.67)
Year 2:	65%	50%
Year 3:	75%	60%
Year 4:	85%	75%
Year 5:	100%	90%
Journeyman	($19.70/hr.)	($21.68/hr.)

In addition, the pension contributions and insurance coverage of participants in these programs closely parallel those of journeymen. As in most unions, all members of UA 136 pay monthly dues ($16) and a 3 percent work assessment (for first-year apprentices working the expected two thousand hours, this comes to approximately $520.20). Many unions also deduct a nominal amount from an apprentice's paycheck to pay for the instructional program (22 cents per hour in the carpenters' program outlined above, for instance).[25]

By contrast, the salaries of most graduate student teachers increase very little during the years they spend as TAs, typically less than one thousand dollars from first year to last, a disturbing trend that further corroborates the premise of the Ohio State graduate handbook: what graduate students learn as teachers only supplements their formal instruction. And clearly the learning curve diminishes as a graduate student teaches the same small cluster of courses for the umpteenth time. Yet, as I have mentioned, at many institutions very minimal increases in salary distinguish a TA on his or her first day in the classroom from one walking in after as many as four or five *years* of teaching. At the University of Tennessee–Knoxville, for example, graduate students in several humanities departments receive more or less the same salary regardless of teaching experience; the most advanced graduate students in English at Indiana earn about nine hundred dollars per year more than a beginner; and at the University of Florida senior graduate employees in English receive about three hundred dollars per course more than their newest colleagues (this varies by department and is based on .50 FTE [full-time equivalent position]). If students really learned their crafts incrementally over a period of time — as apprentices in the skilled trades do — then it would seem to follow that their salaries would increase *significantly* as they refined the skills necessary to teach independently. This generally isn't the case.

A more problematic analogy exists between graduate student employment and apprenticeship in terms of the period of time one occupies such a status. That is to say, apprenticeships in the trades are carefully defined, measured either in years or hours of paid "on the job training."[26] As Cynthia Young discusses in her essay, Yale attempted in 1989–90 to shorten the time needed to complete a Ph.D. by restructuring its financial support and sharply delimiting the period of funding. Things apparently didn't work out so well. According to the plan that outlined this process, known locally as the Kagan-Pollitt plan, dissertation fellowships, in themselves desirable funding instruments, were to be made more widely available at the same time that a six-year rule was enforced (i.e., no support after the sixth year). In Young's view, the plan might have indeed sped up Ph.D. production, but it did not "facilitate doctoral work" because these fellowships came at the expense of the teaching budget and TAs lost their jobs.[27] This problem is not unique to New Haven, for as the American Research Council's *Research-Doctorate Programs in the United States: Continuity and Change* (1995) makes abundantly clear, virtually no program in the humanities graduates *even half* of its students in less than seven years. In English, only Princeton has a figure of less than seven years in the statistic "median years to degree": half of Princeton's Ph.D.'s graduate in less than 6.8 years; half take longer. Yale is 7.6 years; California–Berkeley 10.1 years; the University of Chicago 12.1 years; and so on. Graduate students in such fields as German and comparative literature generally take even longer.[28] This is not to suggest that students cannot graduate in, say, six years; of course, many do. But a huge number do not, which begs the larger question of what rate of production should obtain in the present market (and, yes, such an allusion to supply and demand, as if graduate students were mere products to be manufactured, is disturbing).

Obviously, this topic becomes much more pressing when the supply of jobs is consistent, one reason why time to degree is such an important factor in William G. Bowen and Neil L. Rudenstine's *In Pursuit of the Ph.D.* (1992), which begins with the assumption that colleges and universities will experience "severe staffing problems by the end of the 1990s."[29] By "staffing problems," Bowen and Rudenstine clearly meant difficulties finding qualified doctoral-holders in the humanities, business, and physical and social sciences to fill tenure-track positions vacated by an aging professoriat and necessitated by a larger body of incoming freshmen. But even starting from this prediction, one especially inaccurate insofar as traditional humanities disciplines are concerned, Bowen and Rudenstine reject what they term the "British model" of a "term-limit" degree, which unrealistic funding programs implement in de facto fashion, as an extreme alternative that should not be considered unless all "other efforts to improve outcomes" (i.e., get students through doctoral programs more expeditiously) "fail."[30] Have such efforts failed? And have we reached a point where we as faculty can no longer — *should* no longer — participate silently in an institutional exploitation that even tried-and-true metaphors like apprenticeship can no longer conceal?

Of course, to return to Nelson and Bérubé's point, the job market and the ratio of journeymen to apprentices also wrench the metaphor completely out of the orbit of rationality. Given not just a generally disastrous job market but Yale's unremarkable placement rate as reported in numerous accounts of the grade strike,[31] it is hardly surprising that high on the list of strikers' "demands" — there's that word again — is more formalized "teacher training."

(One should always approach placement statistics with caution, as often the data tell only part of a story: How many job-seekers participated fully in the process? Did students accept all the jobs they were offered? What jobs "counted" *as jobs* in the first place? But I shall assume that student demands for teacher training reflect a sense that low placement rates are related in part to inadequate teaching experience and preparation.) Herein resides the irony that anyone who has ever been a TA must surely have pondered at some point: while universities rationalize low wages by underscoring the vocational training graduate students receive, many of these same graduate students recognize that they really don't receive adequate preparation as future teachers. The quality of teacher training varies from school to school: in English departments, typically, this ranges from the one-week orientation/department picnic or cocktail hours held just before classes begin to semester-long "proseminars" in the teaching of writing or literature. In addition, many programs employ experienced graduate students as consultants to advise their younger colleagues. By contrast, as I have indicated, labor unions provide highly structured learning programs made possible in part by the comparatively large number of journeymen to apprentices. That is, on most union sites the number of journeymen far exceeds that of apprentices, because a homeowner, for example, won't buy a house built, plumbed, or wired by beginners. By comparison to plumbing or electrical systems, college degrees, no matter how expensive they get, are simpler contraptions.

The inherent inadequacy of the metaphor of apprenticeship, to conclude this point, constantly emerges in the slippages in administrative discourse whenever the topic of graduate student teaching is concerned. So, in a letter of February 20, 1996, responding to one of my colleagues' protests over Yale's handling of the strike, Levin remarks:

> We regard the withholding of grades, however motivated, as an inappropriate action *for a teacher.* When one person takes on the power to evaluate another person's work, he or she takes on the responsibility to judge the performance fairly, objectively, and in a timely manner, and not to let external considerations interfere with the evaluation process. *That one group of students chose to penalize another group of students in furtherance of its own aims lent additional inappropriateness to this action.*[32] [my emphasis]

Bracketing for the moment the questionable issue of some Yale faculty's referring to the strike in letters of recommendation (participating in a strike is somehow intrinsic to academic "performance" and thus part of a "fairly" and "objectively" delineated evaluation?), the strategy of this rejoinder seems clear: graduate students are teachers when the administration wants them to be and students when it is more convenient to regard them as such. Hence, the "penalizing" of undergraduates, in Levin's rhetoric, is all the more egregious because it is caused by fellow students. One thing, though, that students clearly aren't is apprentices. Universities do not compensate graduate students as if they were indeed involved in an ongoing training *necessary* for independent teaching, and in some cases they do not even encourage students to regard teaching as sufficiently valuable to constitute the focus of their endeavors. So what are they? And what are the institutions at which they labor, literally and metaphorically, remembering that we "live by" the latter as much as we inhabit or live in the former?

Life, of course, is lived not only within the vehicles of dilapidated metaphors but also in the apartments, dormitories, and houses of college towns and big cities. And while universities in Boston, New York, Los Angeles, and other major metropolitan areas might be ill described by the metaphor I shall develop below, I wondered while talking to graduate students how apt an analogy between the contemporary (or, as Bill Readings prefers, "posthistorical") university and "company towns" might be. In the law, in such cases as *Illinois Migrant Council v. Campbell Soup Company* (U.S. Dist. Ct. 1977), a "company town" is defined as a "community organized on private property by a private enterprise and so used that it becomes the functional equivalent of a municipality, so that, when a 'company town' exists, infringement of First Amendment Rights by those who administer town functions constitutes 'state action' " (438 *F. Supp.* 222, 1977). In this case, agents and employees of the Illinois Migrant Council, a nonprofit corporation funded in part by the federal government and devoted to adult education, especially English language instruction, and health services, were denied access to a community owned by Campbell and filed a petition for relief. Universities, of course, aren't all privately owned, nor do they necessarily form the "functional equivalent" of municipalities. But like company towns, today's agricultural ones and yesterday's coal mining communities, they provide workers not merely with employment but with many of the necessities of everyday life. Mushroom pickers at Campbell's Prince Crossing Farm near West Chicago are provided with "houses in which to live, a store from which they purchase company products, a cafeteria [that serves three meals a day if desired], and a recreational area within a multi-use building" (226). Universities provide these as well. And unlike other kinds of employment, that in company towns — and many universities — brings everyday or private life squarely within the ambit of the employer; unlike most other kinds of employment, that in company towns — and universities — entails both compensation for labor performed and *repayment* to the employer for services provided.

For the purposes of this essay, the quality of services employers like Campbell and American universities afford their employees is not at issue; the cost of those services or the amount of repayment required of graduate student employees — and coal miners and field-workers — is. For what has changed since I began graduate school in the early 1970s is that universities, like the one-company mining towns and the produce industry that often exploit their labor force, *knowingly* compensate graduate employees at a level inadequate for many to live on without slipping into debt. For this reason, the metaphor of the company town and its infamous "company store," as described by John Mellor in his study of Cape Breton coal miners earlier in the century, might be more accurate than comparisons of graduate employees to apprentices. Consider the similarity of economies:

> At the end of every week, [miners] received their pitifully small wages along with an account known as a "Bob-tailed Sheet," which showed the total amount of deductions for rent, coal, light, water, doctor, hospital, church, blasting powder, and company store purchases of food and dry goods. More often than not, they were left with little or no wages after deductions, especially when employed on short time with only two or three days' work each week.[33]

Central to this economy and the miners' lives was the company store, which, while often providing quality goods and open lines of credit, led miners into debt that effectively bound them to the company, at times for life. As Mellor explains, miners who organized to protest these conditions were fired and, at times, blacklisted to ensure that they would never cause trouble again. This generation of graduate students understands these economic and institutional realities all too well.

Because salaries of graduate employees have not kept pace with inflation, it is now almost impossible for many student-employees to begin graduate school the way I did in the early 1970s. To anyone familiar with the 1996 congressional debates over raising the minimum wage from $4.25 to $5.05 per hour, my hypothesis will be totally unsurprising: at present, the minimum wage of eighty-five hundred dollars per year, a figure comparable to what many graduate students earn, is at a forty-year low when adjusted for inflation. In 1973, a minimum-wage earner's salary of under two dollars per hour was worth almost six dollars when adjusted for inflation, or nearly 50 percent more than these workers earned in 1996 when making $4.25.[34] Hence, the tuition scholarship and $278 I brought home each month for teaching two courses per semester, too much teaching for a brand new M.A. student, paid for all of my living expenses — such as they were. Lacking both a car and any semblance of cooking skills, I needed to live on campus, so I moved into a single, cinder-block, ten- by fourteen-foot dormitory room with all meals provided at a nearby cafeteria. In those days, needless to say, personal computers didn't exist (an old manual typewriter and a gallon of liquid paper were the requisite technology); I didn't own a television; and new graduate students felt no pressure to run up their credit cards to attend conferences halfway across the country (which I did in later years). A room, shower down the hall, television lounge, and cafeteria — these were all I needed, and $278 easily paid for them. This stipend left enough to buy books or the occasional pair of jeans, to go to the theater and cinema, and to phone home on Sundays, calling collect. The salaries teaching assistants made then might not have allowed them a lavish lifestyle, but neither in most cases did it necessitate their borrowing much money.

Most students today could not lead this "life of Riley" — living in a dorm room, eating at the cafeteria, and riding their bicycles whenever they needed transportation — without borrowing money or bringing funds with them into graduate school. Graduate students in English at Indiana, for example, earn approximately $875 per month (ten-month contract), netting $750 after federal and state taxes are deducted. To live in a single dormitory room like the one I occupied, students pay between $3,005 and $3,481 for the school year and between $1,728 and $2,344 for meals (depending on type of plan). Taking figures for the cheapest room and best meal package (nineteen meals per week), my choices in the 1970s, a student's expense for the academic year would be $5,349, leaving about $2100 from the stipend for expenses. And these begin right at registration. A graduate student employee at .50 FTE receives a tuition scholarship worth thirty hours per year, but must pay $18.66 in fees for each hour taken. If a student takes full advantage of the tuition scholarship, then, taking twelve hours per semester and six research hours or additional course work in the summer, the cost would be $559.80. That leaves a graduate student employee around $1500 for the rest of the year. And then there are technology fees, student activity fees, student health fees, and so on, not to mention transportation, telephone, books, clothing, computer costs, and the enormous cost of merely looking for a job for those who survive this process. And this list doesn't even include the big-ticket item on many graduate employees' budgets: health insurance.

Like the owners of company towns, universities already know before a graduate student signs on the dotted line that such stipends are inadequate. The Indiana University Office of Student Financial Assistance estimated that for 1995–96 a graduate student living on campus needed at least $9,052; off campus, the figure rises slightly to $9,292. Yet most stipends in the humanities fall short of both figures. As reported in the *New York Times* (January 17, 1996), Yale administrators like Thomas Appelquist acknowledge that although the school provides "enormous amounts of financial aid . . . , it should not be expected, and it was never promised, that we will cover all costs." In the same article, the shortfall between stipend and cost of living is calculated at some $3,000 to $4,000, so the $2,000 raise requested by Yale's GESO members seems almost modest given the university's (corporation's?) own financial analysis. Why would universities purposefully pay graduate student employees less than a living wage? For the same reason, perhaps, that in her letter to the MLA Annabel Patterson objects to the term "living wage" in the first place: because Yale provides significant fellowship support to its students, they really "perform no service" at such times and thus aren't working in the first place? Fellowships, though, aren't awarded out of the goodness of a university's corporate heart, and it is disingenuous in the extreme to suggest that they are. Fellowships serve graduate programs as recruitment tools, pure and simple, as Patterson implies when acknowledging that not all students receive them because of the keen "competition for entrance." During the fifth year of many humanities programs, she notes, for those not on dissertation fellowships the "privilege" of teaching two courses during the year is "extended." No one could deny that Yale's fellowship support is impressive, yet the dean of the graduate school does not deny that the funding is insufficient to live on. It is precisely for this reason that the GESO grade strike at Yale was so important, for it showed with unusual clarity the harsh economic realities of graduate students enrolled in one of the nation's best-supported, most prestigious institutions. Given more time than many graduate employees to conduct their research and pursue their intellectual projects, they are also afforded the "privilege" of substandard wages and taking additional loans, just like everyone else.

And then there's the matter of insurance, which, according to Patterson, costs students $696 per year (Yale graduate students put the figure at $767). As is the case at many universities, students at Yale foot this bill for health insurance, and this includes the $1800 per year stipend a student with a dependent must pay. In the last half-dozen years or so, affordable, high-quality health insurance has been perhaps *the* most consistently sought goal of labor actions and graduate student organizations across the country. At UCLA, for example, graduate employees have won an institutional payment of an approximately $159-per-quarter insurance premium as a result of a strike at California–Berkeley in 1989. At the University of Iowa, where graduate student employees are organizing as COGS (Committee to Organize Graduate Students) with the assistance of Local 896 of the United Electrical Workers, improved health and child care are among the top priorities. (So, too, is a revision of a "bob-tailed sheet" of debits that includes the substantial deduction of tuition from employees' salaries.) As a result of organizing efforts in 1993, the university now pays $55 of the $66 per month insurance premium, but students with dependent(s) must still pay $112.20 per month, which many simply cannot afford. But in Iowa City, the cost of insurance is not the only issue; the quality of

The following table compares the UI Student Insurance Plan with the insurance available to UI faculty*, unionized state employees (including half-time clericals at UI) and unionized graduate employees at UW-Madison.

Health Care Plan Comparison

	Insurance Available to UI Students	Insurance Available to UI Professors and Professional Staff	Insurance Available to UI Merit Staff and Unionized State Employees	Insurance Available to Unionized UW-Madison Graduate Employees
	UI Student Insurance Plan	UICare	BC/BS Program II	GHC
Cost/year to employee for individual plan	$110 (Student Health Center is an additional $84/year)	$0	$0	$0
Out of Pocket Limit	No limit. Insured pays up to $1000 per hospital admission.	Insured pays no more than $1000 per year for an individual, or $1,500 for a family.	Insured pays no more than $500 per year for individual or family.	No limit, but most medically necessary procedures covered at 100%.
Pre-existing Condition Waiting Period	365 days	none	11 months	none
Available to Domestic Partner	Yes (but then pay $1138/year)	No (but other plan available)	No	No
Preventive Care				
Routine Physical Examination	Insured pays 100%	Insured pays $0	Insured pays 10%; limit 1 per year	Insured pays $0
Oral Contraceptives	Insured pays 100%	Insured pays $0	Insured pays 100%	Insured pays $4 for 3 month supply
Immunizations	Insured pays 100% ($0 children under 7 years)	Insured pays $10 per visit ($0 children under 7)	Insured pays 10%	Insured pays $0
Well Child Care (routine checkups, immunizations)	Insured pays $0 (up to 7 years old)	Insured pays 10%	Insured pays 10%	Insured pays $0

***Because faculty, state employees and UW-Madison graduate employees each have several plans to choose from, the plan thought to be the most popular one was chosen for comparison.**

Figure 30. Health care plan comparisons. Furnished by Iowa City UE Local 396-COGS

coverage for graduate students is vastly inferior to that offered faculty and unionized state employees. Even with group coverage, for example, the university plan provides no limit on "out-of-pocket" payments for student employees; hence, a single hospitalization

Vision Care				
Routine Eye & Hearing	Insured pays 100%	Insured pays $10	Insured pays 100%	Insured pays $0
Eyeglasses & Hearing Aids	Insured pays 100%	Insured pays 100%	Insured pays 100%	Insured pays 100%
Dental Care				
Routine Dental Examination & Cleaning	Insured pays 100%	Insured pays $0 (maximum annual benefit of $125)	Insured pays $0 (2 visits/year)	Insured pays $0 (2 visits/year)
Fillings and other Oral Surgery	Insured pays 100%	Insured pays 50% (maximum annual benefit of $500)	Insured pays 20%	Insured pays $0
Dental Accident Care	Insured pays $0, but 100% of follow up after 72 hours	Insured pays 10%	Insured pays 10%	Insured pays $0
Outpatient Care				
Non-Emergengy Medical Care	Insured pays $10/visit. After Blue Cross pays $500 in one year insured pays 100%	Insured pays $0	Insured pays 10% for services not covered under another category	Insured pays $0
Prescription Drugs	Insured pays 100%	Insured pays $7 or 25% whichever is greater	Insured pays 10%	Insured pays $4 generic, $8 brand name
X-ray and Lab (including routine pap smear)	Insured pays $0, but there is a max of $1000 per year	Insured pays 10%	Insured pays 10%	Insured pays $0
Chiropractor	Covered for 90 days following emergency or accident. Otherwise it is Non-Emergency Medical Care	Insured pays $10 per visit	Insured pays 10%	Insured pays $0
Physical Therapy	Covered for 90 days following emergency or accident. Otherwise it is Non-Emergency Medical Care	Insured pays 10%	Insured pays 10% after other covered services deductible	Insured pays $0
Allergy Treatments	See Non-Emergency Medical Care	Insured pays $0	Insured pays 10%	Insured pays $0

Figure 30 (continued)

could wipe a student out financially. Nor does it cover *any* portion of routine vision or dental care, the cost of eyeglasses, routine physical examinations, or check-ups for children over the age of seven (see fig. 30).

And, of course, Iowa and Yale are not exceptional cases in this regard; graduate student employees across the country want pretty much what a largely Chicana workforce wanted in 1986 and 1987 during the Watsonville, California, produce workers' strike: to "know that they can take their children to the doctor when necessary."[35] I don't offer this analogy frivolously and indeed am not the first to compare graduate student employees with workers in America's fruit and vegetable fields. Before 1980, graduate research and teaching assistants in the state of Florida, along with federal/state fruit and vegetable inspectors, were specifically exempted from the definition of "public employee" (section 447.203, Florida Statutes). In June of 1980, graduate student employees gained the status of bargaining unit represented by the UFF (United Faculty of Florida). Even so, a single student in the humanities pays a premium of $507 per year for health insurance; a graduate employee with a dependent pays $1,242 per year, all of this on a stipend of between $8,800 and $10,000. And one might say that collective bargaining in Florida still has a way to go, as graduate students in English routinely earn their salaries by teaching three courses during the academic year and one during a six-week summer term.

But for now, anyway, however imperfect, collective bargaining and graduate student insistence upon the term "employee," not "apprentice," seem far better than silence or passive endurance. In October 1994, graduate employees (GTAC) at the University of Kansas, with the assistance of the Kansas Association of Public Employees, won the title "public employee," and perhaps with it the possibility of securing something better than a benefits package that at that time contained no health insurance of any kind. Graduate student employees at the University of Tennessee similarly receive no health insurance coverage, even though many of them teach the same teaching load as faculty. In April 1996, nearly one thousand teaching assistants at the University of Michigan participated in a two-day boycott of classes, and subsequently the university announced it would raise TA salaries over the next three years by the same percentage as the average faculty salary raise in the college of arts and sciences. From any perspective, these are modest gains. But in today's company towns or, rather, posthistoricist corporations of higher learning, modest gains like the ability to take children to the doctor when they are ill or to have something left of a salary after the bob-tailed sheet is presented at the end of the month are worth struggling for. In addition to their perhaps mythic capacity for revelry and "synging," apprentices have a distinguished history of such activism.

NOTES

1. Josh Goldfoot, "Home Front," *Yale Herald,* January 19, 1996, 6.

2. "Big Labor Goes to Yale," *Omaha World-Herald,* January 13, 1996, 10.

3. Patrick Stephenson, "Bull Moose," *Yale Herald,* January 19, 1996, 7.

4. In February 1996, members of the Modern Language Association received a letter coauthored by Sandra Gilbert, president, and Phyllis Franklin, executive director, explaining difficulties inherent in the drafting of Resolution 6, a censure of the administration at Yale. The letter and copy of recent resolutions were accompanied by four letters from Yale faculty and administrators, all of which aimed either to explain the conditions of employment at Yale or, in the case of the letters from Linda Peterson and Ruth Bernard Yeazell, Annabel Patterson, and Margaret Homans, to refute specific language in the MLA Delegate Assembly's resolution, in part by impugning the motives and integrity of striking graduate students. I am quoting from these letters.

5. My point here is that it is one thing to call the strike "childish," "unconscionable," and "completely reprehensible," as Thomas Appelquist is reported to have done in the *Yale Daily News* (December 13, 1995); it is quite another to vilify one's students. It should also be noted that undergraduate columnists were not alone in relying upon analogies between the grade strike and terrorism. In the story cited above, Associate Dean Jonas Zdanys called the strike an attempt "to hold the academic process hostage," and history professor Linda Colley accused graduate students of taking "others' written work hostage."

6. Emily Eakin, "Walking the Line," *Lingua Franca* (March/April 1996): 52–60.

7. I do not wish to insinuate here that all writers in the *Yale Herald* endorse the opinions cited above. Nicholas Allen, for example, complains that the administration did everything it could to "bludgeon" GESO into ending the strike and that it, not GESO, "is injecting politics into the classroom" ("Union Bashers and GESO Critics Ruin Yale Public Image," February 2, 1996).

8. I want to thank all the graduate students who generously provided me with information: Michele Glaros (Florida); Will Murphy, Ed Fox, Sheila McDermott, Jack Musselman, and Brook Remick (Indiana); Leslie Taylor (Iowa); Johanna Frank (Ohio State); Kathy Newman (Yale); Beth Tollers (Tennessee); Mik Johnson (Kansas); and Chris Thinnes and Mike Miller (UCLA). I also want to thank Heather Riemer, UE Local 896–COGS, Iowa City; Nonie Watt, Indiana University Law Library; and Jeffrey Williams for their assistance; and Pat Brantlinger, Don Gray, and Paul Strohm for their suggestions on earlier drafts of this essay.

9. As I have discussed in "The Human Costs of Graduate Education; or, The Need to Get Practical," *Academe* 81 (November/December 1995): 30–35, graduate student debt has soared in the 1990s. At Indiana, for example, the average debt of those graduate students who borrow was $16,314 in 1992–93; in 1994–95, it was $26,798; and these numbers are clearly on the rise.

10. See Harry Castleman and Walter J. Podrazik, *Watching TV: Four Decades of American Television* (New York: McGraw-Hill, 1982), 75–78.

11. Bill Readings, *The University in Ruins* (Cambridge, Mass.: Harvard University Press, 1996), 11.

12. In *Nomadic Subjects* (New York: Columbia University Press, 1994), Rosi Braidotti describes a homeless, nomadic polyglot that in several respects resembles graduate students. For instance, Braidotti discusses the "migrant," a member of the "most economically disadvantaged groups," within the "new class stratification in contemporary Europe" (22). Are graduate students in America part of such a new class stratification, highly educated and unemployed, potentially rootless, and constantly on the move?

13. Slavoj Žižek, *The Sublime Object of Ideology* (London: Verso, 1989), 36.

14. Here I am alluding to the title of George Lakoff and Mark Johnson's *Metaphors We Live By* (Chicago: University of Chicago Press, 1980).

15. Ibid., 10.

16. "Graduate Associates," *The Ohio State University Graduate School 1995–1996 Handbook* (Columbus, 1996), 67.

17. Cynthia Young, "On Strike at Yale," *minnesota review* 45–46 (spring 1996): 178.

18. Cary Nelson and Michael Bérubé, "Introduction: A Report from the Front," in *Higher Education under Fire,* ed. Nelson and Bérubé (New York: Routledge, 1995), 20.

19. Lucy Toulmin Smith, "Introduction," in *English Gilds,* ed. Toulmin Smith (1870; reprint for the Early English Text Society, London: Oxford University Press, 1963), cxxxiii.

20. In a front-page story on July 24, 1995, the *New York Times* reported that since 1984 the Yale Corporation endowment had grown from $1.1 billion to $3.6 billion, averaging a return of 15.5 percent in each of these years. This brought the endowment to somewhere near $4.2 billion by midyear 1996.

21. Smith, "Introduction," cxlii.

22. Paul Strohm, "'Lad with Revel to Newgate': Chaucerian Narrative and Historical Meta-narrative," in *Art and Context in Late Medieval English Narrative,* ed. Robert R. Edwards (Suffolk: D. S. Brewer, 1994), 164, 166.

23. I say "striking" graduate employees here because it is important to note that not all TAs joined the strike. In *Lingua Franca,* Emily Eakin reports that of the 695 GESO members in the "months leading up to the strike," about 230 "graduate instructors in the humanities and social sciences resolved to hold back their students' grades" ("Walking," 53). Young puts the number of strikers at "approximately 250 on 2 January," which, ten days later, was reduced to about half that number. Young also reaches a conclusion similar to mine about many Yale faculty's functioning as management during the grade strike: "The faculty proved that, in order to maintain academic hierarchies, it was quite willing to be interpellated as an arm of the university administration" ("Strike" 192).

24. In "Lesson in Limbo," *New York Times,* March 31, 1996, sec. 4A, George Judson cites the average salary of an English professor at the University of Illinois as $47,500 and that of a TA as $10,336 (plus a tuition waiver).

25. My thanks to James Pittsford of Local 136 of the United Association of Journeymen and Apprentices of the Plumbing and Pipe-fitting Industry of the US

and Canada, Bloomington; and David McNeely, Coordinator of Apprenticeship Programs, Central Indiana Carpenters Unions, Indianapolis.

26. The Seattle Area Masonry Joint Apprenticeship and Training Committee, for example, stipulates six thousand hours of on-site, compensated work; Local 32 Plumbers and Pipefitters in Renton, Washington, offers a ten-thousand-hour program for plumbers, steamfitters/pipefitters, and refrigeration fitters. Information on these and other apprenticeship programs is available on LABORNET.

27. Young, "Strike," 179.

28. See Marvin L. Goldberger et al., eds., *Research-Doctorate Programs in the United States: Continuity and Change* (Washington, D.C.: National Academy Press, 1995), 257, 264, 254.

29. William G. Bowen and Neil L. Rudenstine, *In Pursuit of the Ph.D.* (Princeton, N.J.: Princeton University Press, 1992), 2.

30. Ibid., 288.

31. In her essay in *Lingua Franca,* Eakin notes that only two out of fifteen job-seekers in English found tenure-track jobs ("Walking," 57); Young claims that in 1994–95, ten humanities departments at Yale taken together placed only 27 percent of their job candidates ("Strike," 182).

32. Richard C. Levin, Letter to Milton T. Fisk, February 20, 1996.

33. John Mellor, *The Company Store: James Bryson McLachlan and the Cape Breton Coal Miners, 1900–1925* (Toronto: Doubleday, 1983), 15.

34. These and other similar figures have been publicized throughout the popular press. I have taken mine from John F. Dickerson, "Give 'Em a Raise, Bob," *Time,* April 26, 1996, 62. See also Simon Head, "The New Ruthless Economy," *New York Review of Books,* February 29, 1996, 47–52. Head notes that, as in the 1930s, the present economy is creating "more losers than winners" (52). Specifically, wage earners, "production and nonsupervisory workers" qualify for the former category; since 1973, their weekly earnings when adjusted for inflation have fallen some 18 percent. Eight out of ten Americans, according to Head, are losing in this economy (47), and this majority includes graduate students.

35. *San Francisco Examiner,* June 7, 1987, as quoted in Ana Castillo, *Massacre of the Dreamers: Essays on Xicanisma* (New York: Plume Books, 1995), 56.

Chapter 12
The Scarlet *L:* Gender and Status in Academe

James D. Sullivan

> *One American University greeted 1995 by advertising a new kind of position — a tenure-track lecturer in English, not eligible for promotion. In other words, after the probationary period, tenure would be granted but not promotion. The teaching load would be set at four courses per semester; salary is negotiable, but I was told by the chair of the search committee it would probably be in the mid-20s. Finally, to avoid embarrassing tenured faculty of higher rank, occupants of lifetime lectureships would be actively discouraged from publishing in areas other than pedagogy. I did not ask whether lecturers would have to wear a scarlet "L" on their jackets. Nor did I ask whether these positions were devised in dungeons replete with instruments of torture. To that question I already knew the answer: the jobs were crafted in the bright light of the university's new identity as corporate boardroom.*
>
> — Nelson 1995, 127

Of course, it was Hester Prynne who wore the scarlet *A* in public, not Arthur Dimmesdale. But when a comprehensive university in the Midwest advertised the job that Cary Nelson describes, I applied for it. The job offered the lowest of tenurable ranks, the lowest pay among tenure-line faculty, four lowest-level classes a semester, not only no funding for but actual discouragement of any professional development other than attendance at teaching workshops, and no chance of promotion, ever — but in the current academic job market, it's better than nothing. There should be little surprise, however, that when the hiring was done, several Hesters sewed the *L* onto their jackets, but no Arthurs.

But I wanted that job. With the twin handicaps of finishing my Ph.D. in English in the 1990s and marriage to another academic (a tenured associate professor in another department at the school in question), my job prospects were limited, most especially if I wanted to avoid a commuter marriage. I'd been doing exactly that job described above, without the job security, as a temporary full-time instructor there, on and off since I had finished my degree at a nearby state university in 1991. I knew the job; I already did it well; it would have been perfect for my family situation; and, if it would make them happy, I would call my research in literary history a hobby and never associate the university's name with my own when I published. But when this rank of lecturer was created, I found myself bumping up against two apparently contradictory truisms: (1) hierarchical structures tend to privilege men and oppress women, and (2) sexual inequality can harm men, as well as women.

The first is, of course, a commonplace in the feminist critique of patriarchy. The second may appear to have the ring of whiny, antifeminist backlash or perhaps of the men's movement yearning to break free of the constraints of modern masculinity. Well, maybe so, but it is also a strategic principle that Ruth Bader Ginsberg used in the 1970s as a kind of ethico-legal jujitsu: by bringing to court some quirky cases in which the application of biased statutes deprived a man of equal protection under the law, she made the federal judiciary take seriously the problems of legally sanctioned sexual inequality. The university decided to create an academic underclass, and they hired women to fill it. The gendered structure of this hierarchy left me out in the cold.

I am not implying, of course, that this new rank was created with the specific intention of hiring only women for it, nor am I implying any sexist intent at all on the part of anyone at the university. There is no cabal of sexist administrators designing a new way to keep women down. In fact, for several ranks directly above the new lecturers in English, women hold the administrative positions: chair of the English department, dean of arts and sciences, and provost.[1] The hiring patterns in academe simply typically reflect the hiring patterns in much of the rest of the society, with men usually overrepresented at the higher levels and women usually over-represented at the lower levels. Nationwide in 1988, across all disciplines, part-time faculty, the group with the lowest prestige and compensation of all faculty, were 67 percent women (Burns 1993, 21). In the 1994–95 school year, 59 percent of those with the rank of full-time instructor and 56.5 percent of those with the rank of full-time lecturer were women (West 1995, 27). This female majority at the lower ranks is especially striking given that, in 1994–95, only 31.6 percent of all full-time faculty are women ("Ray of Sunshine" 1995, 27). That is, at the ranks of assistant professor and higher, men hold the overwhelming majority of the jobs, and the lower ranks are mostly women; the lower the status, the more likely the school will hire a woman to fill the job. A new assistant professor will, in most cases, be a man, and a new lecturer will, in most cases, be a woman. No one at the university consciously intended to create a low-status job that would be specifically female, but when one creates a low-status job in academe, that is what one gets.

So what were the motives for creating this new rank? For a few years, the then-provost had been pushing the university senate to create these lecturer positions, but the senate had resisted. He was selling these jobs as a solution to the sticky legal problem of "temporary" full-time instructors in a couple of departments who had been rehired and (technically) fired year after year well past the time their professorial-rank colleagues would be up for tenure review. Creating these new positions, he said, would be a way to grant those employees officially the de facto tenure they already had. English did not have anyone in this situation, but the new rank was further sold as a way for English and some other departments with a large burden of freshman-level courses to fulfill those responsibilities. People hired in these positions would be eligible for tenure, but they would be judged only on teaching and service. The job was designed for people with master's degrees. Though applicants with doctorates would still be eligible, they would generally be considered overqualified. Supporters of the policy felt it necessary to deny that saving money was in any way behind the proposal but also insisted that, since these people would have lower professional qualifications than their professorial colleagues, they should be paid less.

Designing jobs specifically for people with master's degrees is, in the 1990s, not quite ethical. When there is a surplus of Ph.D.'s, as there is now, a national search conducted in good faith will fill those positions with applicants who have earned doctorates. Advertisements for such jobs may once have meant a desire to hire people qualified to teach lower-level classes so as to free up the talents of better-qualified faculty to teach upper-level courses. But as the job market has soured, such lower-level searches discover candidates as qualified as any new assistant professor. Any justification for such positions based on the argument that they help optimize the professional skills in a department no longer holds. Now, the creation of such jobs is just a way to pay some people less.

After much debate and spirited opposition, the proposal finally passed the university senate in the spring of 1994 and was to be implemented the next year. There were to be three lectureships in the English department, and I applied for the job. I had been around since 1991, when the English department had hired me as a temporary full-time instructor to teach four sections of composition and introductory-level literature classes each term. That year, due to a number of leaves, resignations, and sabbaticals, the English department had an unusually large number of full-time temporary instructors: seven. Among the characters who will appear later in our story, this group included me (the only Ph.D. in the group) and two women who had received their master's from the university and who had taught there part-time for some years before these positions opened up.

One further reason for hiring all these temps: the English department was discontinuing the long-standing, widespread practice of using graduate assistants to teach some of the composition classes. It seems that for several years, some people at the university, in their capacity as enthusiastic recruiters, had been telling prospective undergraduates that all classes at the university were taught by faculty, never by graduate students. This was not true, but the year I arrived, the administration of this tuition-driven institution saw that as a good selling point for the university as a whole and decided to make it policy. As most of us within the academy are aware, graduate assistants can often provide some of the most innovative and enthusiastic instruction, and anyone who has ever attended any sort of school knows well that faculty status does not necessarily imply excellence in the classroom. But an institution with a weak endowment can survive only by convincing enough families to fork over more than ten thousand dollars a year, and it must, therefore, worry more about the image it projects to potential customers than about the quality of the actual product. The professional insult to the graduate student employees — the implication that their work is inferior — is trivial compared with the advertisable benefit of dumping them.

That year, my first article in print, I found the job market shrinking, and I failed to find a tenure-track job. With hirings and returns from leave, the English department needed only two full-time instructors for the next year and advertised for them in the department mailboxes. Well, it was pretty clear who would get them. Laudably, the search committee wanted to reward the two women who had received their master's degrees there for several years of part-time work they had done before they were hired for these full-time gigs. Some friends lobbied on my behalf as the applicant with the most impressive qualifications, but they were told that, for a low-level job such as this, teaching composition and introductory literature classes, my breadth of teaching experience before I arrived, my doctorate, and my interest in continuing my research were all strictly irrelevant. At the last minute, however, an assistant professor in a commuter marriage landed a job at the school where her husband teaches. And so, they rehired me.

Next year, another article in print, the job market still worse, two instructorships were advertised in the mailboxes (guess who got them), and I was out.

So I finished my book and taught part-time at two schools, getting nine hundred dollars a course from a community college English department, twelve hundred dollars a course from the university's English department, and, curiously, seventeen hundred dollars a course from its history department, all of which are, of course, far less than they paid me per course as a full-time instructor. The job market is even worse now. But for the 1994–95 school year, the university's English department needed four instructors (again advertised only internally), and I landed one of them, as did the two perennial instructors and another of the department's own M.A.'s. Married now to a tenured associate professor in another department, I limit my job searches to the state.

That year was clearly to be the end of my career at that university. The department chair made it clear to me that she considered me a poor candidate for the newly instituted lecturerships because I had intellectual interests beyond pedagogy. Completely oblivious to the current job market and my experiences in it, not to mention the impossible position academic couples are in these days, she told me she didn't even understand why, with my qualifications, I would want such a low-status job.

The English department did not publish advertisements for the lectureships but instead mailed announcements to other English departments around the state. The other departments that were to use the lectureships to resolve problems of de facto tenure accepted applications from presumably sincere applicants and then, with varying degrees of anxiety over the honesty of the whole procedure, hired the women who had already been working for them for many years. The administration's hands were clean. If these women received tenure now, it would be through a defined procedure rather than through either the embarrassment of administrative fiat or the expense of a lawsuit from an instructor fired, after ten years, without a tenure review. And if the departments were presented with the ethical dilemma of either conducting a search in good faith or, after years of tenuousness and ambiguity, finally rewarding their drudges with job security, then the administration, at least, had as its ethical alibi the legal fiction of the official search procedures through which the internal candidates simply happened to rise to the top. What had been legal and ethical embarrassment now glowed with the bright, clean sparkle of official procedure.

The English department, as I've said, did not have that particular dilemma. It had something more like a real job search on its hands. Well, for one of the slots, anyway: only the search committee pretended that two of those slots were not already sewed up. This is not in any way, of course, to disparage those two women who had had their instructorships renewed regularly; they are good teachers, and they needed and wanted exactly the same thing I did — that university teaching job. Since no one could quite legally say to them (or for that matter to the instructors with de facto tenure in the other departments) that they had a lock on the job, the stakes and the tension were enormous for all the internal candidates, whatever the length of their employment. Since it was very possible some outside candidates would have more impressive credentials, the loyal internal candidates feared that they stood a distinct chance of losing their jobs.

Given the repeated assurances that my qualifications were irrelevant, I actually had less at stake than people with lower qualifications, since I expected to get the boot. This made me angry, but it cut the tension. When the search committee narrowed the field to ten, however, I actually made the cut. Well, of course I did: I had actual experience in that job, and unlike the external candidates, I could tailor my application to exactly what I knew the committee wanted to see. This had the unfortunate consequence of getting my hopes up. When they narrowed the field to the four who would have full-blown campus interviews, I was not among them.

The final four candidates were all women. In contrast, earlier in the year, in a search for a new assistant professor, the English department had brought in, as final candidates for campus interview, three men. Given the gendered hierarchies of academe, it should not be surprising that men predominate as the finalists for the higher position and women predominate as finalists for the position with lower rank, lower pay, and no opportunity for advancement. The absoluteness of the contrast that year, however, was especially jarring.

The four interviewees were the two perennial instructors and two community college teachers. One of the latter has a Ph.D., but she had been working for many years at a community college in another state. She was willing to give up tenure there for a job in our state, where her husband works. Bizarrely enough, it was explained to me that her research in pedagogy — though that is in basic (i.e., remedial) writing, which the university does not offer — and her community college work demonstrated her commitment to teaching and, thus, overcame the overqualification handicap of her education. By any standard, however, this woman was certainly an excellent candidate for the job. In fact, her qualifications only highlight the injustice of hiring at the rank of lecturer, rather than assistant professor. Though the job was designed for a drudge, they ended up hiring a professional peer — at lower rank and pay than she deserves. The compensation for this, in practice, all-female rank was to have no relation to merit.

Yes, the Ph.D. from out of state got the job, as did the two perennial instructors. Game's over, I lose.

Then, as one of my colleagues said, I was handed a big mug of gall. It was announced at a department meeting that the wife of the new assistant professor had been appointed a full-time temporary instructor for the next year. They both had Ph.D.'s in English and had, for the past few years, been forced to live apart as they both pursued various temporary positions around the country. Finally, he had landed a tenure-track job, and though she had only a temporary appointment, they could finally live together, rather than just visit one another over breaks — it must have been a great relief for them. I was furious. Unlike the temporary full-time instructorships available in the past, this one had been neither advertised nor announced, not even within the department. No one had had a chance to apply for it.

When I talked to the department chair about this, she refused to explain what had happened, reminding me only that my contract as an instructor had always been temporary, and so I had no grounds for complaint if it were not renewed. And besides that, the job was beneath me. Now, as it happens, the lecturer search committee had also had the job of selecting the new instructor, so I asked the chair of that committee what had happened, and to his credit, he was more candid than the department chair. He told me that this instructorship was a surprise to the department because the administration had approved the position at the last minute, and they had moved to fill it right away from the pool of applicants for the lectureship. Another internal candidate and I had been fifth and sixth in line for the lectureship, he said, but we had been passed over for the instructorship precisely because we were internal candidates. It seems there was a policy that temporary full-time instructorships were nonrenewable. If there was such a policy, it did not appear in my contract, nor in the faculty handbook (which the contract refers to as describing the conditions of employment), nor had anyone told me of this policy. The other instructors were also ignorant of this condition of our employment. Furthermore, since some of us actually had received renewals, we had no reason ever to think that there might be any such policy against renewal. The chair of the committee told me that it had always been the policy, but since the department's requests for temporary instructorships were usually approved so late in the spring semester, there just wasn't time, ordinarily, to conduct a search before summer break. If any of us had ever been rehired, it was because the department just did not have the time to follow standard policy. Having this pool of candidates from the lecturer search, it had, for once, a chance to follow the policy.

This policy had been dormant for as long as it might apply to our perennial instructors, and it had been revived only when they were finally safe from it. The department had been developing a reliable professional underclass even before the institution of the lectureships. These women would do a good job and never embarrass the department with achievements that would merit a raise in their status. Applying a nonrenewal policy to them, the department would have been wasting a cheap, reliable resource. This is, after all, the traditional function of a female labor force: to remain reliably subordinate and inexpensive.

By hiring the wife of the new assistant professor and dropping me, they had fudged the question of whether they acknowledged the difficult situations of academic couples. They gave one couple a promise of one year together, at least, but no security thereafter (especially if those in power decided to stick now to that heretofore dormant policy). The English department does, however, regularly offer part-time jobs to faculty spouses—that is, in general practice, to faculty wives.

English departments are staffed with people trained in literary studies, but one of their main functions within a university is to offer composition courses. The literature faculty would, quite naturally, want to spend less time on these grading-intensive courses and more time on literature courses, their area of real expertise and the intellectual passion that got them into this business in the first place. Combine that departmental pressure with budget pressure from the administration, and the desire to create lower-paying positions to staff these classes becomes almost irresistible. One way to fight the further expansion of this academic underclass, however, is to consistently point out the gendered nature of the hierarchy it produces. The lower the status of a job, the more likely a woman will be hired to fill it. Add to that the discouragement of professional development and an actual prohibition on professional advancement, and it should be clear that one of the unintended consequences of creating this rank is a structure of sexual discrimination. Call me naive, but I believe that in academe there is enough concern about sexual discrimination that if proposals for underclass ranks were examined in this light, administrators would be less eager to embrace them.

There is nothing wrong with hiring people primarily to teach composition or the equivalent lower-level service courses in any other department. It is, after all, useful and rewarding work in its own right, and those hired to do it deserve the same professional respect and privileges as their colleagues. New positions, no matter what their course assignments will be, should be offered at the rank of assistant professor, with proactive, affirmative-action policies to guard against perpetuating current gender imbalances in the professorial ranks.

No one should have to wear the Scarlet *L,* but, I swear, I would have worn it with pride.

NOTE

1. The woman who is now provost is not the one who proposed the lecturer policy, but she assumed office soon after it was passed by the university senate. Though she inherited the policy and the responsibility for implementing it, she has gone on record as opposing it because it has implied unforeseen legal and administrative complications not dealt with in this essay — or rather, complications that opponents of the policy had warned about but that the administration only recently took seriously.

Works Cited

Burns, Margie. 1993. "Service Courses: Doing Women a Disservice." *Academe* (May-June): 18–21.

Nelson, Cary. 1995. "Lessons from the Job Wars: Late Capitalism Arrives on Campus." *Social Text* 13, no. 3 (fall/winter): 119–34. Revised and updated in Cary Nelson, *Manifesto of a Tenured Radical.* New York: New York University Press, 1997.

"A Ray of Sunshine? The Annual Report on the Economic Status of the Profession 1994–95." 1995. *Academe* (March-April): 8–89.

West, Martha S. 1995. "Women Faculty: Frozen in Time." *Academe* (July–August): 26–29.

Chapter 13
Disposable Faculty: Part-time Exploitation as Management Strategy

Linda Ray Pratt

A passage in a song by the group Meatloaf captures succinctly part of the daily reality for part-time faculty. "I want you, I need you," the song begins, but there's no way, the passage continues, "I'm ever gonna love you." Don't be sad, the song advises, " 'cause two out of three ain't bad." Of course, if the bill of particulars were to continue, it would not be love alone that's missing in the contract for part-time faculty; respect, a fair salary, benefits, and a role in governance are often equally unavailable.

Part-time faculty employment is one of those abusive situations that is just too convenient for institutions to give up if they don't have to. There are some who argue the value of an inexpensive temporary faculty to institutional flexibility, and some who insist that many people — they especially like to point to women — are really served by the possibility of part-time teaching, but none of these apologists can wash out the undeniable exploitation that accompanies the job, even for those who want only part-time work. "Part-time teaching" often is a slow track to nowhere if you want anything more than the pleasures of having a class and an affiliation with a college or university.[1] The pay scale has been static for several years; the jobs hardly ever convert to regular tenure-track lines; and a record of part-time faculty employment damages one's prospects in the job market. No one who is employed part-time or who employs a part-time faculty will be startled by these statements. The thorny question is why things don't seem to change when everyone knows what the problems are and what might make them less painful to the people and the profession as a whole.

Not only are solutions not taking hold, but the number of people affected keeps escalating. Nationally, the number of part-time workers throughout the economy increased by 88.9 percent between 1969 and 1992. Statistics about the number of new jobs filled suggest that as many as 75 percent of them are part-time. Still, the percent of faculty who are part-time is more than double the 16.9 overall figure for the U.S. workforce.[2] Statistics can only hint at the human costs, but they are compelling measures of the marginalized state of academic employment. According to the most recent data collected by the United States Department of Education, the percentage of faculty members holding part-time positions has risen from 22 percent in 1970 to nearly 45 percent in 1992.[3] The percentage of part-time faculty in community colleges has risen to almost 65 percent. Percentages in the range of 40 to 45 percent of all faculty translate as something close to four hundred thousand people. Constricted funding for higher education, the downsizing of the tenure-track faculty in many institutions, and an increase in the number of Ph.D. degrees granted each year are likely to send these figures higher every year for the foreseeable future.

In the field of English, for example, which employs large numbers of part-time faculty, the number of Ph.D.'s awarded in 1995 rose to 1,080 from 943 in 1994, while the number of tenure-track jobs fell to 234 from 249 the year before; the number of listed positions of all kinds in 1995 was 605, down from 679.[4] If we assume that new Ph.D.'s remain viable in the market for at least three years, the compounding number of job-seekers must be reaching about ten people for each tenure-track position. Put another way, if things continue unchecked, about 90 percent of the English Ph.D.'s on the market in the next few years will not find a tenure-track job. More than 40 percent of recent Ph.D.'s in English won't secure any full-time position. The numbers of recent Ph.D.'s who then seek part-time employment to survive in the profession create an ever-larger pool of cheap labor that only an administrative saint could resist.

In terms of the numbers of aspiring faculty members who will be shoved out of the profession, the situation is desperately bad and getting worse. In terms of those who continue as part-time or temporary full-time faculty, the market will be more flooded with overqualified applicants, though in a few places there are small signs of improving conditions that help to make long-range underemployment more palatable. In terms of the profession, the growing use of non-tenure-track faculty is diminishing the influence of the faculty by reducing the number of tenure-track jobs, the role of faculty in governance, and the general prestige of the academy. From an administrative point of view, these patterns may facilitate the new pathways that administrative organizations such as the American Association of Higher Education want to create. These new pathways include reduced emphasis on research and more emphasis on undergraduate teaching; post-tenure review; erosion of the tenure system; increased evaluation of teaching, especially by peers in the classroom; and greater responsiveness to external communities.[5]

In the presence of efforts to reduce the size of the tenure-track faculty, expand nontenurable positions, and institute post-tenure review, the power of tenure to protect faculty from assaults on their academic freedom and economic stability is under severe attack. Many administrators and their organizations openly expect eventually to eliminate tenure, and the replacement of full-time faculty with part-time faculty is one strategy in this effort. Some tenure-track faculty callously accept the professional advantages that arise from employing an underpaid cadre of part-time teachers, but growing numbers of them are troubled because the link between increased use of part-time faculty and administrative redesign of faculty roles is more apparent now that post-tenure review is an open strategy. Faculty members see their own departments shrinking and their work changing. They are also confronted with their own inability to successfully assist their graduate students in securing a place in the profession.

Areas such as English, math, and modern languages that are typically required for a liberal arts degree have traditionally relied most heavily on part-time faculty to cover beginning-level courses. However, in an era of "downsizing" in which such departments have lost as much as 10, 20, and 30 percent of their tenure-track lines,[6] the part-time faculty is increasingly called on to teach upper-division courses. The failure of most institutions to provide any kind of support for faculty development for part-time faculty is less acceptable as those faculty members take on a wider role in teaching an advanced curriculum. Ten years ago, only about 30 percent of part-time faculty held the Ph.D. degree, and only about 20 percent of part-time faculty sought full-time employment.[7] The increasing number of unemployed Ph.D.'s, the overwhelming majority of whom want tenure-track jobs, has changed all that.[8] Aspiring faculty with the terminal degree, teaching experience, and scholarly activity, often with a list of publications, crowd a part-time market that was once predominantly made up of people with master's degrees and limited credentials beyond graduate course work.

The better the credentials of prospective part-time faculty members, the more apparent the professional debasement of them becomes. Many a graduate assistant, reasonably supported and mentored while in the degree program, has found herself with degree in hand teaching the same courses at the same institution for less pay and no benefits as a part-time faculty member. Many departments provide travel money for Ph.D. students to give papers at conferences as part of the effort to provide responsible graduate training but offer nothing to part-time faculty for the same activity. About half of the institutions provide some medical benefits to employees who work half-time or more, but almost none provides retirement benefits. The future impact of a number of years in the workforce without accruing retirement cannot readily be calculated, but it is potentially an employment liability from which one can never fully recover. After several years of staying alive in the profession through part-time teaching, one of three things usually happens: a few people find a full-time job of some sort and move on with their careers; a larger proportion settles into long-term part-time teaching if another source of family income makes it affordable to work this way; a substantial number, faced with the need for more income and some opportunity to advance, leave the profession. Even those who choose to teach part-time because of partner relationships or other personal considerations are demoralized when performance goes largely unnoticed or faithful service over time does not merit stability of appointment. Eventually, a profession that offers nothing better than marginal employment to those who have met the standards will not attract the most promising young minds.

Stories of the "highway flyers" or "scholar gypsies" who combine two or three part-time jobs in order to make a living are legend, but they are not representative of the large numbers of people for whom multiple academic jobs — even part-time ones — are not a possibility. Many of the biggest universities and best private colleges are not in urban areas where numerous other campuses exist, and many part-time faculty members find themselves in a one-employer market where wages face no competition and an oversupply of degrees floods the local pool. What is "the profession" like for them?

The letter of appointment will also contain the notice of termination. The salary is on a per-course basis, typically somewhere between one thousand and three thousand dollars per section. The average is closer to sixteen hundred dollars. Perhaps you are earning twenty-eight hundred dollars per section in math, but your friend in Spanish is getting eighteen hundred dollars per section. You are teaching six courses a year but are still called "part-time," even though full-time faculty members typically teach three courses per semester — the explanation for what differentiates the two is that the latter also have time assigned to research and service. For teaching six to eight courses in an academic year, the income may be less than ten thousand dollars and rarely more than twenty-five thousand dollars. Private colleges, which often tout themselves as places where students receive personal attention, will probably pay you less than the state university to provide that special care. You will be required to turn in student teaching evaluations, but no one will read them or evaluate your work. Your rank will have nothing to do with your credentials. Many of the people in the department will not know who you are, even as you begin your fifth year with them. The governance structure will provide for student members on committees, but not for the presence of part-time faculty. You will share a small office with three other part-time faculty who are also teaching three or four classes a semester. No typewriter or computer is in the office, and the department does not supply voice mail since the telephone is shared and maybe not in the office at all. When you set up appointments for all the students in a class, you move to a table in the student union for the day since it will be quieter to talk with them there. When the students ask about nominating you for a teaching award, you have to tell them you are not eligible. You give a paper at your own expense at a conference, and the department lists it as evidence of its productivity. Next year, you will have to apply all over again for this job and wait until summer to know if you have it. The final blow is that after a few years of working under these conditions, you'll find yourself stigmatized on the job market as a "part-timer" by those who know perfectly well what the market is like but wonder what was wrong with you that you didn't get a job.

Those close to the world of part-time employment know that this profile, while it varies some from place to place, person to person, is not exaggerated. With pay so low, professional considerations so few, demeaning conditions so prevalent, and unanimity among the professional associations and teachers unions about the need for change, how can this situation go on year to year with so little improvement? First, the profit to the institution is outrageously advantageous. To illustrate, if a full professor in math, English, or modern languages with a salary of $69,750 retires and the department loses the tenure-track line, the equivalent number of courses may be taught by a part-time faculty member for a "replacement" cost of two or three thousand per section.[9] By replacing the tenured line with part-time instruction, the institution may spend ten thousand to fifteen thousand dollars to cover the same number of classes. This is a savings of fifty-five thousand to sixty thousand dollars in salary instead of the thirty thousand to thirty-five thousand dollars that would have been saved had a new tenure-track position been approved. Exact figures will vary in each institution, of course, but the pattern is that replacing a retiring member of the tenure track with part-time faculty will often save as much as three-quarters of the salary, as opposed to half or less of it if a new tenure-track hire is approved. Since the part-time faculty member will not get start-up costs or a full benefits package, the savings are in fact even greater than just from salary.

Beyond its utility for stretching the budget and subsidizing the reallocation of salary money to other purposes, the use of part-time faculty is also valued as a deliberate management strategy. This is more reprehensible than the practice of using part-time employment as a means to balance the budget. Exploitative employment situations are bad enough when they are an unfortunate but necessary budget restriction. Exploitative employment practices as a tactic to redesign — or "re-engineer" — the academy are worse because they coolly calculate the use the institution can make of the economic desperation and despairing ambitions of its potential workers. Higher education is indeed on a tighter budget; state appropriations in the 1990s were down over the increases of the 1980s, and many institutions had zero increases or increases below the inflation rate. But except in a few states, funding was not down as much or as uniformly as some accounts imply. The disastrous cuts in California distort the national figures for funding in the 1990s, which tend to hold at about the rate of inflation when California is left out of the picture (Lively 1993, A29). Many states had small but steady increases over the rate of inflation, and some, especially in the South, had significant increases in funding.

With a generally static budget picture on many campuses, the bruising pinch for funds in part came from changing priorities within the institutions. Higher education now reflects a definition of what colleges and universities must offer students and external communities *in addition to* faculty and classes. At the state universities, reallocation has transferred resources away from academic programs and into expanding management personnel and student services and extending connections to the corporate and civil communities, known in administrative jargon as the "stakeholders." Within the academic programs, classes have gotten larger, the tenure-track faculty smaller, and the part-time faculty and graduate assistant instructors more numerous. A recent sampling of departments around the country for the American Association of University Professors found it was not uncommon for as much as 65 percent or more of instruction in math, English, and modern languages to be in the hands of part-time faculty and graduate students.[10] At the state level, shifts in resources were often away from the more costly four-year institutions to the two-year colleges where instruction is cheaper because it is mainly in the hands of low-paid part-time and non-tenure-track faculty.

Administrators who hire part-time and non-tenure-track faculty at wages less than beginning public school teachers would make have the insulation of not having to see the human situation at the other end of their management objectives. Part-time faculty appointments are largely a hidden problem above the level of the department administration. The department chair may be the only person in the institution who knows who and how many part-time faculty are carrying out what work in the department. Since the nonsalary academic costs of making fewer full-time commitments are largely hidden, delayed, or shifted elsewhere in assessing the real fiscal and educational impact, the immediate profit for an administration in using part-time faculty is an expediency that seemingly outweighs the harm that comes with the gains. The biggest costs are to the overall stability of the academic programs, especially in curricular development and research activity. Some other kinds of costs, unemployment compensation, for example, can add up to a considerable sum in places where part-time faculty are hired in an off-and-on pattern. Part-time faculty can usually qualify for up to twenty-six weeks of unemployment compensation after working for the institution four months. Twenty-six weeks of unemployment compensation may cost the institution as much as it would have paid in salary to keep the employee. I have known part-time faculty members who sustained themselves between appointments in just this way. In metropolitan areas with a large turnover in part-time faculty, these costs can be substantial. Professional employees, because they are an expensive investment in training, increase costs to an institution in numerous ways when it has a high rate of turnover, not the least of which is the cost of expensive graduate programs to train people for nonexistent jobs. But these kinds of cost issues are not usually much considered when making decisions about faculty. Administrators on the fast track to bigger things are more often measured by their ability to cut budgets and produce more with less than by the long-term stability and quality of the academic programs for which they were responsible. Strengthening tenure, investing more in faculty resources, and improving the status of the lowest ranking instructors are not the values that secure career moves for administrators. Studies of "administrative bloat" indicate that proximity is one important factor in determining an administrator's sense of priorities.[11] Just as this bloat produces in them a greater felt need for more midlevel administrators, so, too, does it make the conditions of an almost wholly invisible part-time faculty less real and pressing.[12]

Recognizing that part-time employment is a management tool as well as a budgetary strategy means that merely exposing the wrongs will not lead to remedy. The very attractiveness of part-time faculty for institutions depends on maintaining the status quo.

Thus, despite their growing numbers and the open concern expressed about the conditions of part-time employment by nearly every disciplinary and professional organization, part-time faculty remain largely unseen and unheard in their institutions, which allows the exploitation to go unchecked. Only those strategies that can alter the institutional self-interest are likely to be effective. Faculty members in general, the most vulnerable and powerless faculty in particular, cannot influence institutional directions as long as they are silent, uninformed, or unorganized. The conditions of part-time employment conspire, however, to create a climate in which fear for one's tenuous appointment curbs dissent. One's marginalized position in the profession makes it difficult to know what is happening before it's done, and one's isolation within the workforce makes it difficult to identify others in the same situation. Despite these barriers, some progress has been made. Part-time faculty members at Rutgers and Kent State have successfully organized unions. After an intense and protracted struggle, the Rutgers union negotiated its first contract. The *Adjunct Advocate,* under the editorship of P. D. Lesko, has given a national voice to part-time faculty. The American Association of University Professors (AAUP), the American Federation of Teachers (AFT), and the National Education Association (NEA) have all published thoughtful status reports and position papers that lend credibility to the critical analysis of part-time employment and offer viable guidelines that could improve it. A few institutions, such as New Mexico State, have approved plans that provide non-tenure-track faculty with adequate notice, renewable appointments, equivalent rank, and professional evaluation. In still fewer cases, the institution has agreed to a limit on the number of part-time faculty and a plan for the eventual conversion of such appointments to full-time permanent positions.

The most effective way for part-time faculty to act in their own behalf is through a union, but that is not a possibility in many cases and not a probability in many others. Part-time faculty unions are most likely to succeed where the full-time faculty unions have set a precedent for faculty organizing. Often the part-time faculty will be represented by the same union that negotiates for the full-time faculty, but just as likely, part-time faculty will have a parallel organization. Unions are the best way to take the cheapness and convenience out of part-time employment because they raise the institution's monetary costs and time investment through both the contract and the act of negotiating it. That, of course, is why institutions will fight tooth and nail to defeat unions that may curtail the degrees of flexibility and savings that make part-time faculty desirable. Although collective bargaining offers the only legally protected way for employees to negotiate the terms of their employment, part-time teachers must have other strategies. Whole regions of the country, such as the South and much of the Southwest, deny faculty the right to collective bargaining. Even in states where the right of teachers to bargain is enabled by legislation, the right of part-time employees may be restricted. Faculty members in private institutions have been denied the right to collective bargaining by the Supreme Court's *Yeshiva* decision, which argues that faculty are essentially managers and thus not entitled to unionize.[13] States such as New York, New Jersey, Connecticut, Michigan, and California have extensive faculty collective bargaining, but the majority of U.S. professors are not unionized, unlike their counterparts in much of the rest of the world. Part-time faculty members may find significant legal barriers to unionizing, but there are no laws against organizing, even under the name of an association that may function as a union elsewhere (e.g., the AAUP, AFT, and NEA). An organization of part-time faculty members, armed with the policy recommendations from the disciplinary and professional associations, can give voice to their concerns and purpose to their agitation.

The goal of part-time faculty strategies must be to take the cheapness and convenience out of current practice. This means forcing administrations to put more money into it and more stability behind it, two conditions that negate the attractiveness of part-time over full-time positions. In the long term, this means either restructuring the funding priorities in favor of faculty resources or reversing the marketplace by eliminating the surplus of Ph.D.'s. In the short term, a number of objectives can advance these goals and ameliorate the present situation. One crucial strategy is to establish professional considerations that protect the quality of higher education and the standards appropriate to the profession. These include the use of job descriptions to structure responsibilities and rewards; a formal evaluation of job performance; acceptable standards for working conditions (office space, supplies, basic technology); adequate notice of renewal and termination; access to benefits; rank commensurate with credentials; resources for professional development; participation in faculty governance; and the state-sanctioned protections of affirmative action, equal pay for equal work, due process, and nondiscrimination. In the long term, the profession must balance the supply of Ph.D. degrees with the opportunities for employment, which means limiting graduate school enrollments.

Many of the changes listed above do not require a major financial investment and are patently in the interest of quality education. Yet most institutions have doggedly avoided implementing them. One reason administrations oppose affordable improvements for part-time faculty, such as assigning rank according to credentials or requiring annual evaluation of performance, is that written records of quality work and acknowledgments of credentials legitimize professional status. Recognition of professional accomplishment raises expectations on both sides about the conditions of employment. Written recognition of professional accomplishment opens the door to advancement where merited and grievance where merit is denied. In blunt terms, institutions do not want to be responsible for providing professional situations for part-time faculty, and thus they avoid changes that encourage professional expectations. Administrations may feel that they are acting in the most pragmatic sense of institutional interests in holding down the expectations of temporary faculty. It is, however, a rationale that few would want to defend in a public forum, especially to parents and politicians who think that higher tuition should produce an improved quality of college education. An institution cannot buy instruction on the cheap and still convince the public of its commitment to the high quality of its education, at least, not unless we let them.

As long as the academic labor supply far outstrips the number of positions available, the profession will be vulnerable to the use and abuse of part-time faculty. As long as institutions need the savings and want the management implications derived from a large number of underemployed faculty, they will continue to hire them. Those who worry about creating a two-tier faculty should recognize that it is already here and begin to focus on closing up the distances that harm both tiers and the institutions themselves. Nothing can place at greater risk the status of full-time faculty or the importance of tenure than withholding professional treatment from almost half the members of the profession. The lyrics from Meatloaf's song speak of having the need and the desire but withholding the love. If "love" translates in the world of work as respect, fairness, and interest in the collective welfare of one's colleagues, then the treatment of part-time faculty members today withholds that necessary component to professional soundness. In practice if not in rhetoric, institutions use part-time faculty as an inexpensive and consumable commodity. The disposable faculty. A consumer-oriented society invests in and protects those things it considers too valuable to replace easily. The future academic environment will determine whether faculty members — full- and part-time — are to be disposed of, recycled, or protected. The haunting emotion of Meatloaf's lyrics is that they play their meagerness off the promise of fullness in the original song by Elvis where want, need, and love hold equal stanzaic importance. Unlike that original expression of wholehearted commitment, the revision illustrates the cold miscalculation that unravels all. As members of the profession, we, too, can invalidate all in the denial of essential parts of the whole. If higher education miscalculates its own best interests that badly, it, too, will lose the respect that is its coin of value. And no one needs to remind us what's down at the end of that lonely street.

NOTES

1. "Part-time faculty" is not a fully accurate term since many faculty work full-time some semesters and part-time others, often in the same year for the same institution. Some work on full-time temporary contracts for one to three years and then find themselves back to part-time employment. "Temporary faculty" is also an inaccurate term since the average length of time a part-time faculty member teaches at an institution is almost seven years. I shall use the term "part-time faculty" because the problems associated with the most exploitative aspects of faculty underemployment affect those who do not have full-time permanent positions, even though their appointment in any given year may vary. In that sense, though they may wind up with a "full-time equivalent" (FTE) assignment of courses in any given semester or year, they are situationally part-time in terms of pay, security, status, and, in most cases, benefits.

2. These figures, drawn from several government sources, are published in Robinson 1994, 4.

3. Department of Education data from fall 1992 are the most recent national figures. The data supplied by the National Center for Education Statistics cited herein were presented at the annual meeting of the AAUP in June 1996 by Ernst Benjamin of the national staff. The 1992 national survey of postsecondary faculty estimated the number of part-time faculty at 43 percent. Benjamin's analysis notes

that these figures do not include part-time faculty replacements for faculty on leave. He argues for adjusting the figures upward to 45 percent. I cite his figures because his analysis recognizes more of the variables in how and when part-time faculty are employed.

4. See Modern Language Association of America 1996. The MLA chart cites the positions advertised in the English-language edition of the October 1995 *Job Information List* and the National Council on Research Report 1995. Not all the positions listed are either definite jobs or new ones, and not all positions get advertised nationally. Some jobs advertised are contingent on funds that do not materialize, and others are positions that were carried over from the year before. Some term-contract positions that materialize after the spring publication of *JIL* are advertised only regionally or in the *Chronicle of Higher Education*. I have no statistics about jobs that open after the close of the traditional academic year, but observation and experience indicate that most of these positions will be filled by part-time faculty. These jobs are usually designed to cover enrollment overflow or last-minute changes in the assignment of permanent faculty.

5. The American Association of Higher Education's new pathways project includes publications, workshops, and meetings designed to advance these and other ideas. The Pew Charitable Trust is funding much of this work.

6. My own department has undergone about a 20 percent reduction in the number of tenure-track lines in the last decade; Cary Nelson reports that his department dropped 30 percent in the number of tenure-track lines between 1970 and 1990. Neither institution nor department has had a significant decline in enrollments.

7. Figures from National Center for Educational Statistics of the Department of Education 1987. The data in this survey were extensively analyzed in the "Report on the Status of Non-tenure-track Faculty" 1992.

8. Lomperis's study of Ph.D.'s from 1975 to 1985 indicated that two-thirds of them sought full-time work (see Lomperis 1990).

9. For purposes of this example, I took the average salary for full professors in Category I (doctoral) public institutions as reported in the 1995–96 salary survey of the AAUP (see "Not So Bad," 1996). Given the salary and the kind of institution behind this data, I then estimate the average range of starting salaries in these disciplines and the most frequently reported range of stipends per course for part-time replacement.

10. The sample was part of the work of the AAUP's Committee G on the status of part-time and non-tenure-track faculty. The committee published its extensive "Report on the Status of Non-tenure-track Faculty" with policy recommendations in 1993.

11. The term "administrative bloat" derives from Bergmann 1991.

12. Perhaps a similar sense of proximity of interests explains how administrative salaries in 1995–96 increased by 4.2 percent while faculty salaries increased by 2.9 percent. It was the fourth year in a row that administrative salaries exceeded the rate of inflation (College and University Personnel Association figures as printed in "Administrators' Salaries Outstrip Inflation" 1996, 11).

13. The court's absurd interpretation of faculty governance as the evidence of manager status must seem even more bizarre when extended to non-tenure-track faculty.

Works Cited

"Administrators Salaries Outstrip Inflation." 1996. *Academe* 82, no. 2: 11.

Bergmann, Barbara. 1991. "Bloated Administration, Blighted Campuses." *Academe* 77 no. 6: 12–16.

Lively, Kit. 1993. "State Support for Public Colleges Up 2% This Year." *Chronicle of Higher Education* (October 27): A29.

Lomperis, Ana Maria Turner. 1990. "Are Women Changing the Nature of the Academic Profession?" *Journal of Higher Education* 61, no. 6: 643–77.

Modern Language Association. 1996. Materials distributed at the Association of Departments of English meetings. Summer sessions.

National Center for Educational Statistics of the Department of Education. 1987. *National Survey of Post-secondary Faculty, 1987.*

———. 1992. Unpublished data from 1992 presented at the annual meeting of the AAUP in June 1996.

"Not So Bad: The Annual Report on the Economic Status of the Profession." 1996. *Academe* 82, no. 2: 14–108.

"Report on the Status of Non-tenure-track Faculty." 1992. *Academe* 78 no. 6: 39–48.

Robinson, Perry. 1994. *Part-time Faculty Issues.* Washington, D.C.: American Federation of Teachers.

Steinman, Jim. 1977. "Two Out of Three Aint Bad." *Bat Out of Hell.* Vocals by Meatloaf. New York: CBS Inc.

Chapter 14
Alchemy in the Academy: Moving Part-time Faculty from Piecework to Parity

Karen Thompson

The Logic of Part-time Work

When women entered the industrial workforce in the United States at the turn of the century, they had to accept whatever conditions and positions were offered them just to have work. Sweatshop labor and meager piecework compensation were the rule. Many women in academe today seem trapped in a parallel situation. With 66 percent of full-time lines filled by men, women who want to work in higher education must often settle for part-time assignments. As of 1993, 51 percent of the part-time jobs in academe were held by women. The increasing feminization of higher education — notable in the number of women graduate students — may in fact also increase women's disproportionate representation among part-timers. These marginal positions most often involve low, by-the-course pay and a workload all too reminiscent of the needle trades of a hundred years ago.

This use of contingent labor reflects a widespread trend in the national workforce. Part-time and temporary employment threatens to undermine what little security American employees have earned and learned to enjoy. The largest private employer in the United States today is Manpower, Inc., a temporary employment agency. Such agencies are major employers in many metropolitan areas. In Baltimore, S. E. S. Temps Inc. is second only to Johns Hopkins University in its number of employees. In the general economy, temporary employees, or "assignment employees" as they are now sometimes called ("disposable employees" would be more like it), are responsible for most of whatever economic recovery we have felt. According to the National Association of Temporary Services (NATS), temporary employment increased 17 percent in 1992 (Cook 1994).

Part-time and temporary employees are generally excluded from unions and are extremely difficult to organize. In fact, one of the attractions of hiring part-time employees besides cost savings and flexibility is their likelihood to remain unorganized. A 1988 study (Ehrenberg 1988) suggests that government policy may actually make it more difficult for part-timers to form unions and protect their interests. The only congressional attempt to address the situation of part-timers that I know of, Pat Schroeder's Part-time and Temporary Worker Protection Act, never got out of committee. The temporary industry's association, NATS, however, is moving right along lobbying for restrictive unemployment insurance legislation that would limit temporary employees' ability to receive benefits. As usual, employers are well organized.

The situation in academe, however, is if anything worse than the national pattern, since part-time employees now comprise nearly half of the college and university teaching staff. The part-timer scurrying between colleges, piecing together multiple appointments, never achieving the equivalent of a full-time salary, but juggling more than a full workload, has become a familiar image. Administrations justify this picture by pointing to their "needs" for containing costs in tough times and for flexibility in the face of changing enrollment and student demand, as well as to the easy availability of qualified teachers lined up waiting for the positions. They argue that "market forces," not management, determine the low pay, lack of protection, and disrespect that go with the jobs.

But supply and demand actually has little to do with it, as I observe each year at Rutgers when part-time lecturers who are discouraged all year about future employment become high in demand come September. The fallacy of the "market forces" defense of the exploitation of part-time faculty has been exposed with extensive documentation by Margie Burns in a 1991 article.

Economically, the employment of part-timers in academe has been virtually a fund-raising mechanism. Balancing the tuition income from a part-timer's classes against the content of her paycheck shows consistent gains for the institution. It is actually profitable for departments to budget release time into grants, for example, since the actual expenditure for replacement with a part-time lecturer is so much lower, three or four times lower.

Not only do administrations profit from the use and abuse of part-time faculty in the name of the "market," but they take their economic and flexibility advantages and then blame the victims — part-timers — for lowering academic standards. Piecing together three or four jobs to maintain a professional life, a part-timer is ironically seen as an incompetent or unserious academic. A part-time position can be a stigma on one's vita, although those in this category are frequently doing more than the equivalent of full-time work and are often recognized in their fields. It is not, in fact, uncommon for a part-time faculty member with a teaching assignment heavier than most full-timers in her department to produce publications that are technically not a part of her teaching-only job and that probably will mean nothing in furthering her career. Yet part-timers, devoted to their disciplines and to teaching, continue to pursue both with little acknowledgment or compensation. Meanwhile, calculating hourly wages based on time spent teaching, preparing, and grading, not traveling, can come to less than the minimum wage in some cases.

Accepting a supply and demand explanation for all of these employment practices produces a number of misguided conclusions, as is clear from the December 1995 issue of *Profession,* a publication of the Modern Language Association. One article worries about how many faculty will be available or needed without asking what exactly a "faculty member" might be. Another article concludes, after a lengthy and convoluted statistical presentation, that although we may face a "market that perhaps looks grimmer than anticipated," we must note that "millions of workers in our economy face an alternative . . . that is worse." So we are to take heart in knowing that a Ph.D. *is* still an advantage over a high school diploma. A third article focuses on the importance of graduate students learning "how to make themselves marketable enough." And I cannot help wondering: How marketable is "marketable enough"? Perhaps "marketable" will mean being infinitely flexible and willing to work for free.

If that suggestion seems excessive, consider the case of someone I recently encountered on the Internet who used to be tenured at the University of Bridgeport in Connecticut. She lost her job through a bitter strike when Sun Yung Moon took over the institution. Now she is part-time at another institution and, of course, untenured. It is not typical to switch places so abruptly, but it gave this teacher unusual insight. In a discussion of professional development for part-timers, she was able to point out the exploitative contradiction. While it is flattering and de-alienating for part-time faculty to be asked to serve on committees or take other service assignments, the fact is that it amounts to the extraction of free labor. What our ex-tenured teacher once did as part of her full-time position for a respectable full-time salary, she could now be asked to do in the name of professional development for no pay at all.

Yet the abuse of part-time faculty has effects that extend far beyond the damage done to the part-timers themselves. It can have considerable impact on the quality of education the country can provide. Where we part-timers feel underpaid, our low salaries actually function to hold all wages down, to make it difficult for all university employees to expect annual increases. Where we complain of short notice of appointment or assignment, our students may face less prepared teachers and the whole institution suffers. Where we entreat administrations for office space, others see us as inaccessible and the university becomes more fragmented. Where we crave some form of job security, a new unstable teaching force develops, spreading chaos and poor planning. The list goes on: no role in governance means lost resources for all; no opportunity for promotion makes for a stagnating workforce. At the very least, you have a growing possibility of very low morale.

What makes part-time teaching worth so little? Is it because women do so much of it? Whatever the answer, the only way I know to change these practices in individual institutions is to organize collectively. It is thus my own experience at seeking union representation that I want to turn to next.

Building a Union for Part-time Faculty

My own experience with academic unionism came right out of the concrete expression of my problems as a part-time lecturer at Rutgers. Having taught two or three courses a semester for six years, I found myself not reappointed one year. No one said anything to me or wrote me a letter explaining why. When I inquired, there didn't seem to be much of a reason, and the following fall I did get an assignment, but in the meantime a colleague referred me to the faculty union at Rutgers. The American Association of University Professors (AAUP) didn't represent part-timers at the time, but enough full-time faculty active in AAUP were interested to encourage and support the beginning of an organizing drive. With a committee of a dozen enthusiasts, I spent the next three years methodically building a communication network and preparing for a representation election. The election, in July 1988, was overwhelmingly successful, with 80 percent voting for the AAUP. At the time I remember feeling the problems were insurmountable. Now, I look back and think, "That was the easy part."

Yet in our experience at Rutgers we faced all sorts of predictable problems. Communication between part-time faculty was exceedingly difficult, with part-timers scattered across the state, some without mailboxes and others teaching off campus. Predictably, we received no cooperation from the administration in providing home addresses or telephone numbers. And part-timers were also divided by their widely varying concerns and interests. Many part-timers, moreover, were overworked and too busy to become involved in the organizing effort. Others feared taking action would jeopardize their insecure positions; and so on.

The administration threw up other barriers as well. They invoked a legal precedent requiring us to organize in a chapter separate from the full-timers. This was the first of many "divide and conquer" tactics in the administration's overall strategy to derail bargaining with part-time faculty. The administration hoped to isolate and nullify our bargaining unit by attempting to portray our concerns as separate from and even antithetical to those of our full-time colleagues as well as the students we teach. But we were able to build an active committee of part-time faculty organizers, to secure indispensable support from the full-time faculty and the national organization, and to create a campaign for representation that culminated in a four-to-one election victory.

We were able to unite our immediate constituency of part-timers and make them a cohesive force in a number of ways. Part-timers sent out frequent mailings, including a chapter newsletter. We activated telephone chains and held department and campus meetings. Even the administration's tactics helped build the organizing momentum. Their veiled threats of job loss, their characterization of us as undereducated or inexperienced, and their appeals to false elitism consistently backfired; part-timers were infuriated by the administration's condescension and its indifference to the vital contribution we make to the educational process. Thus we always stressed one issue that united us all — deep resentment over the administration's basic lack of respect.

We learned a number of important lessons through the organizing and negotiating process. One of the most important ones is that part-timers can't make gains by themselves. Without the support of full-time faculty, student organizations, and staff unions, we might have never reached an agreement with the university. Our statewide coalition worked to educate both campus and community in the mysteries of budget trade-offs, divide-and-conquer strategies, and administrative bloat. Of course, in the process, these groups themselves learned the ways in which part-time faculty are exploited, and, centrally, they learned that we *exist.*

Getting support from other groups meant not only educating them but also building alliances with them. Students were generally unaware of the large role played by part-time faculty in undergraduate education; many didn't even know that some of their most admired teachers were part-time; they were shocked to discover the conditions under which we work. We did a number of things to bridge this gap. Our newsletter runs profiles of distinguished part-time faculty members who vigorously assert their dedication to their students, while complaining of the substandard terms and conditions of employment that make teaching difficult. We held a teach-in and discussed the issues in classrooms. We established ties with the activist student organization formed to protest soaring tuition increases, making a financial contribution as well as public statements of support. We spoke at their rallies. They came to our press conferences. We jointly lobbied the legislature and the board of governors. Together with full-time faculty and secretarial and custodial employees, who were all in the midst of negotiating contracts, we showed again and again that salary increases did not have to come from tuition hikes. We emphasized how Rutgers's misplaced funding priorities spent much more on administrators and buildings than on undergraduate education.

Winning over full-time faculty to the mutuality of our interests was sometimes more challenging. Many full-timers also view part-time faculty as underqualified and see us as a threat to their tenure-track lines. We are fortunate that at Rutgers most full-time faculty who are active and outspoken understand that it is in their own interest for part-timers to receive commensurate salaries, benefits, and equitable procedures of notice and reappointment, thereby making part-time faculty less cost effective and stemming the further erosion of full-time lines. But full-time faculty elsewhere may see us as lacking expertise, as a way to lower their workload, or as a threat; so the real challenge is to get full-time faculty to see their self-interest in improving our situations. Our existence as a reserve labor force in higher education gradually erodes the ranks of full-time faculty—we're a cheap labor alternative. As this happens, tenure, academic freedom, and faculty governance become more and more restricted. To turn this around, the economic incentive must be curtailed by limiting part-timers and paying them well. This applies to TAs, postdocs, and temporary full-timers as well. We all need to come together around our common interests.

On the one hand, the alliances we built proved invaluable during the three long years it took to negotiate our first collective bargaining agreement. Students designed and distributed posters about part-time faculty that spoke to the students' concerns. Full-time faculty, other university employees — indeed, people from every segment of the Rutgers community except the administration — participated in a letter-writing drive to the board of governors and a postcard campaign to the acting president. The educational mission of the university is the common interest of all these constituencies, a fact that drew them together even as the administration tried to pit these groups against one another.

On the other hand, we also learned the value of an independent voice. At Rutgers, part-time faculty were forced by the administration into a separate bargaining unit. That necessitated that we do our own negotiations and present our grievances with no direct assistance from the full-time faculty. This means we have to work very hard, but it also means we make our own decisions. We decide the top priority at the bargaining table. We can seek advice, of course, from full-timers, but our public statements and policy decisions are our own. This may sound particularly inviting to some who are struggling with the complications of a large joint unit. But keep in mind that the independent workload is enormous and that our unit is necessarily small and more vulnerable. The optimum situation would probably be a joint unit with clear, strong voices thriving within it.

Negotiating a Contract

Negotiating a contract is where the fun begins. That's where real change can be proposed and implemented, and so that's where administrators dig in their heels. During negotiations, it became clear that the sharpest conflicts revolved around the most crucial issues. When we raised the issue of pro rata salaries and benefits, the administration cut off discussion. We knew that achieving some sort of parity with full-time faculty, compensation calculated on a fraction of a full-time salary, would not only improve our own situations but protect full-time lines by making costs more equivalent. Benefits could also be effectively prorated, based on a percentage and tied to longevity or course load. These factors, in turn, have a tremendous impact on a teacher's ability to perform well, on the actual quality of education. All of these issues are akin to a whole slew of "comparable worth" issues for women in the larger workforce, where women are consistently paid less for equivalent work.

But the administration was not interested in these issues. At one point, they even acknowledged to us that our proposals might be good management practices, would no doubt have favorable effects on education as well as teacher morale, yet in no way would they consider any form of parity with full-time faculty. They couldn't accept pro rata pay rather than piecework because it goes to the heart of our relationship to our work. Almost anything that even suggested a more permanent or respectable connection to the university was contemptuously opposed. I can recall the response that once greeted our reasoned proposal for benefits enjoyed by others. "I'm not going to be lectured at by the likes of you" were the words of the administration's negotiator. Administrators are determined to keep part-timers in a peripheral position, and disdain is a major weapon. For them, maintaining an itinerant, insecure reserve force of teachers is the highest priority. Central to our own long-term agenda, however, must be focusing on issues of equity and turning piecework into parity.

We did manage to negotiate per-credit minimums that resulted in substantial increases for some, an across-the-board increase for those already at or above the minimum, compensation for oversize classes, and percentage increases for everyone in each of the next two years of the contract. So the administration was able to locate some funds as long as we didn't make dramatic changes in our status or the structure of our positions. The respect issue, a sore spot for our folks, was addressed (at no economic cost to Rutgers) by dropping the "visiting" from our previous title of "visiting part-time lecturers." This meant quite a bit to those of us who had been visiting for ten or twenty years.

We were also able to win a grievance procedure and some notice of reappointment, but the measures themselves are very short on real protection and due process. We learned, however, what the central issues are, where we have to begin the next round, and certainly some useful approaches. In negotiating a contract we also realized that compromise can be a step to real change. Our first contract is far from a model, but it does start the negotiating cycle, and it includes basics like salary minimums, annual increases, and compensation for oversize classes. Security remains the touchiest issue: anything remotely suggesting a more permanent or respectable connection to the university was contemptuously opposed by the administration. But the contract is something on which to build, and now the bargaining process begins again. We will see where the second round leads us in these tough times of economic crisis and restructuring of higher education. Our first contract is a first step for us, but it may also be a first step for part-time faculty elsewhere in higher education.

The Part-time Future

The part-time faculty to whom I have referred are actually a rather diverse group. There are a great many part-timers who would prefer full-time positions. These are frequently women, including women who were overlooked or excluded from full-time job searches before the days of affirmative action. There are also significant numbers of part-time faculty who teach their courses on top of their full-time jobs elsewhere. There are high school teachers, executives, lawyers, doctors, computer analysts, even tenured faculty at other colleges seeking part-time teaching to supplement their incomes or stimulate their lives. These tend to be men. One might see a similar grouping in the assorted writers, musicians, and artists who need part-time teaching as a livelihood when performances, poetry, or paintings don't pay the bills. Not surprisingly, these part-timers are more frequently women, women trying to continue their careers and make ends meet. And more and more part-timers are Ph.D.'s seeking full employment but frozen out of a hopeless job market.

In fact the broadest picture might put part-timers together with all of academe's other exploited teachers, which would include graduate teaching assistants teaching while training for nonexistent jobs. Indeed, compared to part-timers, TAs are perhaps in an even more confused situation, being both exploited as employees and misled as future members of the profession. The startling image of a doctoral graduate in cap and gown wearing a sign proclaiming "WILL WORK FOR FOOD" accompanied an article in the *Chronicle of Higher Education* by Cary Nelson and Michael Bérubé, "Graduate Education Is Losing Its Moral Base." The authors don't actually say that Ph.D.'s are as unemployed as steelworkers, but they might as well with a thousand applicants for every advertised position. They neatly outline the ethical problem in an economic context, recognizing that "the collapse of the job market makes the logic of graduate apprenticeship morally corrupt." They make a number of admirable recommendations, including one to "reduce the number of students [graduate programs] admit" and another to "lessen exploitation of graduate students" and "increase their wages and benefits" (Nelson and Bérubé 1994).

I was struck by the similarity between these recommendations and those that frequently arise regarding part-time faculty. Such statements generally recommend limiting the use of adjunct faculty and addressing their lack of compensation and professional treatment. But what's not particularly emphasized in any of these policy statements is the way in which part-time faculty and graduate teaching assistants function as reserve labor forces. This is a point I find myself coming back to again and again. Not only do part-timers and TAs both supply reserve labor, but they actually constitute the same pool, with individuals moving back and forth between the two groups and often simultaneously functioning in both. There *is* a job crisis for graduate students, and they *are* being exploited and treated as expendable, but when those graduate students get their degrees or quit their programs, they become a substitute labor force that is broader than our graduate programs.

An article by Denise K. Magner cites examples of frustrated new Ph.D.'s taking part-time appointments to keep active in their fields or to supplement their incomes. The author points out that "for more and more budding academics, part-time work, one-year appointments, and postdoctoral positions have become the norm" (Magner 1994). So we're talking about an even bigger group of reserve labor: part-timers, TAs, postdocs, and other temporary full-time appointments like sabbatical replacements.

So we see increasing numbers of part-time and non-tenure-track faculty being employed. Usually we hear this explained as a problem of competing interests, of supply and demand, or of marketability. At the same time, the number of full-time, and especially tenured, faculty has sharply declined while the ranks of all levels of administrators have been continually growing for the most part. Frequently given rationales or justifications for all this are the need for economic cost-cutting, the need for managerial flexibility, or the need to bring the "ivory tower" more in line with the real world. We must ask ourselves whose needs these represent. It's not as if we see these economic savings and flexibility channeled into educational programming or student support. Instead we see restrictions in course offerings, reductions in enrollments, cuts in student aid, and an overstressed job market for graduate students. Full-time faculty are finding themselves with heavier course loads, larger class size, diminishing ranks, and, of course, constricted salaries. As their numbers decline, so does their role in governance, their ability to hang on to tenure, and academic freedom. So full-time faculty do not seem to be benefiting from this scenario. Meanwhile, education is rapidly becoming devalued as our public school system is defunded, teaching as a profession is under attack, and students are widely discouraged in many communities.

The key conclusion needs to be stated unequivocally: a reserve labor force performs the same functions in academe that it does in the larger workforce — holding down all salaries, making employees feel desperate and competitive, dividing the workforce, and making organizing difficult. The practical way to prevent this is by pricing part-time and temporary faculty out of the market. They must become too expensive to function as a substitute labor force. The solution seems almost too simple. Providing parity and security eliminates the reserve labor force and limits part-time faculty at the same time it encourages decent treatment. Without the total flexibility and economic incentive, part-time and non-tenure-track faculty are no longer a big attraction, and they are no longer easy to exploit.

Many of our professional associations have developed policy statements speaking directly to these issues. The MLA (Modern Language Association), the CCCC (Conference on College Composition and Communication), and TESOL (Teachers of English to Students of Other Languages) all have very clear positions opposing overuse and abuse of part-time and non-tenure-track faculty. The AAA (American Anthropological Association) and AHA (American Historical Association) (and perhaps others) have endorsed the "Report on the Status of Non-tenure-track Faculty" by the American Association of University Professors (AAUP). We need to get all disciplinary organizations to take similar positions or develop similar policy statements. But we cannot stop with position statements. We need action for change. This is especially evident now that some sectors of part-time and non-tenure-track faculty are demanding a larger role in professional associations, for they are clamoring for teeth in these policy statements.

When reflecting on higher education's failure to confront its treatment of exploited employees, I am reminded of Upton Sinclair noting that "it is difficult to get a man to understand something when his salary depends on his not understanding it." It isn't easy to put forth a line of common concerns, but we nonetheless need to create an agenda that will put education first and that will incorporate our mutual interests as faculty.

To do this we need to go beyond our own disciplines and employee groups to form institution-wide coalitions between faculty, students, and staff and to build national networks to share strategies and success. We are doing some of that in New Jersey, where we have a coalition of unions and student groups from across the state, Challenge 2000, that lobbies the legislature to restore funding to higher education.

But is this enough? We can organize for collective bargaining; we can create alliances and develop networks; but clearly we cannot achieve reforms in the academic labor market without finding funds to finance them. We have to hurdle the final barrier: funding higher education in the face of chronic fiscal crises. The financing of public higher education, and public education in general, is on a shaky foundation, relying on a patchwork of taxes vulnerable to revolt. We need a movement for progressive tax reform that rationalizes the tax structure. And we need to recognize that there is an active conservative movement seeking to disinvest in the public sector, seeking to reduce our commitment to social needs and public services. Education is one of its main targets. In order to build the kind of public support necessary to address these challenges, the higher education work force has to reach out and make broader alliances. This means a unified faculty, working together with other university employees and students, building alliances with constituencies off campus, and taking these issues to the public to defend the public interest.

Works Cited

American Association of University Professors. 1995. "Report on the Status of Non-tenure-track Faculty." In *Policy Documents and Reports*. Washington, D.C.: AAUP.

Burns, Margie. 1991. "Women in Literature versus Women in Writing." *Forum* 2:5–7; *Forum,* 3:1–4.

Cook, Christopher. 1994. "Temps — The Forgotten Workers." *The Nation* (January 21): 125–28.

Ehrenberg, Ronald G., Pamela Rosenberg, and Jeanne Li. 1988. "Part-time Employment in the United States." In *Employment, Unemployment, and Labor Utilization*. Edited by Robert A. Hart. Boston: Unwin Hyman.

Magner, Denise K. "Job-Market Blues." *Chronicle of Higher Education*. (April 27, 1994): A17–20.

Nelson, Cary, and Michael Bérubé. 1994. "Graduate Education Is Losing Its Moral Base." *Chronicle of Higher Education* (March 23, 1994): B1–3.

Chapter 15
Will Technology Make Academic Freedom Obsolete?

Ellen Schrecker

Recently, the administration at Yeshiva University, where I teach, decided to go technological. It spent a considerable sum of money on an electronic classroom with CD-ROMs, huge video screens, and a forty-five-thousand-dollar computerized setup for teleconferencing between the university's two campuses. The subtext was obvious. Because Yeshiva is an orthodox Jewish school, it does not allow coeducation at the undergraduate level and thus has to offer the same separate classes to both men and women. While talmudically correct, the duplicate curriculum is hardly cost effective, and it seemed obvious that some form of long-distance learning would cut costs by combining classes in a way that the local rabbis would accept.

The setup went into operation with what, I assume, the administration considered to be a blockbuster course, team-taught by a well-paid celebrity lecturer who came to campus once a week and an untenured political scientist who specializes in another field. Sixteen students signed up for the course: fourteen men and two women. The women would take the class by teleconference and, through the wonders of modern video and cable technology, would be able to participate in class discussions just as if they were in the same room as the men.

As so often happens, there were bugs in the virtual classroom, and Yeshiva's budget did not include a line for anybody to adjust the equipment. The video camera did not move and focused only on the well-paid visiting lecturer. The sound system was even worse. None of the class discussions were audible over the cable, and only a little of what the teachers said could be heard, a difficulty compounded by the difficulty of obtaining visual clues since the video camera only caught the lecturer's profile.

The defects, it turned out, were systemic, and there was no way to make it possible for the lone woman student (her colleague had dropped the course after the first half-hour of blur and static) to either see, hear, or participate in the class. It was not even possible to videotape the class and let the young woman watch it on a VCR. All she could get was an audiotape. And so she sat in the high-tech classroom all by herself for two and one-half hours a week, listening to the seminar on her Walkman.

I'm sure the virtual classroom, though currently inoperative, will return to Yeshiva. As at other institutions, which are also experimenting with similar set-ups, the search for a technological solution to the cost of instruction is too tempting to forgo.

Only students and teachers will suffer. Electronic education, at least in its current incarnations, has many problems. It cramps one's teaching style, as colleagues at other schools have discovered when they found themselves figuratively chained to the television camera and unable to move around the room as they normally do. The multisited classroom also intensifies preexisting inequalities by offering ostensibly identical, but clearly different, versions of the same course. Only those students at the presumably more privileged home campuses will be able to critique one another's work or interact directly with the instructor. Professors who confront such disparities must either resign themselves to the inequities or else, as some faculty members are already doing, redesign their courses to eliminate the more personalized forms of instruction that they had previously employed. It is hard to imagine that such alterations will improve the quality of education.

Moreover, as so often happens, ostensibly labor-saving technology creates more work for the men and women who actually operate it. In the case of the electronic classroom, the inadequacies of the system are already so obvious that most institutions that use it are looking for ways to ensure some kind of physical contact during the semester. In meeting that demand, on-line teachers may well end up on the road. One three-college consortium with plans for collaborative offerings is contemplating having the faculty members commute to each campus once a week to give hands-on instruction. The techno-dean who described that project gave no information about how the instructors of those courses were to be compensated for their efforts. Just what, one wonders, is being saved?

There are implications for academic freedom as well. Big Brother is already on the Internet. One professor who had been struggling with the technical inadequacies of his multisited classroom joked about it during the class. Within a few days, he got a message from someone in the administration who had presumably caught the show reminding him that such comments would make it more difficult to "market" the program in the future.

The bottom-line mentality that such an administrative intervention reveals is all too pervasive within the academy. We see it in everything from larger classes to smaller photocopying budgets. The implications touch our teaching, our scholarship, and our daily lives. In this essay, I want to look at how this transformation of the American university affects some of the broader issues of academic freedom and our ability to envision a more equitable and democratic society.

There is not much time. Pressures to eliminate the university as we know it increase by the minute. Prognosticators are already describing an electronic academy that would dispense with the entire institutional superstructure of higher education. In this brave new world, students would no longer subject themselves to the old-fashioned technology of teachers, classes, and a four-year sequence of courses. Instead, they would access whatever they needed to learn over the Internet in accordance with the same kind of "just-in-time" inventory control that Japanese corporations employ. Think of it, introductory calculus or political theory as spare parts. Delivered, of course, by private companies.[1]

While this electronic dystopia may still be a gleam in Bill Gates's eye, the imposition of the industrial model upon the nation's universities and colleges proceeds apace. It is transforming an institution that once saw its mission as the creation, production, and transmission of knowledge into one that turns out a product as efficiently and cheaply as possible.

That business categories might not be applicable to the educational process seems to have been overlooked, giving us, just to take one example, a system where the product — an educated individual — is also the market. Nor do the advocates of bottom-line education take into account the fact that the transmission and acquisition of knowledge may well be one of those labor-intensive human endeavors like live musical performances that, by its nature, resists speedups and economies of scale. Such contradictions, however, do not impede the rush toward competitiveness.

Everything is up for grabs.

There is, to begin with, the downsizing that is shrinking faculties, increasing class sizes, and at many schools making it impossible for students to graduate within the traditional four years because the courses they require are either oversubscribed or not offered. There is also the increasingly two-tiered structure of the academy, with elite private and public institutions turning out graduates for the top slots in the economy and the low-end public schools producing candidates for the white-collar jobs high school graduates once took. And, of course, there is the bifurcated professoriat that pits an aristocracy of full-time, full-paid tenured and tenure-track teachers against a displaced peasantry of underpaid, overworked, and insecure adjuncts.

But even this skewed system is in danger.

Tenure may be about to go. It is already under attack from business groups and politicians who question the cost-effectiveness of an institution whose key employees have terrific benefits and only seem to work a few hours a week. Nor is this only talk. A handful of schools — Bennington College among them — have already abolished tenure. And in South Carolina, Arizona, and Florida, state legislators, regents, and other officials have similar proposals under consideration, including the establishment of entire colleges staffed by short-term teachers.[2]

Even within the academy, there are voices calling for tenure's abolition. They use the language both of multiculturalism and of the business world to portray tenure as a bottleneck that prevents the free movement of market forces within the academy and makes it harder for minorities or women to get in. Its elimination would, we are told, offer both faculty members and institutions more choices. One blueprint for reform calls for commodification. Tenure would get an economic value, and professors could presumably convert their "T-notes" into such equivalent goodies as smaller classes or more frequent sabbaticals.[3] The proposal, of course, contains no intimation that the project might contain sticks as well as carrots and could easily splinter an already bifurcated profession even further. Given current trends within academe, the day might well come when senior faculty members would be tempted to give up their tenure in return for the lighter teaching loads or higher pay checks of their less secure colleagues.

The "experts" and administrators who design such programs are obviously scurrying to find a soft way to get rid of tenure before the market imposes a harsher one. The American Association of Higher Education (which not coincidentally is at the leading edge of the movement for the electronic classroom) has gotten federal support for its so-called New Pathways project that will explore the "concrete, pragmatic" alternatives to traditional faculty career paths. Besides my own suspicion of anything with a mushy title that calls itself "new," I can't help being reminded of the apocryphal story about the nationalistic German Jews in the early 1930s who marched in Nazi parades carrying signs saying *Raus mit uns* (Get rid of us).

Still, we should not delude ourselves about the benefits of tenure. Its political value in maintaining the academic freedom of dissenting faculty members has never been particularly strong. At moments of crisis, like the McCarthy era of the late 1940s and 1950s, tenure did not offer much protection against administrators and governing boards who were determined to oust political undesirables from their faculties.[4]

Nor, as the institutional structure that houses the academic profession is crumbling, can we afford too much nostalgia about the traditional university. It was an institution that often reflected and amplified the class, race, and gender inequities of the rest of society. Its stated concern for intellectual freedom and cultural diversity was often more rhetorical than real and almost always limited by an unacknowledged deference to the powers that be.

Most of its operations supported that power structure. It diverted attention from un- and underemployment by keeping large numbers of young people out of the labor pool. It served as a sorting device that recruited athletes for professional teams and credentialed people for middle-class or (at more elite universities) upper-class occupations. And its laboratories tailored their research to the requirements of the state and the corporate sector.[5]

But, at least until recently, it also provided space for some real intellectual autonomy. It was, for example, the last refuge of print culture, the last place in American society where language was still respected and where ideas mattered. Its libraries and presses underwrote serious scholarship. Its classrooms actually opened some students' minds. And the protections that it offered its inhabitants did create space for critical thinking and the conceptualization of alternatives to the status quo.

This space has become very precious. As the nation's political discourse becomes increasingly commodified, the academy has come to shelter most of what passes for political dissent. But the space for that dissent has been shrinking for years, not so much because of open attacks on academic freedom — although that has certainly been taking place — as because of the relentless infiltration of the bottom line into the academy. Funding cuts are the main culprits. But so, too, is the economic insecurity of contemporary students and their increasing vocationalism, as well as the growing emphasis within the academic community on marketing, productivity, and other business functions. The liberal arts — the area that produces most critical thought on key social issues — are the main casualty. Those of us who teach these fields do not, it seems, have a particularly marketable product.

Moreover, much of what we do is being marginalized by the growing conservative attack on the liberal academy. Right-wing foundations fund private think tanks and PR firms to produce and disseminate the wildly distorted stereotypes of multiculturalism, political correctness, and affirmative action that enter the mainstream as realistic portrayals of university life.[6] As a result, contemporary scholarship is losing both its apparent legitimacy and its general audience.

Nor is it only the practitioners of trendy literary theories and ethnic studies who are under attack. As the recent battle over the Smithsonian's *Enola Gay* exhibit revealed, even such staid pursuits as diplomatic and military history can now become vulnerable, criticized by partisan subgroups and uninformed politicians as elitist and unresponsive to the need for a more celebratory view of the past. In my own field of post-1945 American history, right-wing foundations are backing the efforts of scholars like Harvey Klehr and Ronald Radosh to use Soviet and other recently released documents to prove that American Communists were spies.[7] These people's scholarship is highly tendentious, all to one side: the work they produce not only supposedly refutes the research of an entire generation of scholars (though few of us ever claimed that Communists *didn't* spy) but also, by identifying communism so ineradicably with espionage, serves to delegitimize the entire American Left.

The consequences extend far beyond the academy. In this all-out ideological campaign to make the world safe for capitalism, the very notion that there are other human values beyond the marketplace is fast disappearing. Instead we confront a society permeated by twenty-first-century technology and nineteenth-century values. We can either fight back or else submit to the new order, embrace the individualist ethic of social Darwinism, and throw ourselves into the competition for part-time consulting jobs at Microsoft.

But, if we resist, we must embrace collective action. Individuals as individuals simply do not have the power to reverse the inequities that the business community has foisted upon American society. After all, despite its rhetorical adherence to individualism, the corporate sector has operated collectively for years. Its solidarity in the face of all threats to its power is, in fact, quite remarkable. Would the Yale administration be quite so hard-nosed in dealing with GESO and its other unions were it not supported by and supportive of the business community's broader antilabor agenda?

The graduate students who went on strike at Yale are thus, in more ways than one, the future of the academic profession. The ferocity of the administration's response to these students' demands for representation points to the importance of their struggle. Were no larger issues at stake, Yale's administration might well have appointed a committee and tried to co-opt GESO's leaders. But there *are* larger issues at stake, and here we come back to the concept of academic freedom, to the recognition of the organic connection between free speech and the defense of collective action. The university's attempt to punish its students for their organizing activities is in line with a long tradition of antilabor repression. During the early part of the twentieth century, when it was as risky to organize a union in a steel mill as it now is to do so in a university, corporations and local government routinely violated the political rights of union organizers. And it is of some interest that the most highly publicized academic freedom case in Yale's history involved the 1937 dismissal of the head of a national teachers union.[8]

Now as then, the nation's universities are in a state of crisis. Yale's troubles are not unique. There are strikes — of both support staff and teaching fellows — throughout the academic community; and the move toward organizing some kind of resistance to academic privatization and downsizing is spreading. These struggles mirror those outside the university. Their success may well depend as much upon the efforts of the presumably reenergized labor movement in revitalizing public support for unionization as on any individual campus victories.

Those of us who are professors and who support such efforts have a special responsibility for articulating the connections between the restructuring of the nation's universities and the restructuring of its economy. We need to explain to our colleagues, our students, and ultimately to whatever audience we can reach just how the assault on labor, on liberal education, on welfare, and, ultimately, on anything that does not enhance the profitability of the nation's corporations affects us all. Our jobs and our ability to speak out are both on the line. Fragile at the best of times, academic freedom (or any kind of substantive free speech) will soon be as ephemeral as a well-paid industrial job. Or a tenured radical.

NOTES

1. Michael Prowse, "Endangered Species," *Financial Times* (London edition) 20 November 1995, 16.

2. Denise K. Magner, "Tenure Re-examined," *Chronicle of Higher Education* (March 31, 1995): A17.

3. The trade-off of tenure for more sabbaticals has already occurred at Webster University in Missouri. See "New Pathways: Faculty Careers and Employment in the 21st Century," project description, American Association for Higher Education, n.d. (probably 1995).

4. For an account of the academy's capitulation during the McCarthy period, see Ellen W. Schrecker, *No Ivory Tower: McCarthyism and the Universities* (New York: Oxford University Press, 1986).

5. Within the past ten years, historians of science have been exploring how federal, and especially military, involvement actually shaped such fields as physics. See, for example, Stuart W. Leslie, *The Cold War and American Science* (New York: Columbia University Press, 1993); Daniel Kevles, "Cold War and Hot Physics:

Science, Security, and the American States, 1945–56," *Historical Studies in the Physical and Biological Sciences* 20, no. 2 (1989): 239–64.

6. See Ellen Messer-Davidow, "Manufacturing the Attack on Liberalized Higher Education," *Social Text* 36 (fall 1993): 20–80.

7. Harvey Klehr, John Earl Haynes, and Fridrikh Igorevich Firsov, *The Secret World of American Communism* (New Haven: Yale University Press, 1995) and Harvey Klehr and Ronald Radosh, *The Amerasia Spy Case: Prelude to McCarthyism* (Chapel Hill: University of North Carolina Press, 1996).

8. For a useful overview of the political repression directed against the labor movement, see Jerold S. Auerbach, *Labor and Liberty: The Lafollette Committee and the New Deal* (Indianapolis: Bobbs Merrill, 1966). On the case of Jerome Davis at Yale, see Schrecker, *No Ivory Tower,* 67–68.

Contributors

Stanley Aronowitz is professor of sociology at the Graduate Center of the City University of New York. His recent books include *Science as Power; The Jobless Future* (coauthored with William DiFazio); and *The Death and Rebirth of American Radicalism.*

Michael Bérubé is professor of English at the University of Illinois at Urbana-Champaign. He is the coeditor of *Higher Education under Fire* and the author, most recently, of *Public Access: Literary Theory and American Cultural Politics* and *Life as We Know It.*

Daniel Czitrom is professor of history at Mount Holyoke College. He is the author of *Media and the American Mind: From Morse to McLuhan* and coauthor of *Out of Many: A History of the American People.*

Barbara Ehrenreich has written widely on feminism, socialism, and other progressive topics. Her books include *Hearts of Men: American Dreams and the Flight from Commitment; The Worst Years of Our Lives: Irreverent Notes from a Decade of Greed;* and *Fear of Falling: The Inner Life of the Middle Class.*

Robin D. G. Kelley is professor of history at New York University. His books include *Hammer and Hoe: Alabama Communists during the Great Depression* and *Race Rebels.*

Duncan Kennedy is a professor at Harvard Law School. He was one of the founders of the Conference on Critical Legal Studies and teaches legal theory and low-income housing law and policy. His book *Sexy Dressing Etcetera* collects a number of his essays on cultural politics.

Cary Nelson is Jubilee Professor of Liberal Arts and Sciences at the University of Illinois at Urbana-Champaign and the author, most recently, of *Manifesto of a Tenured Radical.* His recent work also includes the coedited collections *Madrid 1937: Letters of the Abraham Lincoln Brigade from the Spanish Civil War* and *Disciplinarity and Dissent in Cultural Studies.*

Kathy M. Newman is in her final year of the graduate program in American studies at Yale. When she is not working on her dissertation ("Marketing Identities: Broadcast Advertising and Consumer Activism in Postwar America"), she organizes unions, teaches, writes a biweekly column for the *Yale Daily News,* and publishes a cartoon about graduate student life called "Ph.D."

Linda Ray Pratt is chair of the Department of English at the University of Nebraska–Lincoln. She is also a past president of the American Association of University Professors. She chaired the AAUP's national committee on the status of non-tenure-track faculty that in 1993 issued a major report with policy recommendations for improving the status of part-time faculty. She has spoken and written widely about issues in higher education. She also publishes in the areas of Victorian literature and early modern poetry.

Corey Robin is a Ph.D. candidate in political science at Yale. He is currently writing his dissertation, "Fear and Modern Politics: From Hobbes to the Cold War."

Andrew Ross directs the American Studies Program at New York University. His recent books include *Strange Weather* and *The Chicago Gangster Theory of Life.*

Ellen Schrecker is professor of history at Yeshiva University. Her books include *No Ivory Tower: McCarthyism and the Universities,* the edited collection *The Age of McCarthyism,* and the coedited *Regulating the Intellectuals: Perspectives on Academic Freedom in the 1980s.*

Michelle Stephens is a Ph.D. candidate in American studies at Yale. Her dissertation is titled "New Ethnicities and the Politics of National Identity: Anglophone Caribbean Intellectuals in the U.S., 1920–1990."

James D. Sullivan is the author of *On the Walls and in the Streets: American Poetry Broadsides from the 1960s*. He has been a visiting faculty member and an unemployed Ph.D. He is currently teaching part-time.

Karen Thompson has taught part-time in the Department of English at Rutgers University since 1979. She is currently the president of the part-time chapter of the American Association of University Professors at Rutgers and also chair of the national AAUP's Committee G on part-time and non-tenure-track appointments.

Stephen Watt is professor of English at Indiana University. He has also served as director of graduate studies for his department. His books include *Joyce, O'Casey, and the Irish Popular Theater* and the coedited collection *Marketing Modernisms*.

John Wilhelm is general secretary-treasurer of the Hotel Employees and Restaurant Employees International Union, AFL-CIO-CLC. A 1967 magna cum laude graduate of Yale University, Wilhelm was business manager for HEREIU's Local 35 at Yale from 1978 to 1986; for the last six of those years he was also organizing coordinator for Local 34. From 1982 to 1996 he was HEREIU's vice president, while also serving as chief negotiator for citywide hotel contracts in Boston, San Francisco, Los Angeles, Las Vegas, and New Haven.

Rick Wolff is professor of economics at the University of Massachusetts–Amherst. A New Haven resident since 1964, he received an economics degree from Yale in 1969 and was the mayoral candidate of the New Haven Green Party in 1985, receiving 10 percent of the vote. His books include *The Economics of Colonialism* and *Knowledge and Class*.

Index